Choreographer
and Composer

Twayne's Dance Series

Don McDonagh, Editor

Choreographer and Composer:
Theatrical Dance and Music
in Western Culture by Baird Hastings

Denishawn: the enduring influence
by Jane Sherman

George Balanchine
by Don McDonagh

Choreographer and Composer

Baird Hastings

Twayne Publishers

Choreographer
and Composer

Baird Hastings

Published in 1983
by Twayne Publishers
A Division of G. K. Hall & Company
70 Lincoln Street, Boston, Massachusetts 02111

Printed on permanent/durable
acid-free paper and bound in
the United States of America.

First Printing

This book was designed by
Barbara Anderson and typeset
in Garamond by Compset, Inc.
with Snell roundhand display type supplied
by Typographic House.

0-8057-9600-2

To Lily

Contents

Editor's Foreword

Music, which has been the handmaiden of dance throughout its history, has rarely been commented upon intelligently in that context. The fact is less due to a conspiratorial silence than to lack of authoritative scholarship among writers who can both see and hear. Far too often, musical writers have perceived dance as an intrusion or an imposition upon a particular score, and dance specialists rarely are sensitive to musical values other than the egregious one of poor playing. When George Balanchine first choreographed his sublime "Serenade" he used three of the four movements of Tchaikovsky's "Serenade in C for String Orchestra" opus 48. Seven years later in 1941 he added the "Russian Dance" to use the full score, and commented that none of the reviewers seemed to notice the addition. At least none commented on it!

Choreographers themselves, with the rare exception of Balanchine, are frequently ignorant musically and few make any effort to correct the condition. They certainly recognize and respond emotionally to music that appeals to their kinetic sense, but are surprisingly unaware of the technical aspects of any given score, including those that accompany some of their finest creations.

It is a particular pleasure, then, to have the current volume by Baird Hastings, himself a conductor and perceptive observer of theatrical dance. He modestly refers to this searching historical survey of both music and dance as an essay, but it will be obvious to readers that it is far more. It is an examination that has not previously been made of the relationship of the two arts from a sound historical perspective.

The seventeenth-century world of Louis XIV saw the rise of court ballet and its spread throughout Western Europe. It was also a transitional period in which the professional dancer began to assert supremacy over the accomplished but amateur nobility. The Renaissance ideal of expert facility in several fields still had its influence, and men such as Jean-Baptiste Lully and Pierre Beauchamps flourished. Lully was not only the most accomplished musician of his time but a dancer of discernable skill and experience. Beauchamps's abilities as a ballet master were accompanied by compositional skills to a degree unknown in our own time, where the roles of choreographer and composer are so clearly divided.

By dealing with such figures in the context of their own time, the author has clarified the extent of their achievements and the logic of their own artistic development. In the presence of artistic genius we are frequently blinded as to its antecedents. It is one of the chief measures of the present volume's importance to have consistently dealt with major and minor figures as artistic representatives of a cultural world with its own aesthetic assumptions and boundaries.

Inevitably, as specialization became the artistic rule rather than the exception, music and dance began to follow the internal logic of their individual means of expression. The ballet master's role eventually focused on choreography and/or teaching with less and less emphasis on musical proficiency, although even as late as the 1930s the distinguished teacher/dancer and choreographer Nicholas Legat regularly conducted his classes from the piano.

The division of roles has reached its logical limit in the work of Merce Cunningham and his longtime musical associate John Cage. While they share an obvious aesthetic outlook, Cunningham's choreographic designs are frequently developed without reference to a preexisting musical score. Cage does not compose a score after the dance is completed. The two artists agree on the emotional "climate" of the work and its duration, and each proceeds to develop movement and sound independently. Often the two are first heard and seen together at the premiere performance of the work. It is obviously a working method far removed from that of seventeenth-century composers' and choreographers', but its logic stems from our theatrical conventions.

The important point that is emphasized throughout is that the working relationships of composers and choreographers have evolved in response to the specific needs of the times. The reader will find no hard and fast rules or theories expounded restricting the boundaries of creative excellence. He will find sympathetic and intelligent appreciation of accomplishment either as a result of direct collaboration between living artists or the fruitful encounter of a choreographer with a score from existing musical repertory. It is no more and no less than each deserves.

Don McDonagh

Preface

Music and dance are two art forms of expression and communication that come from "where dreams are made." Each has its mystery; each has its concrete structural and technical elements; each has its language and its dialects, its charms, and its forms. Dance communicates through the eye, while music communicates through the ear. Evidently interdependent elements of lyric theatre, together they may employ similar patterns and figures that build a convincing, combined art form, or they may simply provide structural units that do not clash with those of their sister arts. As Lincoln Kirstein stated in *Dance,* "Art is not an imitation of nature. It involves synthesis, intensification and repetition of observation." Even Richard Wagner, for whom art was life and life was art, would agree on the need for synthesis, intensification, and repetition.

In this essay (which was originally entitled "Scales and Five Positions") we discuss the nature of working relationships between composers and choreographers: the dance that choreographers have created to theatrical music, and the music composers have written that choreographers use. Music history books do not pretend to give dance its rightful place in the large grouping of the arts. Dance history books usually are so concerned with particular sequences of steps, and the cult of the personal, that they cannot pretend to devote adequate time and space to related musical problems. While considering the cultural context, we discuss significant and fascinating interrelationships in perspective, based on the most recent information. Each major area is presented in its own historical frame rather than in a frame into which it might be thrust arbitrarily. The participants are discussed in the light of their particular strengths rather than shortcomings so that we have a clear idea of what they were trying to achieve and can thus evaluate their work and importance with greater appreciation. Indeed there are some significant heroes—Beaujoyeux, Lully, Noverre, Petipa, Stravinsky, and Balanchine—creators who have molded and expanded both music and ballet.

Traditional tunes and improvised steps had an anonymous beginning, but became cultural ornaments, primarily in Western courts, churches, outdoor festivals, and circuses of France, Italy, Spain, Germany, and England. Until at least the waning of the Renaissance, religion and the arts were inextricably related, developing as part of culture together with Western social history and philosophy. The dance was alternately damned and utilized by the church; and the secular music of the troubadours, trouvères, and "courts of love," whose poetry and manners provided a frame for artistic development, grew and nourished throughout the Middle Ages.

Scales—major, minor, modal, pentatonic, and so on—are fundamental to music itself, and positions—feet, arms, body, and the like—provide necessary structure for steps, movements, and choreography in all dance. Scales existed as soon as melody, rhythm, and phrase were created. Positions were at the origin of all movement. The five positions of the feet suggested by Arbeau and his contemporaries in the sixteenth century were codified about one hundred years later by Beauchamps; the positions of the arms were codified only about the beginning of the twentieth century.

Although history is at the basis of almost our entire essay, we are not discussing the history of music or of dance. Our object is to consider how choreographers of Western theatrical dance have used music in producing their works, and how musicians have composed works for dance performance. Most choreographers begin to work with themes or ideas, not with forms or with music. But when they actually design dances to express a theme, they have forms to work with that often influence the manner in which it is developed (as we will note when we discuss the relations of Gluck with Noverre and with Angiolini, for example). Choreographers also have interpreters whose participation influences many aspects of ballets in their unique ability to perform with virtuosity and artistry, and decorators also exert their influences. In addition, the infinite variety of melody, harmony, rhythm, and texture involved in ensemble music helps provide an entire structure for all theatrical dancing, whatever theme or mood it presents.

Our presentation discusses major collaborations of musicians and choreographers over a period of six centuries. I have avoided gossip and hearsay except as they related directly to our subject, and have reinforced my own perceptions—study of all the scores involved, and seeing just about every work that is still performed—with those of Cyril W. Beaumont, Edwin Denby, B. H. Haggin, Lincoln Kirstein, G. B. L. Wilson, and others who are credited in the text or bibliography. In the selective discussion of certain outstanding ballets, I have attempted to draw attention to the many problems involved in their authentic presentation, and provide some insight into solutions. I have tried to avoid terms that might be too technical for nonprofessionals as I explored pertinent concepts in particular masterworks. Throughout I have attempted to use the correct modern spelling of terms or titles; I have translated foreign words or phrases only when needed for clarity. The length of my discussions of particular works and particular figures should not be construed as a value judgment on my part.

In discussing scores that have been pivotal or definitive in the development of lyric theatre, and particularly theatrical dancing, I have chosen representative works; I make no pretense of completeness. My choice is based on applied study, and it can serve as a summary and introduction to a vast, fascinating subject.

The first two works singled out for notice in our historical presentation, the secular *Robin* and the sacred *Daniel,* certainly are fine examples of lyric theatre; although they contain elements of ballet, they cannot pretend to be ballets. Beaujoyeux's *Le Ballet Comique de la Reine Louise* was called a ballet, although some opera historians have claimed it as the first opera. Lully's secular works were almost exclusively theatrical. His ballets, comédie-ballets, tragédie-lyriques (operas) all included important dancing. As he was an excellent dancer himself, and given his position and his personality, his complete control of balletic aspects (assisted ably by Beauchamps) was inevitable.

While Lully in the seventeenth century and Stravinsky in the twentieth dominated the music of theatrical dancing, and thereby both its form and content, in the eighteenth and nineteenth centuries, outstanding choreographers were in control of the production of ballets. In the eighteenth century the greatest figure in the dance world was Jean-Georges Noverre, who worked with such composers as Gluck, Jommelli, and Mozart, but whose major choreographic works were created to music by such musicians as Granier, Rodolphe, Aspelmayr, and Starzer. In the field of nineteenth-century ballet, we place particular emphasis on *The Sleeping Beauty,* which Marius Petipa choreographed to music by Tchaikovsky in 1890. As mentioned above, the music of Igor Stravinsky (much of it choreographed by George Balanchine) stands preeminent among works in the field composed in the twentieth century.

Although they have developed and grown somewhat more elaborate in recent years, most of the basic forms in music and in dance have existed for about two hundred years. How Western composers and choreographers have used the forms and structures they have created and inherited is the subject of this essay.

Before we consider the work of major choreographers and musicians in each of several periods, we must acknowledge the background to theatrical dance as it developed from medieval dance dramas, and also acts of itinerant entertainers. We must note the anthropological basis of early dance cultures prior to the emergence of Christian dances. Even before Salomé performed for King Herod the dance was an important part of Western culture. Each period and each culture has had its own traditions, its own horizon, its own forms. Each major figure has contributed to the artistic structure that is still growing. Progress is not a good word to use in the arts. Change is.

Acknowledgments

The bibliography contains, either in itself or in generations of bibliography, the major sources of inspiration and erudition. Were I to burden readers with all the details, the length would be excessive.

It has been my privilege to live at a time when many creative persons worked, and I have profited greatly from experiencing their work, and very often knowing them as well. Through many documents, we can be thankful the past lives, as well as the present, and the future.

For particular guidance in the preparation of this book I wish to thank Don McDonagh. The staffs of the Harvard Theatre Collection, the New York Public Library, the Juilliard School have been most helpful.

For special favors, I am grateful to Valerie Van Winkle of American Ballet Theater, Anita Legalt of the Martha Graham Company, David Vaughan, and Michel Sobotin.

For the sins of commission or omission I assume full responsibility.

Chronology

1230   Birth of the trouvère Adam de la Halle, whose *Play of Robin and Marion* (Naples) is the earliest secular spectacle-entertainment extant, just as the anonymous *Play of Daniel* (from a slightly earlier period in France) is the earliest religious spectacle-entertainment to survive. These popular productions are further illustrated by Philippe de Vitry's *Roman de Fauvel* of nearly a century later.

1453   The fall of Constantinople caused artists and scholars to flee westward.

1478   Lavish court pageants and entertainments were produced in Florence by Lorenzo de Medici, establishing a tradition in which such artists as Leonardo da Vinci participated.

1558   Elizabeth I, Queen of England until 1603. During her reign most of Shakespeare's plays were produced and the important series of masques was begun.

1581   *Le Ballet Comique de la Reine Louise* produced in Paris—"the first ballet," performed the same year Vincenzo wrote his historic *Dialogue of Ancient and Modern Music* (presaging the Baroque). *Le Ballet Comique* was followed in 1588 by the publication of Thoinot Arbeau's *Orchésographie,* the most important early dance manual.

1618   Beginning of the Thirty Years' War.

1637   First public opera theatre, in Venice.

1653   Jean-Baptiste Lully (1632–1687) composer active at the court of Louis XIV (1638–1715).

1725   Publication of *Le Maitre à Danser* by Pierre Rameau.

1761   *Don Juan* (Gluck-Angiolini, with stage designs by Giulio Quaglio) produced in Vienna.

1778   *Les Petits Riens* (Mozart-Noverre) produced at the Paris Opéra.

1797   *Flore et Zéphyre* (Bossi-Didelot, with decors by Liparotti) produced in London, made pioneering use of wires to create a flying ballet.

1801   *The Creatures of Prometheus* (Beethoven-Vigano, with decors by Platzer) produced in Vienna.

1813   Birth of Richard Wagner and Giuseppe Verdi, two giants of lyric theatre in the nineteenth century.

1832   *La Sylphide* (Schneitzhoeffer-Taglioni (Filippo), with decors and costumes by Ciceri and Lormier)—a poetic ballet in which toe dancing was for the first time artistically combined with flying—produced in Paris.

1841   *Giselle* (Adam-Coralli and Perrot, with decors by Ciceri) produced in Paris.

1842   *Napoli* (Paulli, Helsted, Gade, Lumbye-Bournonville, with decors by Christensen) produced in Copenhagen.

1845   *Pas de Quatre* (Pugni-Perrot) produced in London.

1862   *La Fille du Pharaon* (Pugni-Petipa) produced in Saint Petersburg.

1870   *Coppélia* (Delibes-Saint-Léon, with decors and costumes by Cambon, Despléchin, Lavastre, and Lormier) produced in Paris.

1877   *Swan Lake* (Tchaikovsky-Reisinger, with decors by Shangin, Valts, and Groppius) produced in Moscow.

1895   *The Sleeping Beauty* (Tchaikovsky-Petipa, with decors and costumes by Levogt, Botcharov, Shishlov, Ivanov, and Vsevolojsky) produced in Saint Petersburg.

1909   *Les Sylphides* (Chopin-Fokine-Benois) produced in Paris as a feature of the first of twenty seasons of the Ballets Russes de Serge de Diaghilev.

1917   *Parade* (Satie-Massine, with decors and costumes by Picasso) produced by Diaghilev in Paris.

1928   *Apollo* (Stravinsky-Balanchine, with decors and costumes by Bauchant) produced by Diaghilev in Paris.

1930   *Le Sacre du Printemps* (Stravinsky-Nijinsky) (1913, Paris), given its American premiere in Philadelphia, in a new version by Massine with Martha Graham.

1931   *Job* (Vaughan Williams-de Valois-Raverat) produced in London.

1932   *The Green Table* (Cohen-Jooss-Heckroth) produced in Paris.

1934   *Four Saints in Three Acts* (Thomson-Ashton-Stettheimer) produced in Hartford, Connecticut.

1938   *Saint Francis* (Hindemith-Massine, with decors and costumes by Tchelitchew) produced in London.

1942   *Pillar of Fire* (Schoenberg-Tudor-Mielziner) produced in New York.

1946   *The Seasons* (Cage-Cunningham-Noguchi) produced in New York.

1957   *Agon* (Stravinsky-Balanchine) produced in New York.

1972   The New York City Ballet presented a Stravinsky Festival in which Balanchine and Robbins choreographed *Pulcinella*, Balanchine created seven ballets, and twelve other new ballets to music by Stravinsky were prepared by Jerome Robbins, John Taras, Todd Bolender, John Clifford, Richard Tanner, and Lorca Massine.

1982   The New York City Ballet presented a Stravinsky Festival in which twenty-five ballets were presented, including twelve new works by Balanchine, Robbins, Taras, Martins, d'Amboise, and Lew Christensen.

1

The Beginnings and Medieval Times

Theatrical dancing, or ballet, as we recognize the term, began in the sixteenth century; however, its roots and the roots of the music involved extend far back to primitive cultures and tribal ceremonies in prehistoric times. The religious circle and linear ensemble dances executed by aborigines to music of drum, fife, and perhaps other accompaniment contained the germ of theatrical quality that became more evident in the Hellenic and Christian eras. Curt Sachs and Lincoln Kirstein have discussed motivations and early developments of dance in their excellent surveys.

Theatrical performances involving dancing were part of feudal ceremonies and "triumphs," yet their essential quality and artistic unity blossomed only when musicians (composers, instrumentalists, and singers) all began to be professionals, as they did in the later Middle Ages. From this time on charades, pageants, and masques, as well as religious ceremonies, began to lose their improvisational and somewhat amateur aspect in favor of true artistic achievement. Dancers, however, only began to be fully professional in seventeenth-century France, under the general supervision of Lully.

In prehistoric times, and even today in a few remote areas, dance was primarily ritualistic, often with aspects of erotic symbolism. Serving to invoke magic and healing and to propitiate the gods, solo dances were performed by medicine men or a select group of warriors. Often the women had their separate dances. It was the Greeks who developed the dance as an art, an expression of beauty celebrated in the writings of Lucian. The Christian church generally opposed dancing, theatrical or other, because of the "obscene" elements it contained and encouraged, but despite this in about 1300 certain polyphonic instrumental and sung dances began to furnish foundations for various sacred and later secular performances.

Medieval Times

Before the fifteenth century there were numerous court spectacles and masked balls, and various popular entertainments and church ceremonies; they were generally produced anonymously. The dance element was prominent in these loosely structured feudal shows, both religious and secular, indoors and out. There was little specialization among performers, except perhaps for singers and instrumentalists. The producer was generally a noble, as were most of the participants, except in popular outdoor entertainments in which the lower classes amused their peers with juggling acts, dances, and acrobacy; vaudeville, if you will. In the religious pageants and ceremonies a churchman would direct subordinate clerics. At the close of most court spectacles (usually very long affairs), the spectators, including royalty if present, joined with the performers in dancing a moresca, which often led to the entire company dancing the night away.

The church ceremonies, which involved scenes from the Bible inserted as tropes in the service to be interpreted and acted out, also included dances and processions. The popular entertainments, mostly in the village square, involved many folk dances and mime scenes, which usually were much freer in structure, treatment, and subject matter. It is problematic to realize accurately the true sociological and theatrical place of the dance, despite the survival of tapestries and occasional prints and accounts, partly because of lack of more precise documentation of the early spectacles. Our reconstructions of the Dance of Death, the folk fairs, court balls, and religious ceremonies depend on manuscripts and artifacts that have to be interpreted by scholars.

We can, however, discern a beginning of lyric theatre in the spectacle-entertainments found toward the close of medieval times in the surviving manuscripts that give us appropriate dance tunes and rhythms, even if the tempos are rarely explicit. Without rhythm there can be neither music nor dance. Without melody there can be no real form, merely monotonous (if effective) repetition. The apparently infinite variety of melody and rhythm, harmony, and texture involved in ensemble pieces provides an appropriate starting place for a discussion of music and theatrical dancing in Western cultures. (The original impetus of dance in primitive cultures, which we noted is not primarily theatrical, is perhaps more animal in both sound and rhythm; also, primitive dance is more participatory, whereas Western theatrical dance has the indispensable element of observation.) In the late medieval period incipient professionalism in music began to encourage development of lyric theatre. By the Renaissance the improvement of instrumental techniques and the expansion of forms, as well as the move toward the diatonic tonal system that involved major and minor scales, all contributed to the structures into which theatrical dancing would fit, closer and closer, until the seventeenth century when codification generally occurred.

Dance tunes, which often were sung, have existed since time immemorial. Their incorporation into theatrical dancing and into differentiated forms of spectacle-entertainments has been a gradual process from the tribal dances, Roman games, Christian ceremonies, and secular "routs" of medieval times to the numbers of Renaissance ballets, and on to ballet as we know it in the twentieth century.

In Western Europe the dance forms available for medieval theatrical use included various ensemble caccia, hymns, marches, estampies (the Spanish ones often influenced by Arabic melodic ornamentation) in triple and duple time,[1] for court and church, and various solo steps such as popular gigs, which really only flourished in the Renaissance. The rondel was a medieval three-voice composition offering many possibilities of movement; it began as a fugue type, although later it emphasized the principle of alternation and as such was a forerunner of the rondo and the rondeau. The dance rhythms were controlled tightly by the straitjacket of the classic rhythmic modes (TIDAST, see below), modeled after Greek poetic forms. (All were variants of traditional church-favored triple rhythm except spondaic, which was duple.) Some rhythms were simple, repetitious, and possibly to our ears monotonous. But this was the style of the period, and slowly yet surely the forms of the dance tunes were developing. The rhythmic modes that controlled rhythm, and often tempo, were as follows:

Trochaic ♩♪
Iambic ♪♩
Dactylic ♩♪♩
Anapest ♪♩♩
Spondaic ♩♩
Tribrachic ♫♫

For centuries, monophonic melody prevailed, but by the thirteenth century polyphony had earned its place. The adaptable conductus (of the twelfth century) was a vocal processional march that was used in many contemporary church works such as the anonymous *Play of Daniel* and *Play of Herod*. It provided the producer with ample opportunity to make use of the dance in the gothic cathedral spectacles, and soon the form was adopted for use in secular spectacles as well.

In the twelfth century, a kind of pre-Renaissance renaissance, there were several important developments fundamental to the origins of both opera and ballet as lyric theatre began in the shadow of the Catholic church. Already for a number of decades there had been incubating within the church a form known as Latin liturgical drama, performed as tropes (inserts in the religious service) at Easter time (*Quem quaeritis?* "Whom do you seek?" was probably the earliest of which we have documentation) and during the Christmas season. Subjects included the Resurrection, the birth of Christ, the raising of Lazarus, the conversion of Saint Paul, legends concerning Saint Nicholas, and the Last Judgment. These productions in France were mostly in Latin, while in Italy the vernacular was used.

The twelfth-century Beauvais *Play of Daniel* (like *Hilary* before it) foretells the coming of Jesus Christ. The trials and tribulations of Daniel at the courts of Belshazzar and Darius are retold most poetically. Performed with pomp and pageantry before the Te Deum of Matins, the sixty-two numbers of the *Play of Daniel* have fifty different tunes, mostly sung in Latin, with a few French and other phrases; the many effective short scenes include a dozen sumptuous courtly processionals. According to the meager information we have, the following instruments were used: rebecs, positiv organs, vielles, recorders, bells, drums, finger cymbals, and ancient trumpets. Most of the texts are set powerfully in syllabic style (one note per syllable) in the manner of the sequence (repeated melodies beginning successively on different notes), although there are also moments of ornamentation and of repose. The women's roles originally were taken by men and boys. In this full lyric work, the earliest we know, forty-four of the sixty-two numbers are in varied triple rhythm, thirteen are in some form of duple rhythm, and five are free. The hour-long *Play of Daniel* makes abundant use of known secular trouvère melodies, but dresses them up, sometimes providing elementary harmony. There is little tonal variety; most numbers are in C major, while a few are in F major and G major. Even when seen in the twentieth century the *Play of Daniel* is a unique experience. How extraordinary it must have been to audiences in the twelfth century is difficult to imagine.

The trouvères of northern France were the most sophisticated solo musicians of the medieval period, although their art was only a few short steps away (culturally and geographically) from that of the provençal troubadours and the early wandering popular minstrels. Among the best known of the trouvères was Adam de la Halle (ca. 1230–1287), a wandering musician who helped develop lyric theatre as a secular art by extending a favorite form of the dramatic ballad, the pastoral, relating the romantic affairs of a knight in his unsuccessful courting of a comely shepherdess who remains true to her love. Ornamented with monophonic songs of a folk nature written in the notation of the Gregorian chant, and accompanied by similar but fewer instruments than those used in the *Play of Daniel,* Adam de la Halle's masterpiece was entitled *Play of Robin and Marion.* First performed at the French court of Naples in 1285, this famous work, beginning with a rondeau in triple time to be sung and danced, has a total of twenty-nine numbers—sixteen in triple time and thirteen in duple time. Several tonalities are used. Our records show the tonal center is G major.

The *Play of Daniel* and the *Play of Robin and Marion* are forerunners of opera and of ballet. Most of the numbers are sung; most are solos; most have provision for movement, that is, dance or procession. Until the eighteenth century most ballets continued to have many sung solo and ensemble pieces; even such recent works as Stravinsky's *Pulcinella* have sung sections. Many operas, even today, have ballets.

Following these lyric productions in the thirteenth century, as well as the "Laudi," which Ranieri Fusani organized in Perugia, Italy, in the fourteenth century there were several lyric theatre forms, what with the coming of the *ars nova* to replace the rather constricted formulas in music of the *ars antiqua* and also the move away from improvisation. The restrictions in tempo and dynamics imposed by the Greek poetic forms were not followed so strictly, and even the music used in masses and other religious ceremonies took on some variety. The madrigale, ballate, caccie, trottas, and carols were all sung, but very often they were danced also, and the dramatic circumstances of their performance began to dictate their tempos, their use of solo and group numbers, and orchestra size. We note that many of the dance forms originated in Italy, but that soon they were used at the French courts in literary and artistic productions as part of spectacle-entertainments.

We cannot conclude our consideration of the origin of classic theatrical dancing without further reference to pageants and tournaments. This area of spectacle-entertainment, which frequently has an acrobatic or military aspect to it, often brought an invigorating contrast to the art when it threatened to become effete. The purely physical aspect of mass display may be anathema to the artist, yet without appropriate exploitation of resources of both disciplined muscles and mind, the performer, no matter how inspired, becomes like Bunthorne in Gilbert and Sullivan's *Patience*—"an aesthetic sham." Thus the feudal jousts, the Renaissance horse ballets (and even today the Lipizzaner dressage at the Viennese Riding Academy), the musketeers of Louis XIII, the Olympic Games from Greece onward, even the Medranos, the Tildens, the Babe Ruths and Joe Louises, and on and on, are all in some way related to our story, as they are part of spectacle, which when it is refined, we call art.

As a transition from our discussion of theatrical dance in largely anonymous medieval era to the freer, more experimental, and more personal Renaissance times, it is appropriate to define the earliest European forms, noting also that gradually the solo dances separated from the ensemble dances, pantomime dances separated from processional and figure dances, and duple rhythm eventually became more prevalent than triple time. (See: Appendix 1.)

2

The Renaissance

Court Festivals and Celebrations, and Popular Entertainments

The excitement of living in the Renaissance may well have been comparable to that enjoyed by many of the young and young at heart now living in the planetary age. The rediscovery of a glorious past, which had been veiled (though by no means extinct) for more than 800 years; the experience of life as an adventure rather than a cruel and all-too-brief interlude between cradle and grave; the promise of the future as new worlds in ideas and in physical reality were exposed to many: these new perspectives began to make it a new world indeed for all despite its many limitations. During the Renaissance the themes of lyric theatre spectacle-entertainments and pageants changed from Christian (as they had been in the Middle Ages) to pagan—to Hercules, Jason, Greek mythology, and hedonism, with allusive overtones praising the reigning princes rather than the Prince of Peace.

We have noted that court celebrations, church ceremonies, and popular entertainments have contributed to the spectacle-entertainments that in the 1400s embraced drama, song, and dance. Beginning in Italy and gradually spreading northward, the movement involving exploration of the arts and sciences of the ancient Mediterranean world, as well as the nature of man and his surroundings, was called the Renaissance. Progressively, the cloak of anonymity was removed from the artist-craftsman; the genius of Shakespeare, Monteverdi, and Beaujoyeux enabled drama, music, and dance to begin to assume individuality, although often to this day they have used similar procedures and parallel forms.

7

Although the mass was still the major artistic form, slowly in the Renaissance music began to develop away from direct supervision of the church, though by no means totally away from its influence. The ornate polyphonic style of much Renaissance music, which was virtuosic and exciting on its own terms, would present problems for both forms of lyric theatre—ballet and opera. The solution of some of these problems by court producers such as Beaujoyeux and by musicians such as Monteverdi was what began to make possible the individual development of the sister lyric arts. Before we come to the genesis of these separate forms in the late 1500s, we must investigate the conditions of their gestation.

The 1400s saw the flourishing of exploration and rediscovery, which coincided with a birth of nationalism in England, France, and later in other countries. With the gradual secularization of many institutions, lyric presentations began to move slowly in the direction of specialization. The beginning of printing, first of the Bible and religious works in ancient languages and then of literature in the vernacular by Gutenberg and his successors, and of music by Petrucci in Venice and soon various French printers, helped encourage expansion of the arts in France and Italy. The French in their drama, as in most facets of their lives, appeared more reasoned, stately, Apollonian, and choreographic, all in appreciating divertissement. The Italians were more inspirational, florid, Dionysian, and vocal. The lavish courts of such Italian dynasties as the Florentine Medici and the Mantuan Gonzagas, as well as those of Paris and Burgundy (soon to be reunited in the French kingdom) contributed greatly to all the developing arts. During two centuries of the Renaissance in Europe, various elements of lyric theatre were perfected, until finally under the Valois in France in the 1580s a model "ballet" was produced, the excellence of which was recognized immediately.

After the constant trials and tribulations of medieval times, which included plagues, the chained-in blinders of the feudal system, and the lack of opportunity for individual expression, it was a wonderful relief for the inhabitants of fifteenth-century Florence to have carnival time during the reign of Lorenzo de Medici celebrate "triumphs" in the style and tone of Ovid. In the Renaissance the poet Petrarch composed "triumphs" of love, time, and of death. These works were an inspiration for the processional celebrations that were both fantastic and based on antiquity.

It was a characteristic of the Renaissance that the idea of a unified spectacle-entertainment (including music, dance, drama, and decors) began to take precedence over the medieval plan of alternating pantomime and procession, solo and ensemble, comic and tragic while incorporating the most effective ideas of the earlier loose forms. Although it would be almost the 1600s before the full impact of the creative French logical approach would prevail (even in theory), there were numbers of representations in many courts that contributed to the emergence of ballet as an art form in Paris in the last years of the Valois dynasty, before the coming of the Bourbon monarchs and of professionalism under Louis XIV, Lully, and Beauchamps.

In the matter of the theme (book, story, libretto), the work of a succession of Italian poets was all-important: Dante, Petrarch, Tasso, Ariosto, and Politiano whose *Orfeo* of 1471 was a model for many a subsequent *Orfeo* and related pastorals. In France there was François Villon (1431–1489) above all others. Meanwhile, the political and social changes set in motion by the fall of Constantinople to the Turkish invaders in 1453, with the attendant scattering of Hellenic learning westward, also contributed widening horizons of dramatic action available to producers of spectacle-entertainments.

In music, there was gradual expansion from the traditional set dances whose main dimension was repetition (with elements of variation) to more than twice as many, also capable of variation and including differentiation and specialization. Composers such as Darius Beverini (ca. 1400–1480) brought social dances and various pantomimic and non-pantomimic dances into the spectacles at several courts. The choreographers preceding Beaujoyeux generally are anonymous, although there are several Italians virtually contemporary with Beaujoyeux (originally named Belgiojoso), some of whose work is known to us through contemporary accounts.

In the matter of costumes we have documentation through many paintings of very brilliant marriage celebrations that displayed wonderfully lavish habiliments. One painted by Gozzoli was of Lorenzo de Medici and Clarice Orsini, another was included in the Primavera of Botticelli. The settings—the seven gyrating planets featured in Leonardo da Vinci's *Paradiso,* produced at Pavia, or the decors for various Milanese extravaganzas on which he collaborated—must have been marvellous to behold, as were Rafaelo's imaginative designs in 1519 for Ariosto's pastoral drama, *I Suppositi.* All were successors to earlier pageants and celebrations chronicled by Cranach, Burgkmair, Crivelli, and many other artists.

Court ballets of the fifteenth century were festive occasions with loose sequences of dances based on steps of the conventional ballroom repertory performed in costume, either as divertissements or representing an overall theme. Gradually, the decorations became more and more elaborate and somewhat unified, as did the musical accompaniment. In the early sixteenth century the intermèdes, pageants, and carousels began to be merged with courtly dances, and the relatively brief masquerades were expanded and developed into dramatic entertainments.

One of the many considerations of creative artists and lords of the Renaissance was recovery of the past. In the process of doing this some members of the noble courts began to acquire the notion of history and the conviction that the achievements of their own time were often worth preserving. It is true that it was the seventeenth century before the practice of multiple performances, touring, and revivals of successful works began to be observed, yet concern for the beauties of the time was necessary before the establishment of archives could be considered. In Ferrara in the latter fifteenth century flourished one of the first dancing masters of whose name we are certain—Domenico of Ferrara (ca. 1430–1490). His contemporary Guglielmo Ebreo (di Pesaro), also possibly known as Giovanni Ambrogio (1435–1495), collected a number of Domenico's dances and also at least two from Lorenzo de Medici; he published these with his own dances along with a number of popular tunes in a manual we have today in the Kinkeldey edition. Ebreo's contemporaries and successors included Antonio Cornazano (ca. 1431–1500), Diobono (ca. 1530–1580), Cesare Negri (ca. 1546–1605), and Fabritio Caroso (ca. 1530–1600). The last two and Angelo Gardano published their versions of numerous dance forms, many of which we will discuss shortly, particularly those published by Arbeau in his *Orchésographie* of 1581.

We have found that banquets forming parts of festival celebrations provided occasions for major secular productions designed to contribute to the pleasure of the guests. One famous banquet, the Oath of the Pheasant, was held in Lille in February of 1454; its many pleasures have been chronicled by Olivier de la Marche and Mathieu d'Escouchy. Three huge tables were placed in the banquet hall. On one there was a church with a bell and four singers, who performed with a positiv organ. On the second table there was an enormous pastry containing twenty-eight performers on various instruments, including shawms (early oboes). At the main table three small children and a tenor sang a chanson, and then a shepherd played on a bagpipe. Two mounted trumpets sounded a fanfare; four other trumpets played from behind a green curtain. The adventures of Jason were enacted for the guests of honor: Philip the Good and the Knights of the Golden Fleece who had vowed to undertake a crusade against the Turks. After performances by the groups of the tables, a "stag" was led in ridden by a boy who sang the upper part of a chanson while the "stag" sang the lower part. Also performed were pieces by Dufay (1400–1474) and Binchois (1400–1460) on harp, lute, and flute, some of them mimed with accompaniment. In 1489 Duke Galeazo Visconti of Milan produced another famous ballet of Jason, among many other spectacles.

In the Renaissance, as we noted earlier, many new aspects of living were tolerated and achieved. As gradually the church lost total control of all forms of life and art, the spectacle-entertainments became freer in every way, and the set forms they used became more varied.

Although by the 1500s the sequences of steps in the court basse danse had become fixed in France and in Spain, in Italy they remained somewhat freer as well as more extended and longer. The melodies of the basse danse in Italy were written out, but they were used as an underlying cantus firmus, which could either have a new set of upper parts composed for each new dance use with varying rhythmic patterns, or be accompanied by upper parts that were newly improvised each time the melody was used. Generally, the upper parts were performed by several shawms, while the lower parts were played by the slide trumpet; on some occasions strings also took part. Often the melodies were sung. In Italy, four different rhythms characterized the four general types of the basse danse; a pair of dances was formed with the basse danse and the saltarello, as in France a pair was formed by the basse danse and the pas de Brabant. Also, in Italy the dance masters added the rapid, structured piva and the slower saltarello tedesco, to be used occasionally for contrast in the free dances, balli. Whereas in Italy and France the basse danse was a court social dance, the ballo was a freer dance often used to accompany dramatic action and pantomime.

Meanwhile, what with cultural exchanges expanding as the artistic effects of the Renaissance spread, in 1512 Henry VIII was able to introduce the diverting Italian masque to England (a fact not lost to Shakespeare when he wrote his play on Henry VIII). In France, during the reigns of the vigorous François I and his less effective successors, there was a move toward artistic unity, the themes of dramatic entertainments often featuring the championed lady. Among the creative poets of the period were Du Bellay, Daurat, and Ronsard (1524–1585); among the court musicians were Jannequin, Goudimel, and Gervaise; among the decorator-artists were da Vinci, del Sarto, Clouet, Cellini, and Titian; and the most important producer of festivals was Etienne Jodelle (1532–1573). Together these artists fashioned the early ballet-de-cour, developing it into a suite of entrées with contributing choruses, social dances, and gay and dramatic masquerades performed to music.

What other background do we need to understand the importance of the historic *Le Ballet Comique de la Reine Louise,* which in 1581 epitomized ballet in the Renaissance and at the same time pioneered in the unification

Opening scene from *Le Ballet Comique de la Reine Louise* (Paris, 1581).

of a theme and its presentation balletically? The literary and linguistic work of Jean Antoine de Baïf (1532–1589) has a significant place in the development of structure in the arts, including modern performing arts. He founded the Académie de Sainte Cécile ·in 1570, with the aims of reforming the French language according to rules of the Greeks and of achieving an equilibrium of drama, verse, and dance in theatrical entertainment. This undertaking was patronized by Catherine de Medici, the powerful widow of Henri II and Queen Mother of François II, Charles IX, and Henri III. In French history the name of Catherine de Medici (1519–1589) is particularly unfavorably associated with the divisive wars of religion that took place between the Catholics and the Huguenots during the latter half of the 1500s. However, this cultured Italian consort of Henri II loved to dance, and in 1581, during her ascendancy as Queen Mother, ballet's famous founding work was produced.

One of the main results of Baïf's Académie and the work of the Pléiade of French poets was that musicians began to learn the laws of verse and prosody and apply them in such a way that their accompaniments foreshadowed the dramatic scenes and recitatives of Lully, who was to make mastery of vocal and instrumental articulation a main element in both his ballets and his operas. In addition to the more than thirty set social dance forms that were available to composers and choreographers in the latter sixteenth century, and which could be used with or without singing, there were also the extremely flexible balli or balletti, all of which now helped make possible the production of ballets with dramatic themes that were more tightly and more logically structured than ever before. In France, Baïf helped reinvent the "renaissance of the classic spectacle," the technical part as far as dance forms were concerned, which had been inherited from Arena, Diobono, Ebreo, and others, and which in turn was passed on to such successors as Caroso, Negri, and Gardano. Gradually, the French preference for masquerades and dancing asserted itself in the production of "ballets" during the second half of the sixteenth century, while in these closing years of the Renaissance the Italian preference for singing led to staged madrigals and eventually to opera. In the music of both types of lyric theatre there was much use of imitation and a gradual movement toward polarization of harmony. With these changes the rhythm could be followed more closely, and a melody could be used by the dancer or singer who was a dramatic and lyric protagonist of the choreographer and librettist. At the same time, the significant dominant-tonic cadence in harmony began to influence the development of musical structure and form as such.

The components of early ballets-de-cour were récits (generally vocal solos at the beginning of each act); vers (couplets for various characters, ensembles, and choruses); entrées (elaborately costumed and masked performers executing large maneuvers, or exotic dances, within the frame of the theme); concluding with the "grand ballet."

Familiar from her youth with the Florentine trionfi, Catherine de Medici often sponsored lavish productions and fêtes. The very night the 1572 Massacre of Saint Bartholomew erupted as the most infamous of the French religious catastrophes, the court had enjoyed *The Defense of Paradise* at the Louvre palace that she helped to build. A year later, at the Tuileries, Catherine entertained the Polish ambassadors who had just elected her second son, Henri d'Anjou, king of Poland. The ballet was entitled, appropriately, *Le Ballet des Polonais;* it was a collaboration of French poets and the distinguished international musician, Orlando di Lasso (1532–1594), who provided dances following Italian models of figures and steps developed in the previous hundred years.

Produced in a large temporary theatre with spectators on two sides and King Charles IX and his retinue at one end of the long salle, *Le Ballet des Polonais* began with three entrées—performed by ladies of the court *France, Peace,* and *Prosperity.* Next Silenus and four satyrs pushed forward a large gilt rock on which were perched sixteen of the queen's ladies in waiting, representing the French provinces. Following a brief verse in Latin, the ladies descended from the rock to perform a dance. After a presentation to the king, there was general dancing. The performance took about an hour, and also featured a group of thirty violinists playing while the sixteen ladies paraded through their various figures. Slow and fast dances alternated; the divertissement was given unity by the verses recited between brandos, balli, and balletti. (As a footnote to history we note that fortune, ever fickle, decreed that Henri d'Anjou would be king of France, rather than of Poland, and unfortunately not a very good king, at that.)

Many of the French dances had been imported, modified, and codified in several stages. The social dances and figurations of the steps formed a source of ballet manners and deportment as we have come to know it, particularly as dramatic and artistic meaning and tradition added aesthetic layers to the originals. The producer-choreographer of *Le Ballet des Polonais* was Baldassare di Belgiojoso, soon transformed to Balthasar de Beaujoyeux (ca. 1530–1590). He had come to France as a professional violinist in 1555 in the train of Marshall de Brissac, who a few years earlier had brought the Milanese dancing master Diobono to the French court, along with several other Italian artists (Bracesco, Palvello, and Gallino). In addition to being an excellent musician, Beaujoyeux turned out to be clever and quite agreeable, which contributed to his having thirty years of success in France. The geometry of the choreography in ballets of this period, at times resembling soldiers drilling in military formation, was symbolic in its foundations. The square, representing four seasons or four directions, signified the earth; while the endless circle signified heaven, the octagon signified a fusion of heaven and earth, and a fountain signified purity. The dance language emphasized precision and elegance. Despite a few jumps and turns, widespread use of speed and elevation was over a century away.

While fifteenth-century court banquets had elaborate entremets in which dancing, singing, and drama were combined, and various fêtes during tournaments featured the courts of love and the championed lady, it was only later when these diverse elements were combined under humanistic concepts and principles of structure in the sixteenth century that the ballet-de-cour was born. Baïf, Courville, and the members of his Académie formulated a law involving the equal duration of steps and notes, which we find described by Arbeau (1519–1585). The danse mesurée that resulted could thus be set to musique mesurée. In the sixteenth century these ballets had secular stories, more than mere themes, which usually contained a moral. The composers often composed or arranged the music into a unity that was no longer improvised, and they directed trained musicians. Although generally there was not yet a theatre with a proscenium, the decors, costumes, and sets began to be integrated under the direction of producers, and not improvised as previously. Only the dancing was still in the hands of amateurs (gifted though they often were), under the general supervision of the noble producers who often were the librettists as well.

On Sunday, October 15, 1581 at the grande salle of the Palais Bourbon beginning at 10 P.M. *Circé, ou le Ballet Comique de la Reine Louise* was produced. Beaujoyeux called his presentation a *ballet* because it presented geometrical arrangements of an ensemble of dancers accompanied by diverse instruments and voices; *comique* because of the lovely tranquil, happy (as opposed to tragic) conclusion, and because of the quality of the characters who were mostly divine. The immediate occasion for its production was the marriage King Henri III had arranged for his favorite, the Duc de Joyeuse, and Marguerite, Princesse de Lorraine, sister of King Henri's consort, Queen Louise. Beaujoyeux combined elements of the drama of the balletti, the precision of the figured dances executed by leading nobles who had been thoroughly prepared, the performance by professional musicians, and the fantasy of the entremets, and parodied them after the manner of Tasso's pastoral (which, in turn, was an imitation of Virgil). In Tasso's *Aminta* of 1573, which many educated persons of the time already knew, the author compared the bloody state and its factions with the peaceful countryside and its shepherds. Now Beaujoyeux produced his pastoral story of Circé aided by La Chesnaye, the king's almoner who wrote the verses in French; Lambert de Beaulieu, Thibault de Courville, and Jacques Salmon, who composed the music; and Jacques Patin, who managed the decorative elements; the production was chronicled by Clouet. The language and the taste of *Le Ballet Comique de la Reine Louise* were quite French, but the thematic ideas sprouted from Italian sources. (A word here about the decorative element in spectacle-entertainment, first provided by floats. When lyric theatre began to have permanent theatres, the decorative element not only included sets, but "machines" which originated as huge cranes used to transport gods to and from earth as might be appropriate to the action. The Italian artist Brunelleschi was an important pioneer in this field. These magical machines we still have with us.)

We are told that *Le Ballet Comique de la Reine Louise* took about five hours to perform, although this may have included intermissions and the time spent in social dancing after the conclusion of the dramatic action. The improvisational state of theatrical machinery as set in the Salle des Cariatides of the Palais Bourbon made it inevitable that the dramatic action was interrupted while the scenic dispositions were changed. Only three instrumental and nine vocal musical numbers to the work are extant, while probably five numbers are missing, including the overture and one interlude. The total musical performance could not have taken much more than one hour; however, there were several spoken interludes.

This work has been claimed as a ballet by ballet historians and as an opera by opera historians. No one doubts that it was lyric theatre, including singing, dancing, and drama. In any event it does belong to the history of ballet, just as do such other early lyric pieces as the religious *Play of Daniel* and the secular *Play of Robin and Marion*. Even today ballet has not totally abjured singing; even today opera has not turned its back on theatrical dancing. Each uses the comprehensive resources of the performing arts as appropriate in particular works.

The existing numbers of *Le Ballet Comique de la Reine Louise* are rather short and not as sophisticated as we normally expect from this period, though the very fact that many of the performers were amateurs may help explain this fact. (Compare, for example, contemporary madrigals by

Marenzio and Vecchi, which were used in stage productions, and one can note the differences.) For one thing, most of the melodies are simple. Then, the sense of tonality and the architecture of the harmony is not very developed: only four tonalities are used in the twelve remaining numbers. The orchestration is quite developed, however, what with flutes (recorders), cromornes (oboes), trumpets, cornets, trombones, harps, lutes, lyres, snare drum, organ, and five strings (usually three violins, a viola, and a bass)—more than thirty instrumentalists, plus singers. It is appropriate, while speaking of the texture of the ballet, to observe that the versification follows the principles of Baïf, which contributed to the audience's comprehension of the story. We have noted the heterogeneous standard of the performing abilities of the participants, which probably deterred the creators from a greater variety in the roles they imagined. The music in itself is generally homophonic, and though it is naively charming, it lacks progression and definition.

At one end of the salle sat Henri III and his family. The main floor surface was for the performers; however, reputedly more than 9,000 persons were crowded around the salle and its balcony. On Henri's right hand the Arbor of Pan was constructed, including a grotto and illuminated trees. On his left hand was placed an arbor for the musicians, "the Golden Vault," which was framed by clouds. At the other end of the salle from the king was placed the garden and chateau of Circé, the enchantress. At the corners there were passages that permitted dancers, personages, and floats (cars) to pass in and out. From a recent printing of the 1582 souvenir edition of *Le Ballet Comique de la Reine Louise* we can learn why this grand spectacle entertainment is so important in the history of Western lyric theatre.

After the playing of an overture, performed dolce, the prologue began as a terrified Sieur de la Roche came fleeing from the chateau of Circé. This gentleman in waiting to Catherine, clothed in silver, caught his breath and addressed Henri III in verse, "L'Harangue du Gentilhomme Fugitif." After a few thoughts on the nature of vanity and the hope of happiness, he enquired of the King of Peace and Abundance whether His Majesty had seen Circé, and if so would His Lordship please save him from her wiles. He no sooner disappeared than Circé (Mlle. de Saint-Mesme) came forward, reproaching herself for permitting her "dear de la Roche" to cast off his enchantment as an animal and resume his human form, following which she retired to sulk in her garden.

The action continued with six verses of a marchlike song performed by parading Sirens and a Triton, their tails being gathered on their arms. The chorus in the Golden Vault responded. When the Sirens and the Triton left, a large float was brought before the king by a group of Hippocampes. On the float, which featured a working fountain, Glaucis and Thétis were surrounded by twelve golden, jeweled noble nymphs, including Henri's Queen Louise and the new bride (her sister, Princesse Marguerite de Lorraine) as well as the duchesses de Guise, Nevers, d'Aumale, and Joyeuse. Accompanying this moving fountain were the twelve marching pages illuminating the entrée and the eight marching Tritons who performed on the lyre, lute, flute, harp, and other instruments, and who also sang. The Tritons replied in chorus as the divinities, Glaucis (bass) and Thétis (treble), engaged in a dialogue of eight verses.

The rapid melody of the premier ballet was played by two lines of five violinists dressed in white satin enriched by gold pieces, and the twelve pages danced with the twelve Nymphs. The Nymphs took their decorative positions during the first part of the instrumental interlude; during the second part they turned toward the king and performed the figures of their dance. The Nymphs began in three lines, with Queen Louise as their focus—three in the front, six in the middle line, and three in the rear. This first entrée had twelve separate geometric figures. At the point in the scene when the spectators heard the bell song (based on an old folk tune), Circé fumed out of her garden, and touched the dancers, now in two lines en croissant, with her magic wand, making them rigidly immobile. Then she returned to her chateau.

In the entrée de Mercure the part of the messenger of the gods was performed by Sieur du Pont (bass), gentleman of the king's bed chamber. In his hand Mercury held the caduceus, his hat had gilded wings, his cape was a violet cloth of gold, and his costume of Spanish satin incardine had gold finishings. Following a clap of thunder, Mercury descended from a cloud and delivered a flowery speech. Then he sprinkled the Nymphs with a holy herb, which enabled them to continue their dance. In the finale of part I Circé returned to philosophize and mesmerize the dancing figures again including Mercury himself, as she led them in a column marching two by two like marionettes into her garden, which was already full of courtiers she had transformed into animals.

At the beginning of part II is the sixth extant musical number—the deuxième intermède—an entrée of eight Satyrs conducted by the Lord of Saint-Laurens. Their parade was accompanied by "new and gay" music played by flutes. An extant engraving testifies to the producer's knowledge of Hellenic costumes found on archeological cups and sarcophagi. After the Satyrs toured the salle, with the chorus of the Golden Vault singing responsively and with echo effects after each of their couplets, there began the entrée of the Dryads (in an action anticipating Shakespeare's "Birnum Wood come to Dunsinane" from *Macbeth*). Within a small forest on the float sat four pastoral virgins. The Satyrs and the Nymphs both sang. The Nymph Opis sang a solo to King Henri and then addressed Pan, who promised to help rescue the captives from Circé. In the troisième intermède four Virtues (in long dresses covered with gold stars) serenaded King Henri; two ladies played lutes and two sang. After each of the seven verses, twelve instrumentalists in the Golden Vault played a ritornello. Then a large serpent drew in the chariot of Pallas. Pallas called for Jupiter, who appeared from heaven on an eagle, as the deus ex machina, accompanied by joyous singing and the instrumentalists from the Golden Vault (number 10). In number 11 Pan led a group of Satyrs armed with sticks, as the assembled company attacked the chateau of Circé. (The organ music accompanying the beginning of this scene has been lost.) In the finale (number 12) played by the violins, Jupiter presented his prisoner to King Henri and introduced Minerva and Mercury to the monarch. The Dryads danced joyously, and brought the Nymphs from Circé's chateau, and the entire company rejoiced in a grand ballet with many figures.

Two by two all the dancers came to the center of the salle, first Queen Louise and her sister (Princesse Marguerite). After each of the fifteen figures executed by the large company, all turned their faces to King Henri III. This was an "overture" to a large ballet of forty geometrical figures[1]—squares, circles, and triangles—following which the dancers presented symbolic medals to the great personages. Queen Louise offered her King a dauphin (coin) to receive an heir, and there were other presentations of a witty nature, reminding one of ritual give and take in medieval celebrations. Presumably, after the moresca there was a long night of social dancing.

Of the seventeen numbers of *Le Ballet Comique de la Reine Louise* that exist or are accounted for, thirteen were vocal. Although only three numbers actually specifically involved elaborate ballet figures—squares, triangles, circles, etc.—every entrée made use of parade and march elements of ceremonial choreographic design and movement, and there were some exotic scenes. Duple rhythm was in the majority.

The verses sung by Circé were influenced by characteristics of the French poets of the Pléiade, including themes of allegory and moral ideology. The familiar figure, Circé, represented the spirit of evil; the nymphs, made up of natural forces, represented the spirit of good. Circé changed into monsters the four who gathered herbs: earth, air, fire, water.

Le Gentilhomme Fugitif is both Ulysses and the eternal wandering soul. By keeping Ulysses captive and having children with him, Circé gives birth to the Four Seasons. In all this variety, Beaujoyeux kept in mind a unity that most masquerades, pastorales, tournaments, festivals, and the like did not attain and he was widely praised for the success of this spectacle. Yet there were no immediate successors to this extravaganza, partly because of the uncertain state of the body politic in France, and also because of the enormous cost of the production, which was performed only once.

It is necessary once again to emphasize the importance of the publication in 1588 in Langres of Thoinot Arbeau's (Jehan Tabourot) *Orchésographie*. In dialogue form not unlike that of the Roman author Lucian, Arbeau gives clear directions to his young student for the performance of thirty social dances of the time. By 1588 many of these dances were already in the repertoire of stage dancing, many of the others were to be adopted by the stage, and a few were obsolete holdovers from a previous era.[2]

Theatrically, the two centuries of the Renaissance proper formed an exciting period in France, Italy, and England, as well as other Western countries: for the discovery of printing and engraving, the rediscovery of single vanishing point perspective, the emergence of artists from anonymity, the beginning of the commedia dell'arte, the modern theatre in Ferrara and the Palladian theatre at Vicenza, and for the model of *Le Ballet Comique de la Reine*.

Ballet came to be known by various names—ballets-de-cour, ballets-comiques, ballets-mascarades—all of which added up to confusion (just as French politics did). The important point is that no definitive forward steps were taken, despite Beaujoyeux and the success of *Le Ballet Comique de la Reine Louise*, until Lully and Beauchamps came on the scene. All the Renaissance spectacle-entertainments tended toward divertissement. Generally, the lack of a central organizer meant that even if the dramatic theme was carefully selected, there was little unity between the work of several producers, decorators, composers, and dancers, despite the presence of musicians who were professionals. (For the dance forms, see: Appendix 2.) (While Catherine de Medici was presiding over French destiny, Elizabeth I was ruling England, and in the historic year of 1581 entertained her unsuccessful French suitor, the Duc d'Alençon, with a masque entitled *The Four Foster Children of Desire*.)

3

The Seventeenth Century

The Early Baroque

Coming between the Renaissance and the period of Classicism, the Baroque Era, named after elegant extravagance (or perhaps extravagant elegance), covers the century and a half after 1600. During the early part of the seventeenth century the producers of spectacle-entertainments were still diverse, and their presentations were not often focused. But during the long reign of France's great monarch Louis XIV (1638–1715) there emerged a great artist whose contributions to the lyric theatre have been felt ever since, Jean-Baptiste Lully (1632–1687). The French ballet of the early Baroque involved a number of experiments that merged gradually into the still vaguely defined ballet-de-cour, best exemplified by the many brilliant collaborations of Lully the musician and Pierre Beauchamps (1631–1719) the choreographer. When joined by Molière, the masterful comic playwright, this imaginative trio produced a series of immortal comédie-ballets. The death of Molière and other circumstances led to Lully's development of tragédies-en-musique, always with the full cooperation of Beauchamps. In the period after Lully's early death there developed in France the opera ballets and ballet operas of Campra and Pécourt, followed by productions of Jean-Philippe Rameau, whose brilliant stage works profited from the first of many outbursts of ebullient virtuosity that dancers were to display once they became fully professional under Lully and Beauchamps.

In the first half of the seventeenth century, court feste and pastorales in Italy, court ballets in France, and court masques in England all attempted to unify the arts, most particularly the lyric theatre. To achieve this, the forms gradually were separated into opera (with dancing) and ballet (usually with singing), with both for a time retaining some dramatic scenes. It can be said that the ballet-de-cour was the principal forerunner of modern ballet, whereas the pastorale influenced the evolution of opera as we know it. By the middle of the seventeenth century there were also other than court entertainments that assumed increasing importance, for example, the effective Venetian and Neapolitan operas (often comic in subject matter, they made small use of the dance and the chorus), and popular theatre. During the period of the late Renaissance, Luther's reform movement against the religious establishment caused political, moral, physical, and artistic losses, which were only partly recovered during the decades of the seventeenth century Counter-Reformation. Budding nationalism was often at odds with the cultural elitist and autocratic centralizing, unifying ideals of Lully and his patron—though while Louis XIV reigned individuality was directed toward what was politically *and* culturally valid.

Italy was a purveyor of leaders in the early Baroque years just as it had been in the Renaissance, in art, literature, music, and spectacle. Among the poets who contributed to lyric theatre were Tasso, Politiano, Striggio, and Ottavino Rinuccini (1560–1621). Rinuccini, who attended the performance in 1581 in Paris of *Le Ballet Comique de la Reine Louise,* in 1608 at the Mantuan court produced a lavish *Ballet de la Nuit,* which effectively employed the new elaborate cloud effects for which Italian decorators and engineers became famous, along with other new theatrical devices. Several of Rinuccini's collaborations with Monteverdi were important artistic achievements.

In France and Italy during the seventy-five years between Beaujoyeux's productions and those of Lully, there were a number of important court fêtes and ballets. For these spectacle-entertainments (remember that in 1741 Handel called his own *Messiah* "a grand entertainment"), mostly performed by members of the nobility, many of the collaborators were anonymous, but we will give credit to those whose contributions can be traced. The character and quality of the dancing in these spectacle-entertainments varied from stylized to folk, from slow to fast, from noble to comic to vulgar, and from solo to group. Until after the middle of the seventeenth century, however, there was no "school," no tradition.

Published evidence has the five positions of the feet as established by 1725.[1] Yet although we know they did not exist in 1581, in the decades before 1700 they were in the process of formulation. They may not have been codified in 1652 when Lully began his long and productive association with Beauchamps, but they most certainly existed well before the end of Lully's life in 1687. Pierre Beauchamps is generally regarded by his pupils Feuillet and Rameau as the dancer who codified them, though Feuillet and Rameau were the first to publish these positions in the early eighteenth century as the basis of all ballet. Scales, by which term we indicate major or minor tonalities in all their variations, also were fully established on a diatonic basis essentially within Lully's lifetime.

While some Italian early Baroque composers (Gallilei, Vecchi, Caccini, and Peri) were ingeniously "bending" the madrigal and also inventing recitative, Monteverdi (1567–1642) turned his talents to dramatic intermedii, balli, favole, and dramma per musica, with themes from Ovid and other classic poets beautifully rendered into operatic libretti. He saw immediately the need for a new approach, and his unifying efforts on behalf of the emerging lyric theatre provided a dramatic aesthetic for ballets and operas that his colleagues and followers made more specific in their own lyric theatre. Altogether, Monteverdi's expressive use of the entire range of music and spectacle created a serious basis that Lully and his successors would embellish and develop. Using both the stile antico and the stile moderno, Monteverdi deployed a variety of musico-dramatic procedures in a continuum of recitative-arioso-aria-chorus into which he also introduced a more idiomatic and specialized writing for particular instruments, which he named specifically in his *Orfeo* and on other occasions.

Monteverdi's effective musical sequence, which worked so well in *Orfeo* (1607), became a recognized procedure for a number of ballets, and in fact nontheatrical forms as well. It was during Monteverdi's lifetime that the famous Cremona group of instrument makers began to give their instruments modern shapes and modern sonorities. Monteverdi used the new stile concertato, and he emphasized use of harmonic polarization involved in basso continuo that was to help guide composers toward providing melodies and rhythms for expressive solo and ensemble dancing. He also appreciated the twin importance of dramatic dance and divertissement in spectacle festivities, and used dance scenes and songs effectively in various parts of his operas as well as in such other works as *Il Ballo dell'Ingrate* (1608). Although he was not the first composer to use this technique, certainly he was extremely effective. In a number of instances we have letters from Monteverdi to the producers of his works for the lyric theatre in which the composer (like Gluck and Wagner after him) described stage action he considered indicated and appropriate.

In addition to the many contributions Monteverdi and his followers made to the tonal and musical-dramatic development of the lyric arts, we note that Italy was also the center of important activity in the theory and practice of defining theatre space itself. The process involved republication of the classic work of Vitruvius, construction of Vicenza's amazing Teatro Olimpico (1582), development of the proscenium, clever devices for lighting, and initiation of the science and art of the great theatre machinists, including Torelli and Rivani who followed in the footsteps and developed the seminal ideas of Brunelleschi.

Vigorous activity in the performing arts in Italy continued at the several ducal courts of Milan, Mantua, Ferrara, Turin, and Florence. On the occasion of the marriage of Fernando Gonzaga, Duke of Mantua, with Caterina de Medici (sister of Cosimo II of Florence) on February 6, 1616 there was a magnificent festival in the Teatro Ducale of the Palazzo Uffizi entitled *La Liberazione di Tirreno e d'Arnea, Autori del Sangue Toscano*. We are fortunate that the accomplished French artist Jacques Callot (1592–1635) has chronicled this spectacle decorated by Giorgio Parigi (with music probably by Marco Gagliano), in which Amor rescues the couple imprisoned by Circé, and the pair then goes on to found the Italian state of Tuscany. (Callot's inspired chronicles of such commedia dell'arte types as Scaramouche are further mementos of seventeenth-century spectacle.) The language of the performers was Italian, but predictably the mythic theme of *Tirreno e Arnea* came from the golden age of Roman letters, from Virgil and from Ovid. At the finale the spectators rose and joined with the protagonists in social dancing, a custom that would continue at court spectacles until the reforms of Lully and his collaborators.

At the wedding celebration in 1600 in Florence of the French King Henri IV and Marie de Medici there was presented a pastoral, *Orfeo,* words by Rinuccini and music by Peri and Caccini. To judge from the music and other surviving documents, this very attractive work was rather a more interesting precursor of Monteverdi's Italian opera ballets than a successor to such French works as *Le Ballet Comique de la Reine Louise.* Among Monteverdi's many followers and successors in the lyric theatre were Heinrich Schütz (1585–1672), whose *Orfeo* (1638) was a German landmark: P. F. Cavalli (1602–1676), whose forty operas for Italy and France included *Giasone, Serse,* and *Ercole Amante;* Luigi Rossi (1598–1653), famous for his *Orfeo;* Francesco Sacrati (1590–1650), best known for his opera *La Finta Pazza;* P. A. Cesti (1623–1669), whose grandiose *Il Pomo d'Oro* (1667) was seen first in Vienna; and, later in the century, Alessandro Scarlatti (1660–1725). Most of these operas were on serious classical themes, mythological or historical, although Scarlatti also adopted stories from Boccaccio and other literary figures of the Renaissance.

The age of Louis XIV has been justifiably hailed as a period of great cultural achievement in Western Europe, and the codification of ballet during the long reign of the Sun King is certainly not the least of its many accomplishments. Yet even Lully and Beauchamps and their many splendid collaborators probably could not have produced what they did without the continuous fertile developments during the seventy-five years between Beaujoyeux's *Le Ballet Comique de la Reine Louise* and the accession to the French throne of the forceful, pleasure-loving monarch whose wide-ranging activities provided models for the rest of Europe in almost every conceivable area of activity. During the reigns of Louis XIV predecessors, Henri IV and Louis XIII, such musicians as Filippo d'Aglié (1600–1667), Antoine Boësset (1587–1643) and his son Jean, Etienne Mouliné (1600–1670), and Jean Cambefort (1605–1661) collaborated with G. B. Balbi (1600–1655) and other successors of Beaujoyeux, as well as French and Italian artists and machinists such as LaBelle and Torelli. Their grand ballets had as many as thirty entrées[2]; other typical ballets of the period had about twenty[3]; the ballets masquerades were somewhat shorter.

We have already noted that in the Renaissance the themes of the spectacles were no longer church-inspired, but were usually adapted from classical mythology or from history, with allegorical overtones. We have observed the gradual increase in the use of professional musicians to create, direct, and perform the music. Finally, trained ballet masters began to replace noble functionaries or poets as producers of ballet. The new forms of social dancing of the time were used in theatrical entertainments. These were greatly expanded from the four or five dance forms originally sanctioned by the church, to over thirty different pantomimic and figured dances performed to instrumental or sung accompaniment. The designers in the new theatres, backed by huge court budgets, brought an end to improvisation by offering a series of dramatic stage pictures that fit the time and action.

During the first decades of the seventeenth century the structure of the ballet-de-cour in France assumed some stability and musical forms began to have greater variety. Just as composers realized they could use elements of the past and/or their own imagination, and as the expressive possibilities of the major and minor scales were recognized, the role of the choreographer was strengthened and defined. Then as the five basic positions of the feet were employed and their possibilities, technically and expressively, began to be explored, that role was expanded.

Cloud effects were used effectively to enhance the theme of the approach, reign, and flight of Night and its attendant pleasures in productions designed by Francini and other descendents of the innovative Florentine artist, Filippo Brunelleschi. There were also divertissement ballets, ballets comiques in which pastoral and mythological subjects were used. These and the ballets melodramatiques, with music by Pierre Guédron (1565–1621) and Gabriel Bataille (1574–1630), such as *Alcine* (1610) and the lavish *La Délivrance de Renaud* (1617), were all forms of the evening-long ballets-de-cour.

The humanitarian Henri IV was assassinated in 1610, just as his self-centered predecessor Henri III had been twenty-one years earlier. This noble, dedicated French king, however, devoted his two decades on the throne to healing many of the wounds resulting from the French religious wars of the previous half-century. The reign of Louis XIII (1610–1643), which began with the regency of his mother Marie de Medici (so well chronicled by the artist Rubens), was one in which the arts once again made considerable advances, often based on Italian models. French rulers used the diverting arts in their seduction of the nobles' leisure time (both as participants in the numerous divertissements and as spectators in the more unified productions), lest the nobles become restless and try to retrieve some of the power they were losing to the newly centralized state. Louis XIII is documented as being extremely involved in the production of ballets, in several of which he performed alongside his dear friend the Duc de Luynes; the king even composed the music for *Le Ballet de la Merlaison* (1635). Among the professional musicians who composed much of the music for ballets during the reigns of Henri IV and Louis XIII were Jacques Maudit (1557–1627), Antoine Francisque (1570–1605), Charles Chevalier (1550–1620), and François Chancy (1600–1656). It was during these years that gradually the professionalism of the musicians began to show results, both in execution and in form, as for the first time an overture was played before the action started.

There were theatres in half a dozen Parisian palaces, although none was very well equipped. The commedia dell'arte was infusing vigorous comedy and new humanity into the classic themes of ballet and drama. France became the center of ballet because the art was favored by royalty, and later because its structure and survival was assured by an active academy. Usually, the ballet plots continued to be rather thin pretexts for divertissement, yet the performers, musicians (vocal and instrumental), dancers, and actors were used with imagination, according to contemporary accounts. For example, the musicians performing the overture would often parade, masked and costumed, across the stage to a vantage point from which they could see as they played, and also on occasion descend to take

La Décoration du Palais d'Apolon.

Representé et Jnventé par Iaques Torelli de Fano en Jtalie, et gravé par Aueline.

Giacomo Torelli's decoration for the Palace of Apollo, a scene from Francesco Sacrati's *La Venere gelosa* (Venice, 1643). Showing dancers, singers, and four cloud machines, this Parisian engraving illustrates Torelli's talents, often used in the theatrical works of Lully. (*Courtesy of the Harvard Theatre Collection*) an active, choreographed part in the spectacle itself. Later, during the minority of Louis XIV, his mother, Anne of Austria (Louis XIII's widow), was regent and Cardinal Louis Mazarin (1602–1661) set an Italian tone in spectacles at the French court, inviting the famous artist-engineer Giacomo Torelli (1600–1678) to supervise lavish productions choreographed by Giovanni Battista Balbi (competing with and complementing other attractive productions by Gissey and Belleville, who were native Frenchmen). The brilliant revival in 1645 on the proscenium stage of the Louvre of Sacrati's comic opera *La Finta Pazza* (four years after its very successful Venetian premiere) was supervised by Torelli; it featured a number of exotic entrées with slow and fast dances in alternation. Two years later some spectators found Rossi's *Orfeo* static and overlong, but the Italian scenic influence continued in French productions supervised by Torelli, and by the machinists, Gaspare Vigarani (1586–1663), and his son, Carlo.

Other important French musicians who continued to contribute to court spectacles despite the Italian artistic invasion accentuated by Mazarin when he succeeded Richelieu as prime minister of France in 1642 were Michel Mazuel (1600–1660), C. C. Dassoucy (1605–1677), Louis de Mollier (1613–1688), Verpré (1610–1665), and Michel Lambert (1610–1696). This last was not only one of Lully's good friends and teachers, he was his father-in-law. However, it was not until Lully and his colleagues applied their combined talents to the form that ballet began to develop Aristotelian qualities of unity that the French theatre and to some extent the English theatre were beginning to embrace. In France this coincided with a rationalist aesthetic characteristic of Descartes.

In the late Renaissance the inspiration of French and Italian poets, which had been based on enchantment, allegory, mythology, and flattery, tended to become formula-ridden and somewhat repetitious. Much of the vocal music declined in vigor, despite new forms inspired by the dance. Not so in England, where the imaginative charades and masques were begun prior to the end of the War of the Roses (1485), during a period when the English court rivaled the Burgundian court as a feudal center of knightly pageantry. When in 1485 Henry Tudor returned to England from exile, he initiated a number of revels, games, entremets, masques, and ballets similar to masquerades and grand ballets he had witnessed in France. His heir, Henry VIII (1491–1547), early on musical, lusty, courageous, and sensitive, delighted in revels of many kinds, and encouraged productions featuring song and dance, drama, and decoration. It was probably Henry's ambition for England to lead in every way that accounted for his sponsorship of the Italian masquerade at epiphany of 1512.

Henceforth the English court masques were popular for more than a century. Although their lavishness faded due to budgetary priorities, they were reputed to have pleased Queen Elizabeth greatly. We know from the Fitzwilliam Virginal Book and other manuscript collections of the age of the many musical forms that were available to the composers of the English masques, and we know from eye-witness accounts the names of those that were danced. The pavane, gaillard, gigue, allemande, volta, and courante were found among them, yet the surviving manuscripts do not tell us much about the dances themselves. In the 1590s Gray's Inn had a tradition of presenting masques, and one shrovetide *Proteus and the Adamantine Rock* was performed for Elizabeth. It featured a prologue of song and speech, followed by the masqued entrée, the dances of the masque, the revels (a sort of grand ballet interlude in which the entire assembly participated), a concluding speech, and a chorus for the performers, which brought the spectacle to a close. In 1600 a Mrs. Fiske led a Wedding Maske before the queen, in which, according to a witness, first eight ladies danced, then eight more, with the music provided by "Apollo."

In *The Court Masque,* Enid Welsford has compared and clarified a defining element in French and English theatrical dance at this time (see Bibliography). The English grand masque was the main feature of the performance: in it one or more disguised nobles would execute a specially prepared dance. The grand masque was placed near the center of the evening's entertainment, to be followed by general revels (social dancing involving the entire assembly), then by the concluding dramatic speech and song, and perhaps after this a final dance of the masquers. In France, however, the elaborately costumed grand ballet usually came as a climactic finale, after which the entire company of performers would join in the moresca, and general social dancing followed.

In 1603 Ben Jonson (1572–1637) became the poet of the royal Jacobean revels, and composed a classic, enchanted pastoral, *Satyr.* Two years later began his incomparably brilliant series of masques created in full partnership with the architect Inigo Jones (1572–1661).[4] Together with young Ferrabosco, Thomas Campion, Matthew Locke, and other composers, they elevated the genre to a height probably never again equaled. Jonson, a younger colleague of Shakespeare, and Jones, who had learned considerable of the art of Callot, the Parigi, della Bella, Serlio, Palladio, and Peruzzi, reintegrated into England the wonderful plastic imagination of the late Italian Renaissance.

The same James I who was responsible for the pioneering, grandly sonorous, and, for its time, very scholarly version of the Bible had as his consort Anne of Denmark. Because of her wish to appear in a performance the

Masque of Blackness was presented in 1605. The story of this brilliant masque by Jonson and Jones is as follows: Oceanus and Niger arrive at the English court. Niger explains how his daughters (played by Queen Anne and her train) fell into despair when they heard of the great beauty of a group of nymphs living elsewhere, and how they have been wandering, hoping to be cured of their "blackness." The Moon goddess appears to inform the spectators that they have arrived in Britannia, where the King's rays are of a force to blanch an Ethiopian. For the delight of the audience Jones provided a varied landscape and also an exciting ocean, through and over which the travelers journeyed.

　　In successive years Jonson and Jones imagined a series of beautiful and dramatic masques, and the form was successful right down to the English Revolution. Among the most notable were Milton's *Comus,* with music by Lawes, presented in 1634, and the Jones-Davenant *Britannia Triumphant* of 1638. One of the final Whitehall masques, sponsored by Charles I, was the extremely handsome, though complicated, *Salmacida Spolia,* produced in 1640. The English Rebellion and Cromwell's Commonwealth in the middle of the seventeenth century probably had some salutary effects, but overall, the arts suffered a setback for many decades. Eventually, George Frideric Handel (1685–1759) brought English opera (in Italian) to a supreme pinnacle, and John Weaver (1673–1760) profited from the work of Beauchamps to give character to English stage dancing.

Lully and Beauchamps

Returning to developments in France, we come to the lyric theatre's central figure in the seventeenth century—Jean-Baptiste Lully, born in Florence as Giovanni Battista Lulli. His artistic career can be divided into three periods of activity. The first comprised eight years as a developing ballet composer; the second, eight years as a master composer of comédie-ballets with Molière; and the final period, fifteen years as a composer primarily of tragédie-lyriques (operas). Some seventeen ballets, fifteen operas, and about seventeen other lyric works form Lully's impressive legacy to the performing arts. His position as the musical and performing arts dictator in France was consolidated only in 1672, but from the time he first met Louis XIV in 1653 his multiple talents were appreciated and began to be rewarded. Quite simply, Lully knew how both to please the king and to proclaim his glory in artistic terms. He earned his position, and his reputation has been well deserved. Lully was not only a fine musician and a clever dancer. He was a good judge of talent and an

Lully. From a painting by Pierre Mignard in the Musée Condé, Chantilly.

excellent producer and administrator. Both by his personal leadership and by his foresight in strengthening L'Académie Royale de Musique and L'Académie Royale de Danse he solidified France's position as the great exponent of ballet and opera, a position it has aspired to ever since, even in periods when it was rightly claimed by other nations.

Lully's influence on all forms of the performing arts was profound. He set an example by being a hard worker, both in his works for the stage and in his other music. Our records show him fully occupied with producing premieres from 1653 until his death, with only 1663 unaccounted for. In almost every one of his stage productions he was assisted by the choreographer Pierre Beauchamps, a true collaborator. There is an interesting parallel to be drawn from the careers of Beaujoyeux and Lully. Both were Italian musicians brought to the French court, one in the sixteenth century, the other in the seventeenth. The difference in their accomplishments lies in the high quality of Lully's collaborators, in the very strong support he received from Louis XIV, and in such imponderables as his adaptability.

Lully was brought to France in 1646 to serve Mademoiselle Montpensier and to converse with her in Italian. His remarkable musical gifts were soon recognized, and he became a member of the royal string orchestra, rising to be its conductor by 1652. Although he had quickly and jealously been given the pejorative appellation "le Florentin," Lully abandoned many of his personal and artistic Italianisms, and became more French than most of the native-born French composers. (In later years it was said he accused his rival Marc-Antoine Charpentier of being too influenced by Carissimi.) Lully drilled his chamber ensemble until it was famed for its precision, always a hallmark in the performances he conducted. In 1653 he collaborated with Cambefort and Boësset to compose parts of the important production, Le Ballet de la Nuit, and also took part as a dancer, performing at the side of Louis XIV himself. The king's debut as a performer (in the first of twenty-eight ballets, mostly to music by Lully) had taken place in 1651. Louis XIV, who was six years younger than Lully, loved to dance, and he appreciated Lully's many gifts and wit. Soon Lully was named court composer, with other honors and responsibilities to follow, including ennoblement. As a particular compliment to Lully, the king danced the leading role in Le Ballet de la Galanterie du Temps (1656), the first work for which Lully composed all the music. It is important to note that Louis XIV's long reign brought considerable stability to a country that needed it; however, his political and artistic pretensions cost large sums. Raising the necessary funds entailed burdensome taxes that weakened the French economy and reduced incentive in the commercial areas, which badly needed encouragement.

Generally, until after 1660 the music for the spectacles was composed by several musicians, and this disunifying practice was even continued in many theatres into the eighteenth century and beyond. Gradually, however, Lully achieved both unity and expressivity. He created the celebrated French style, using bolder harmonies than many of his predecessors, more colorful orchestration, notes inégales, and a variety of forms that seem monotonous today only because we have lost touch with the true performance practice of his time. His overtures—in ABA form, slow–fast/ fugal–slow—were the models of the French overture. His logical development of the récit-song-dance continuum was an effective extension of Monteverdi's procedures. His dance tunes were well constructed, flowing yet exact, melodious, graceful, supported throughout by harmony that clearly knew where it was going. They were not over-ornamented during his lifetime; this was done only by later interpreters, whose efforts completely changed the works' character.

In his ballets Lully used the following forms, in order of frequency: bourrées, minuets, sarabandes, gavottes, canaries, chaconnes, courantes, gaillards, and loures. When in the 1670s he turned mostly to composing tragédie-lyriques, Lully's favorite dance form became the minuet, though the bourrée, sarabande, canaries, march, and chaconne were also frequently heard in his operas. In the 1650s a new style of ballet had begun, which was the result of the collaboration of the poet Isaac de Benserade (1613–1691), working with the choreographer Beauchamps, the producer Saint-Aignan, Molière, and Lully. Charles Silin's admirable study, *Benserade and his Ballets de Cour* (see Bibliography) discusses a number of these imaginative works, noting that Benserade brought not only a new brilliance to the text, but also a witty touch of sarcasm, which has always pleased the French public.

Part of Mazarin's celebration of final victory over the rebellious nobles of the Fronde, the aforementioned *Le Ballet de la Nuit* was first performed in 1653 in the Salle du Petit Bourbon, and was a very successful, grandiose work that had to be repeated six times; it is the earliest extant ballet with music by Lully. In addition to the king, who performed his favorite role, that of Apollo, a number of nobles and seventy-two professional dancers (more male than female) participated, including the choreographer Beauchamps, Mollier, Verpré, and Lully. A large number of professional musicians played. From overture to finale, Le Ballet de la Nuit lasted almost all night, which we have seen was not unusual for major events. Ballets provided excellent diversion, and excellent distraction. Organized in four parts, it was made up of mimed entrées, dances, recitatives, solos, choruses, and the grand ballet involving spectators as well as the aristocratic and professional performers. The forty-three entrées were divided into four acts, or "vigils": dusk to 9 P.M., with fourteen entrées; 9 to 12 P.M., with six entrées; midnight to 3 A.M., with thirteen entrées; 3 to 6 A.M., with ten entrées. In the second part there were old-fashioned forms such as courantes and branles, as well as exotic forms such as Spanish sarabandes. There were mythological entrées, mimed entrées, a series of transformations showing Paris, nightmares, and a return to reality. Then, as Night completed its cycle, glorious Dawn, represented by Louis XIV himself, arrived surrounded by Honor, Grace, Love, Courage, Favor, Renown, and Peace.

At the Salle du Petit Bourbon in 1654, in the ballet of the opera *Les Noces de Pelée et Thétis,* Louis XIV and thirty nobles, along with a similar number of professionals, performed ten entrées as divertissements between the acts of Carlo Caproli's opera on a mythological theme of Ovid, which Mazarin had imported from Italy. The ballet was produced by Benserade and Saint-Aignan, with the attractive visual elements again designed by Torelli. Beauchamps was the ballet master, and Lully took part in a number of capacities. The king danced in six of ten entrées, appearing as

Apollo. The theme of the opera and the ballet was the travails Thétis and Pelée underwent before they could be wed. Because of his enthusiasm for the lyric theatre, in the next few years the king had other royal halls adapted for ballet and opera so that lavish spectacles could be presented properly. These were the Palais Royal, the Tuileries, the Luxembourg, Vincennes, Fontainebleau, Saint-Germain, and Versailles. With the comédie ballets created by Molière, Lully, and Beauchamps, there is clear development away from divertissement toward the ballet d'action of the eighteenth century.

I do not believe we diminish Lully's achievements when we reaffirm his good fortune in his collaborators—Benserade, Molière, Quinault, Torelli, Bérain, and throughout his career, Beauchamps. Yet it was primarily Lully who had the architectural sense of grandeur in the performing arts consonant with that of Louis XIV and his age.

In 1661 the chateau of Vaux-le-Vicomte was the locale of the premiere of the first of a series of nine comédie-ballets and one tragédie-ballet on which Lully, Beauchamps, and Molière (1622–1673) collaborated. Probably it was a result of the fact that the playwright had joined the composer and the choreographer as one of the king's preferred dancing companions. Les Fâcheux turned from Renaissance-type allegories and from dramatic themes of Greek classics used by Corneille and Racine to the comedy of manners. In this witty entertainment, which also called on the talents of the machinist Torelli to make possible rapid scene changes, the hero and the heroine finally celebrate their wedding following a lengthy and exasperating series of interruptions by ten particularly irritating and boring characters. For this play of three acts with a prologue, Lully composed music for ten varied dances, several of which were integrated directly into the dramatic action, and others that served as appropriate divertissements. At the center was Molière's inventively prolific, extremely polished, practical, professional, and often profound, approach.

Although Louis XIV was in the audience when Les Fâcheux was premiered, he is documented as having appeared on stage more than one hundred times up to 1681. (This date marks his "retirement" from performing, which took place in one of Lully's most sumptuous ballets, Le Ballet Royal du Triomphe de l'Amour. This work, which began the eleven-year "reign" of professional ballerina Mademoiselle La Fontaine, had sixteen songs in its twenty entrées, and a number of choruses as well. Its music was well applauded for its ingenious orchestration as well as for its effective dynamic variety.)

During the 1660s Lully by no means confined himself to composing music for comic entrées. In 1662 he wrote ballet music for Cavalli's spectacular *Hercule Amoureux,* which was the seventh and last of the Italian operatic imports organized by Mazarin. During the decade Lully, Beauchamps, and Molière frequently performed together, perhaps most notably in Molière's *Le Bourgeois Gentilhomme,* when the author played the lead and the musician took the role of the Mamamouchi, causing the king to "mourir de rire." For more than four decades *Le Bourgeois Gentilhomme* was the favorite dramatic amusement of Louis XIV, and it has remained a true classic. In 1670 Lully, Beauchamps, Molière, and Carlo Vigarani the machinist produced *Les Amants Magnifiques* at Saint-Germain in a collaboration involving antique and contemporary themes, including burlesque; in his twenty-seventh ballet, once more Louis XIV played his favorite role, Apollo. Mention also may be made of a work in a different form on which Lully collaborated with Molière (and also two other poet-librettists, Benserade and Quinault): *Les Fêtes de l'Amour et de Bacchus* (1672), a pastiche, was Lully's first opera, and though it was not the equal, musically or dramatically, of the composer's later tragédie-lyriques, it was revived as late as 1738.

The part played by Pierre Beauchamps in the development of ballet is of decisive importance. He was old enough to be creatively mature and to guide the young king's enthusiasm for dancing and for the performing arts. Lully found, in Beauchamps, a true ally, with whom he worked on most productions up to his death in 1687. During his long tenure as ballet master to Louis XIV, Beauchamps codified the all-important five positions of ballet. He had been trained by his father and one grandfather who were both professional violinists, and at age 17 young Pierre passed the dancing examination supervised by the musicians' guild. Shortly thereafter he began taking part in court ballets, as a performer, choreographer, and occasionally as composer. With twelve other senior dancers he was a cofounder of L'Académie Royale de Danse in 1661. Raoul Auger Feuillet (who was a disciple) and Pierre Rameau said that Beauchamps gave Louis XIV a ballet lesson daily for twenty-two years. When Beauchamps was asked where he got his choreographic inspiration he replied that he fed the pigeons and observed them scrambling for tidbits. Thus it was that the new haute danse (based on observing choreography from above) replaced the hitherto universal basse danse. Haute danse also involved jumps, as opposed to slides. In his career of making ballets for more than fifty years, Beauchamps made a number of contributions to divertissement ballets. In comédie-ballets he made the necessity of using only a few dancers into a virtue by integrating the dances and dramatic scenes into the main plot of the work, still giving the dancers time to change costumes. For the tragédie-lyriques of Lully's later activity he provided choreography for from six to twenty varied solo or ensemble dances.

Increasingly throughout his theatre work, Lully coordinated a number of elements that were diverse, often following the Aristotelian unities of time, place, and action, while occasionally casting logic to the winds and creating fantasy spectacle. While today neither Lully's music nor the dances of Beauchamps are as widely performed as are the plays of Molière (Molière's fame as a playwright is hardly less than Shakespeare's), in the Age of Louis XIV the comédie-ballets were described as ballets accompanied by action. (O tempi, o mores! In the eighteenth century Mozart's violin-piano sonatas were described as keyboard sonatas with the accompaniment of the violin!) In any case Lully was able to feature his wide-ranging mastery of comic incidents and scenes in the comédie-ballets, all while effectively using his dance-songs (often minuets) in which the same melodies serve dramatically and kinetically. This practice of using dance-songs, noted in the Renaissance, continued later, with Grétry, Mozart, Auber, Rossini, and beyond. The rhythm of a song could dictate the form of a dance, or vice-versa, in Lully's time, as in Stravinsky's.

The reliance of Lully and Molière on the machines for varied effects and quick scene changes led some contemporaries to call their collaboration the age of "tragédies-à-machines," referring particularly to *Psyché,* the Lully-Corneille-Quinault-Molière tragedie-ballet that Lully later turned into a tragédie-lyrique. Both versions of *Psyché,* celebrating the marriage of Amour and Psyché, were highly successful, certainly in part due to the splendid ballets of Beauchamps.

After the period of working with Molière, Lully turned to other collaborators. In the composer's later years, the poet Philippe Quinault (1635–1688) was the most faithful and inventive, for he was malleable, and like Lully, could profit from what was useful in Italian operas while remaining very French.

In 1669 an indifferent poet named Abbé Pierre Perrin and a noble producer, the Marquis Alexandre de Sourdéac, secured patents from Louis XIV to found L'Académie Royale de Musique. Two years later they produced the first essentially French opera ballet, largely free from numerous Italian influences observed on many previous occasions. Although *Pomone* (with music by Robert Cambert and choreography by Beauchamps) was not successful, very shortly Lully realized the possibilities inherent in French opera, and he persuaded the king to give the direction of the Académie over to him. Until his untimely death due to a doctor's ineffective treatment,[5] he ruled the Académie as his private duchy knowing equally well how to flatter the king both in his lyric tragedies and in their personal relations, and how to charm, train, and discipline his artistic personnel. What contributed so much to the effectiveness of Lully's work was not only the formal logical variety he achieved (which is difficult to appreciate merely through reading his music) in recitatives, choruses, and dances, but the musical and dramatic perfection he exacted from each performer.

During the years 1673–1687 Lully composed fifteen operas, mostly on Hellenic themes, all of which included important ballets as part of the action, and in all of which the glory of Louis XIV was lauded. About half of the operas contained six or seven dances, at least one of which was a minuet. The other half contained ten to twenty dances, with two or three minuets. Thus a number of Lully's operas consisted of forty percent dance. In Lully's ballets there was dancing sixty percent of the time, the remainder being devoted to songs and drama. The content of the comédie-ballets on which Lully collaborated with Molière varied greatly; usually the time devoted to music and drama was divided about equally, but in the musical portion singing occupied somewhat more time than dancing.

Although its form was more that of a ballet opera (with a touch of the pastoral-shepherd feeling) than that of an opera ballet, most authorities list *Les Fêtes de l'Amour et de Bacchus* (1672) as Lully's first opera ballet, probably for the rather obvious reason that it was the first of his productions after he took over the direction of the Académie Royale de Musique. The text of this work dealing with country life was the joint work of Molière, Benserade, and Quinault, the dances were by Des Brosses, and the machines were by Carlo Vigarani. The form of opera ballet, or, as Lully called it, tragédie-lyrique (a lyric drama, mostly in five acts), was properly defined by 1673 by his *Cadmus et Hermione* (in which Cadmus, with the help of Amour, rescues and weds Hermione, who had been captured by a giant). Characteristically, this work is interspersed with cogent dance scenes all with choreography by Beauchamps. There are three dances in the prologue. The chaconne is at the center of act I. In act II Amour "choreographs a ballet of gold statues." Act III closes with sacrificial dances. Although there are no dances in act IV, in the final act, celebrating the joining of the lovers, there are several, concluding with the minuet chanté. And, in *Acis et Galatée* (1686) in the finales of acts II and III Lully

Alceste, tragédie en musique by Lully; choreography by Beauchamps (Paris, 1674).
(Courtesy of the Harvard Theatre Collection)

and Beauchamps used the variations of the chaconne and sarabande to frame and generate solos, ensembles, and choruses. Most of the vocal and instrumental numbers are cast in binary form,[6] although for dramatic reasons Lully turned to the French rondeau on occasion.

Generally, Lully's orchestra included flutes, recorders, oboes, bassoons, trumpets, timpani, harpsichord, and strings (in five parts)—some fifty or more players. The orchestration for his *Alceste* (1674) calls for two flutes, two oboes, two trumpets, *four trombones,* harp, harpsichord, *percussion,* and strings. Although Lully was precise in the instruments he needed, it was not really until the time of Beethoven that a composer could count on performances using the full instrumentation requested. It is important to list the instruments of the score as part of each discussion, because it can give the reader an immediate aural image and is just as important as noting dance forms. The four trombones in *Alceste* at once suggest somber brass; if it had been four trumpets it would have suggested festive brass; also, percussion includes more instruments than just timpani. Henceforth readers will note that instruments named in italics indicates that the composer was contributing a particular color to his music, which in turn could help the choreographer in his presentation of dramatic or aesthetic action.

Lully's indispensable collaborators in establishing and perpetuating this development included Quinault and Beauchamps, many of the artists we have already mentioned, and also a number of new faces. Among these were the designer Jean Bérain (1637–1711), the poets Thomas Corneille, Nicolas Boileau, Jean Galbert de Campistron, and Bernard de Fontenelle, and of course new performers. Prévost, Hilaire d'Olivet, L'Estang, Pécourt, and Feuillet were foremost among the men, and La Fontaine and Subligny among the women.

Louis XIV's granting of a charter to found L'Académie Royale de Musique was preceded by several important related developments. In 1637 Richelieu had founded L'Académie Française. Following this other Académies were established, notably that of the Danse, in 1661; its council of thirteen dancing masters (of whom Beauchamps was one) met regularly to codify the court dances and character dances. One of their duties was to instruct the nobles who arranged and performed in the court spectacles. Lully controlled this body as he controlled all aspects of lyric theatre in France. Thus he influenced all forms of lyric theatre throughout Europe, through his collaborators and their colleagues and successors. With the strong support of Lully these excellent ballet masters improved standards among both noble amateur and professional dancers. According to contemporary accounts, their fine training achieved particularly notable success in such ballets as *Le Triomphe de l'Amour, Flora,* and *Le Temple de la Paix* (choreography by Beauchamps). Throughout this period the king steadfastly backed Lully, gradually granting him greater and greater powers over all musical and theatrical performances in France, and making available every needed resource, including the best theatres. Lully responded by creating the finest productions of lyric theatre in Europe.

In reviewing the literary, dramatic, scenic, vocal, instrumental, and choreographic "building blocks" of lyric theatre as it developed in France after 1581, we can appreciate what Lully and his colleagues achieved. First, Lully continued the ballet-de-cour and then brought to definition the comédie-ballet which was a synthesis no one else had been able to make, principally because no one else was fully prepared with the proper vision and had the political power to do so. Second, Lully successfully defined the opera ballet, which was an entirely different achievement; again, because of his vision and his power, and because his artistic talents were matched with creative imagination beyond simply knowing how to compose noble and comic entrées. Lully commanded his colleagues and co-workers throughout his career because he was a good administrator who, while looking out for his own interests, always took care to place the quality of the particular event above personal considerations. (This can easily be verified by readers who consult original documents in French.)[8] Lully's first achievements took him the better part of the 1650s and 1660s, but when he turned his major attention to lyric tragedies he did not by any means abandon his lifelong attachment to theatrical dance. Throughout his career he was steadfast in the maintenance of his ideals. Initially as a means of securing entry into high court circles, Lully showed his personable terpsichorean and choreographic talents alongside the young Louis XIV who loved to dance. An accomplished violinist, Lully soon rose to become the conductor of the Court Chamber Orchestra, but the dance always continued to remain an important key to his artistic power and success.

At the beginning of the 1650s Lully needed the cooperation of a literary figure; Isaac Benserade (1613–1691) was his choice. Benserade's *Ballet Royal de l'Amour Malade* was first performed by the king, his courtiers, and a group of professionals (including, and directed by, Lully) on January 17, 1657. The fact that the orchestra was formed of sixty musicians indicates how elaborate the production must have been. The plot concerns the prescription of two doctors for the curing of the sick patient who, at the conclusion of the piece, confesses that his illness has been assuaged.

Typically, the prologue of *L'Amour Malade* begins with an overture in the form of a suite punctuated by dramatic interludes. The ballet proper, in fifty-two musical sections, opens with its own overture, and proceeds to tell its story in ten entrées of varying length and importance with songs, dances, drama, and interludes: 1. The divertissement of the instruments (we have already noted the popularity of this manner of introduction); 2. Two astrologers seek to capture happiness; 3. Two fortune hunters are tricked by spirits and beaten by hunters; 4. Four men about town fight over two flirts; 5. Eleven doctors listen gravely to a candidate doctor who praises Scaramouche (Lully); 6. Eight hunters proclaim their quest with drumroll accompaniment; 7. Two alchemists attempt to change mercury into gold, only to have six Mercuries appear and pursue them; 8. Six Indian couples parade with parasols; 9. Two men seek to betray four gypsies; 10. A gay village wedding in fifteen elaborate and varied sections. Louis XIV appeared in the first and last entrées of this scene.

For this work Lully used tempos that ranged from slow (in seven numbers), to moderate (in twenty-four numbers), to fast (in twenty-one numbers). The rhythms were duple and triple, evenly matched at twenty-six each. The harmonies were almost exclusively in the tonalities of F major, G major or minor, with a very occasional C, A, or B flat. The entire last section is in g minor, one of Monteverdi's favorite tonalities. In addition to imaginative free forms Lully used the sarabande, gigue, canaries, minuet, gavotte, and gaillard. Even in this relatively early work, Lully's orchestration and sense of form were sure and engaging. His use of the trio as a contrasting section in the middle of a piece worked well both dramatically and musically. We can understand that this fully formed ballet makes sense in any age, Lully's, Noverre's, Petipa's, or Diaghilev's. There is a dramatic plot imagined by Benserade, and singing as well as dances, which are formal and also free. The form is ballet, which is more evident in this work than in certain others for which Lully composed some or all of the music and choreography, many of which were more grandiose, but few so well constructed.

In the decade of the 1660s, the great success of the Molière-Lully-Beauchamps collaborations in comédie-ballets was at least in part due to the fact that Molière based most of his works on the situations and characters of the Italian commedia dell'arte, which he had long observed, and then transferred and transformed them into French types within the appropriate ambiance. Being Italian himself, Lully understood these basic characters very well, and thus was able to compose dance music that expressed the mood. Beauchamps, who had been exposed to the Italian style through the many importations of Cardinal Mazarin, did his part in making the character dances fit the collaboration. Visually, it is easy for us to remember the identifying gestures of Polichinelle, Scapin, Scaramouche, and all through the masterful art of Callot, Tiepolo, and many others. Molière imagined scenes and manipulated his characters in simple plots as the amorous, cruel, lecherous, or silly protagonists enacted their comedy of manners accompanied by Lully's defining music and Beauchamps's dances. The foibles of the French were often reflected by, or contrasted with, those of other times and ages—the exotic Turkish, Chinese, gothic, Egyptian, Spanish, Indian, and the like, which were exploited for their variety, contrast, and comedy.

In the comédie-ballet *Monsieur de Pourceaugnac* (1669), Lully apparently set himself the problem of providing variety melodically, rhythmically, and harmonically within the unifying tonality of G major, whereas in *Le Bourgeois Gentilhomme* (1670) he used eight tonalities, ranging from E flat to D major, which taxed the string players extremely. The music and dance of this work did not actually dominate, no matter how important they were, yet, it is as perfectly proportioned as any of Lully's comédie-ballets. Lully began *Le Bourgeois Gentilhomme* with one of his typically French overtures,[9] and in the play used the following dance forms: march, sarabande, bourrée, gaillard, gavotte, canaries, passacaglia, minuet, and chaconne; choreography was by Beauchamps.

We have already noted that Lully's main activity in his later years was operatic. We can select as an example the greatly admired *Alceste* (1674), which was very noble, yet very French in its clever construction and sardonic wit. The ingenious libretto by Philippe Quinault (1635–1688) was based on Euripides, but added a number of original scenes (including comedy) to increase the scope and the love interest. The majority of the numbers were vocal—recitatives, airs, ensembles—but they were constantly augmented by ritornells that invited choreographic movement. In the matter of tempos, Lully approximated the same ratios he chose in *L'Amour Malade:* twenty percent slow, forty-five percent moderate, thirty-five percent fast. His favorite tonalities were F major, C major, and G major and minor. The rhythms varied between duple and triple. Like Monteverdi Lully was a master at mixing the older forms with the new—the minuet, passepied, march, and loure, along with dance songs and imaginative use of the French rondeau. Although Louis XIV did not appear in Lully's later operas, playing his ballet role of Le Roi Soleil, French culture shone brightly through the brilliance of the performing arts directed with genius and method by Lully. While Lully successfully promoted the principle of professionalism in lyric theatre, there continued to be notable exceptions. Performing his favorite role of Apollo to the measured rhythm of the loure, Louis XIV danced in public at least as late as 1681, dancing alongside of Lully's star pupil Mlle. LaFontaine in *Le Triomphe de l'Amour,* the book of which was by Quinault and Benserade, and the decoration by Bologna's favorite son, Rivani. In 1682 the ballet of Lully's tragédie-lyrique *Atys* was performed by the elite terpsichoreans of the French court, including the Dauphin, the Princesse de Conti, and Mlles. de Tonnerre and de Laval.

Tastes change, however, and styles are forgotten: Bach's music was misunderstood; Mozart's works were massacred; only recently have performers begun to fathom the mysterious magic and spells with which Handel charmed and inspired his enthusiastic audiences. Let us remember that conventions change in every age. What may at first seem to be static rhetoric, ornate formality to us was to earlier audiences passionate, dramatic, idealistic. The formulas of a particular age can speak to any age if they are properly approached by protagonists and audiences. Then we can appreciate their timeless messages. Intense refamiliarization with past glories and standards is necessary if we are to appreciate fully the beauties of Lully and his lyric theatre, as living art rather than lifeless museum effigies of honorable, overdecorated, bloodless merit. The rhythm, melody, harmony, and texture in Lully's music may be related to those of composers whose works we know better, but they have their own special flavor, tempos, and other rules which must govern performance. Lully's expression varies more from modern music practice than the early French language differs from modern French. Its proper performance will lead us to proper appreciation of theatrical dance of the period. A large step in the right direction has been made by Wendy Hilton in her teaching and in her book *Dance of Court and Theater,* which helps unlock a number of mysteries (see Bibliography). Among his own works, *Amadis* (1684) was Lully's personal favorite (possibly because it was, with *Atys,* harmonically one of his most venturesome). *Amadis* was popular with the French public and the artists; in the 1730s both Sallé and Camargo danced in its divertissements. Most popular of all, *Thesée* (1675) played virtually continuously for 104 years.

Lully admired tragedies of the Corneilles and Racine, and in his vocal passages he sought to achieve theatrical verity similar to what he heard performed by Mlle. de Champmesle and other fine actors of his time. His ideal of exactness in slow and rapid musical passages extended of course to the dancers, who were under the personal supervision of Beauchamps and his colleagues. "Following life" was Lully's theatrical motto. As a result his art was not boring.

Formally, Lully's tragédie-lyriques consisted of a prologue and five acts. Depending on the structure of the theme, and on the event for which they were created, his comédie-ballets, pastorales, ballets, and other stage works frequently were somewhat shorter. On occasion Lully employed leit-motifs. His imaginative use of the harmonic resources of the circle of fifths included varied extensions through dominant relationships, and also through seventh and ninth chords. Sometimes he found unity in as much harmonic variety as possible, even in the recitatives and the récits (short songs or ariettes). Lully would vary his rhythms and tempos between duple and triple, fast and slow. He achieved the splendor of the march in *Alceste,* the hypnotism of the extended chaconne in *Psyché,* and the magic of various sleep scenes such as are found in *Armide* and *Persée.*

Neither in his airs nor in his dances did Lully always observe symmetry. Minuets could have three-measure sections as well as the usual four-measure sections. Sarabandes could have seven measures as units instead of eight; however, most of his bourrées and gavottes were built on sections of four measures. Many of Lully's rhythms had anapestic cadences. "Les notes inégales" and double dotting effects helped give variety to his dances. When the rhythmic marking changed from fast 4/4 to 3/2 a slowing of the tempo was indicated. There is little doubt that effective stylistic decoration in tempo was as important as precision and coloring (see Appendix 3).

In each number Lully appeared to vary the tempo, texture, instrumentation, and orchestration. He composed for comedy and tragedy, equally well for solos and ensembles, for human passions, pomp, wit, pathos, and exhilaration, for gods, for Heaven and Hell. In *Armide* his use of the passacaglia enabled him to call on the full resources of the ballet and the chorus in the climactic moment, as Mozart did in *Idomeneo,* and Wagner, Verdi, and Saint-Saëns were to do later. In the lighter *Acis* Lully used a chaconne for a moment of triumph. The fact that triumphant moods could be expressed in minor as well as major tonalities in the seventeenth century enabled the composer to produce particular effects very subtly.

Lully was a professional musician who understood dramatic verity. For him this was essential in the theatre, and he demanded that his artists represent faithfully the emotions of the characters they were portraying. He did not insist invariably that there was only one way to perform his works, though he did always insist that the diction of the performers be impeccable and expressive. In a sense a visionary, a forerunner of Wagner, Lully was always a practical man of the theatre, both musically and visually.

4

The Eighteenth Century:
The Classical Age

The Birth of Rococo

For about one-third of a century Lully had been the brilliant definer and dictator of the theatrical performing arts in France, and, by reflecting the tastes and models of Louis XIV, over most of Europe. With Beauchamps and his other colleagues and his Académies of music and dance Lully presented what was progressive and unifying in the lyric theatre. Even after his death and after that of Louis XIV in 1715, Lully's importance continued in many areas. In music his influence continued to be a very significant factor almost to the French Revolution of 1789.

When Lully died in 1687, Louis XIV had almost three decades to live. During these twenty-eight years a tentative beginning was made toward replacing unified formality in the arts with a more human scale, from artistic unity and absolutism toward diverse ideals. Perhaps this was due to the absence of a strongly motivated, dedicated artistic figure in charge such as Lully, and to the fact that in the second half of his reign Louis XIV himself was no longer the ebullient, confident, extravagant, dance-loving monarch he was in his youth.

In the graphic arts the spacious, formal world of Charles Lebrun (1619–1690) and Ferdinando Bibiena (1657–1721) gave way to the more personal world of Antoine Watteau (1684–1721) and his successors. In similar fashion the measured Lully was supplanted by the bon-vivant Campra, and later the sensitive Jean-Philippe Rameau. The dramatic, ethical world of Corneille and Racine dissolved into the less absolute one of Marivaux and Regnard in the comedy of manners. The rococo—the human and intimate—replaced the grandiose, perhaps for the first time in history.

Every student of Latin is aware of Julius Caesar's categorical division of Gaul into three parts. For our purpose we may divide the Classical Age into three parts: the birth of Rococo and the transition toward decorative divertissement pleasurable for its own sake without unifying structure; the advent of Noverre and his logic in art; and finally a redefinition, a move toward naturalism with the approach of the nineteenth century, which produced the pre-Romantic Period at the time of the French Revolution.

Lully had taken infinite pains to develop a French style in music that was both personal and reflective of the glory of the monarch, but in the eighteenth century the only composers to follow this style fully were Couperin (who did not compose for the theatre) and Rameau. Their music remained rational, precise, and generally without the fantasy of the Italians. With all Rameau's harmonic variety and musical sensitivity, he maintained contact with the Lully tradition in most of his music. Henceforth, some French composers aimed at becoming international in their approach, while others steadfastly adhered to the "French" tradition.

We will have occasion to compare specific points of artistic change and controversy in connection with the attractive, less weighty, somewhat Italianate music of Campra, the newly expressive music of Rameau, and also the more psychological music of Gluck, each of whom took issue with certain ideals of Lully. But even these composers, and also such a unique choreographer as Noverre, were led to consider the unifying principles of Lully as a major force in eighteenth century lyric theatre. Yet as such contemporary figures as Voltaire and Rousseau expressed a new artistic-human-social atmosphere, the air seemed to change. It was called the Age of Reason by the philosophers. In art and in life it was called Rococo, when by about the 1730s it began to replace the monumental Baroque.

Clearly, Lully was the figure in the seventeenth century lyric theatre who made the greatest contribution to ballet. Just as clearly Jean-Georges Noverre (1727–1809) was the most important figure in the eighteenth century.

Despite Lully's death before that of his sovereign, his theatrical works (along with those of Blamont, Colasse, La Coste, Montéclair, Mondonville, Charpentier, and Campra) continued to be performed under the direction of his collaborators and their students at court, the Opéra, and in newer public theatres. Eventually this led to stagnation and call for reform, which was inevitable when the performance practice of Lully's time was forgotten and abandoned and his works were no longer performed in a manner consistent with their creation.

With regard to the genealogy of ballet masters the progression was from

Beauchamps to Pécourt, to Balon, to Dupré. At first ballet did not take into account either the slowly but surely changing social times, calling for the human scale to replace the monumental, or the changing musical scene as classical forms gradually began to influence many traditional forms and dances. Beginning in 1733 the imaginative dramatic music of Jean-Philippe Rameau (1683–1764) (unfortunately, composed mostly to unadventurous subjects) helped prepare for the genius of Gluck and Mozart. On stage the expressivity and charm of new dancers helped prepare for the coming of Noverre. The noble, graceful, but somewhat repetitious dancers such as the delightful Françoise Prévost and her gifted partner Jean Balon were effective in works derivative of the seventeenth century, but the public was ready for something new, either in virtuosity or in subject matter, or both.

During the formative phase of the Classical Age, with the gradual strengthening of professional male and female stars in ballet for the first time, the most successful composer was the prolific Abbé André Campra (1660–1744), whose gracious, somewhat Italianate divertissements bridged the years of the long and gradual decline of Lullyan influence to the ballets and operas of Jean-Philippe Rameau with dramatic new harmonies but static dramatic action (see Appendix 4). This moribund phase continued even after the premiere of Rameau's first great opera ballet, *Hippolyte et Aricie* (1733)—the classic story of Phèdre—and went on until the emergence of the ideas of Noverre and those of his contemporaries Hilverding, Angiolini, and DeHesse. We know the division of history is at best an arbitrary matter, and even before these distinguished ballet masters began to produce their expressive ballets d'action in the capitals of Europe (as opposed to ballets-de-cour, opera ballets, or comédie-ballets), a French dancer named Marie Sallé had preceded them to London, where in 1734 she presented a free and imaginative production of the ballet *Pygmalion,* the touching fable of the sculptor and his sculpture that comes to life. At this time Sallé also appeared in several of Handel's productions, including *Alcina, Ariodante, Il Pastor Fido* (portions of which were also performed separately under the title *Terpsichore,* a 20 minute ballet); she had probably previously appeared in Handel's *Rinaldo.*

While we cannot here devote an entire section to Handel's many contributions to the dance and to the relation of much of his music to dance forms, certainly a brief discussion is indispensable. There can be no doubt that this very great composer (who lived from 1685 to 1759) was cognizant of the many dimensions of lyric theatre, including music, drama, divertissement, and spectacle. For example, the first scene of his early opera, *Almira* (1705), begins with a court ceremony, followed by a ballet of Spanish ladies and gentlemen, a sarabande; subsequently, there is a festive celebration including a courante, bourrée, minuet, and rigaudon; later there is another ballet entrée, and also a second sarabande followed by the choral finale. In his English operas Handel, and others producing opera sung in Italian at London's Haymarket Theatre, from time to time called for spirits, genii, and various nonsinging performers. Dancers performed many of these roles, as well as taking part in processionals and crowd scenes. In *Amadigi* (1715) Handel's stage directions make clear where the ballet should be performed, and he specifically includes a gavotte in act I. In *Admeto* (1726) the first scene includes a ballo, and the scene of the rescue of Alceste by Hercules is danced and mimed. Handel places a gavotte in act I of *Arianna* (1727), and a suite of dances prior to the closing chorus, as, in fact, he did frequently. Ballos, gavottes, minuets, and marches are the dance forms Handel used most in his operas. In each of his instrumental sonatas, at least one movement customarily was a dance form—minuet, gigue, passepied, and the like. The 1734 season was particularly rich in ballets for the Handel operas: *Alcina* had nine dances, *Pastor Fido* had thirteen, and *Ariodante* had six. Handel's typical orchestration called for one flute, two oboes, two bassoons, *two horns,* two trumpets (and percussion), occasionally *harp,* strings, and continuo.

André Campra is reputed to have said about the spectacles being produced in his time, "The way to have a success would be to lengthen the ballets in the evening's entertainment," which is exactly what he did in his lyric compositions, "and to shorten the skirts of the danseuses." Campra no doubt applauded the vivacious Camargo and the audacious Mariette when they did just that in 1730. Camargo daringly showed her legs, partially because of the brio of her haute danse as she performed a solo in the tambourin; however, the actual shortening of the costume had been practiced in certain comic entrées at least a century earlier. Nevertheless, with his characteristic Gallic wit, Campra may well have been completely serious in his aesthetic observation. Uninspired poets such as LaMotte, Danchet, and Fuzelier failed to provide imaginative themes to replace the Hellenistic subjects transferred from Ovid and Virgil on which musicians and choreographers had been counting for more than two centuries. There was a definite need for something new, the ability to move freely, dramatically, musically, and choreographically. For a short period the impetus was provided by the increasing variety and virtuosity of a group of new male and female dancers who emerged from the now established Académie de Danse. Their increased participation even in the court ballets

Tiede aux loix de la Cadence MLLE CAMARGO.   Orginale dans ma dance

Si jeune, au gré de l'art, les pas les plus hardis.   Je puis le disputer aux Rubins, aux Blonde

Marie Camargo. From a contemporary print by Laurent Cars after a painting by Nicolas Lancret. (*Courtesy of the Harvard Theatre Collection*)

crowded out the noble amateurs, who were no longer inspired by the long-time example set by Louis XIV, and by Lully. Beauchamps and his successors, Louis Pécourt (1655–1729), Hilaire d'Olivet (ca. 1640–1700), Louis L'Estang (ca. 1660–1730), and Michel Blondi (1675–1737) had trained an entire new generation of danseurs and danseuses whose increasing virtuosity helped keep alive professional ballet traditions until Noverre could assume artistic responsibility—that responsibility which Lully had taken over from the poets, who had previously assumed it from the lords of church and state. As Beauchamps had been at the center of the codification of the five basic positions and in the training of most of the above dancers, he presided at the creation of a true school of dancers for the first time.

Though Mesdemoiselles Mollier, Verpré, Gerault, and LaFaveur had been members of the earliest Lully-Beauchamps professional performances where the nobility also participated, Marie-Thérèse LaFontaine (1655–1737) and Marie Subligny (1666–1736) were the first leading danseuses followed by Françoise Prévost (1680–1741), a great specialist in the passepied. Among the important danseurs were Raoul Auger Feuillet (1675–1730), who invented a system of notation; Pierre Rameau (1670–1730), the famous author of the classic *Le Maître à Danser,* 1725, which was catalytic in the oeuvre of the English dancing master, John Weaver; Jean Balon (1675–1725), famous for his lightness and his jumps; Louis Dupré (1697–1774), the teacher of Noverre; and members of the Dumoulin family.

Whatever the other vagaries of his character were, apparently Lully never took advantage of his position to exact particular favors from any of his personnel. The aesthetics and ethics of the eighteenth century would seem to have developed different standards, for Campra was well known to be quite a fancier of ballerinas. There is a story, perhaps apocryphal, that the good Abbé was the arbiter of a light-hearted contest of ballerina buttocks, the fine firmness of which was judged by touch. Still, it should not be inferred that Campra was not a fine musician: his sensitive use of the Italian aria da capo in his splendid opera ballets and his effective use in closing even his lighter works with the traditional chaconne in crescendo are examples that show his thorough understanding of procedures of lyric theatre.

During the last years of the seventeenth century and the first two decades of the eighteenth, the most important spectacle-entertainments in France included the following:

1693   *Medée,* opera ballet in a prologue and five acts; music by Marc-Antoine Charpentier; libretto by Thomas Corneille.

1695   *Ballet des Saisons;* music by Pascal Colasse.

1697   *L'Europe Galante,* opera ballet in a prologue and four entrées; music by André Campra; libretto by A. Houdar de La Motte; choreography by Louis Pécourt.

1708?   Act IV of Corneille's tragedy *Horace* presented in mime (at Sceaux) in a production that belonged both to the past and looked forward to the mise en scene of Noverre. Performed to music by Jean-Joseph Mouret (a prolific theatre composer, 1682–1738), Jean Balon and Françoise Prévost took the roles of the brother and sister whose double tragic end is caused by their firm concepts of love and honor, apparently an extremely moving presentation of the ethic of classic tragedy.

1710   *Les Fêtes Venitiennes,* opera ballet in a prologue and three entrées; music by André Campra; libretto by A. Danchet.

1716   The regent of France established opera balls.

In the eighteenth century there were several developments in theatrical dancing in England, Denmark, Germany, and Russia, but most of them reflected the hand of their French creators or the training their creators had received in France. (Thus, our narrative will continue to concentrate on developments in France; we will consider other countries directly only in the last two chapters.)

The world of ballet began to change in the third decade of the eighteenth century as Françoise Prévost relinquished her position as première danseuse at the Paris Opéra to two younger rivals who had been her pupils: Marie Camargo (1710–1770) and Marie Sallé (1707–1756). This rivalry stimulated public interest in ballet at a time when the repertoire was not the raison d'être for going to the Opéra, and it led to a number of new developments, both technical and aesthetic. It was, in a sense, the beginning of the cult of personality that continued later in the century with ballerinas such as La Barbarina and La Guimard, and in the nineteenth century with Taglioni, Elssler, Grisi, and Legnani, on to a legion of names in the twentieth century. As a phenomenon it has influenced aesthetics ever since.

Marie Camargo, whose real name was Marie-Anne de Cupis, was brought up in Belgium by parents who were of Spanish origin. Her debut

at the Paris Opéra probably took place in 1726 in *Les Caractères de l'Amour*
based on a score by Jean-François Rebel (1666–1747) in which the
composer very effectively characterized leading dancers by using leit-
motifs. In the form of a suite of divertissements, with Amour (originally
Françoise Prévost) leading the various brief scenes, the program is as
follows: Prélude—Amour tells mortals to profit from his ability to grant a
wish; Courante—An elderly lover asks to believe himself loved;
Minuet—A girl asks Amour to put her mother to sleep so she can meet her
lover; Bourrée—A shepherdess asks Amour to open the eyes of a shepherd;
Chaconne—A fop requests the reputation of being lucky and rich;
Sarabande—A deceived lover asks advice of Amour; Gigue—A girl asks
Amour for a lover who will dance with her always; Rigaudon—A fool
boasts, as he is rich he can have his choice of loves; Passepied—An
abandoned lover asks to become indifferent, so his mistress will return to
him; Gavotte—A girl asks Amour for the return of the lover she foolishly
dismissed; Loure—A disciple of Bacchus asks to go on drinking, as often
this induces love; Sonate—An orchestral summing up.

This thirty-minute jewel of a ballet-divertissement is scored for string
orchestra and continuo. Eight of the sections are in D major, and the others
use minor tonalities. Seven of the sections are in duple time, and the others
are in triple. Most tempos are moderate or fast.

Camargo's debut at the Paris Opéra in *Les Caractères de l'Amour* had been
encouraged by Françoise Prévost, but after Camargo began to take away
her hitherto unrivaled popularity, Prévost deeply regretted her sponsorship of the younger dancer. Contemporary accounts inform us Camargo
was a light, vivacious dancer whose quick steps, turns, and entrechats
were seen and applauded because she daringly raised her skirt above the
ankle, causing the hitherto unnecessary donning of underdrawers by the
danseuses; although Françoise Prévost had already somewhat shortened
the costume from that worn by her predecessor, Marie Subligny, Prévost's
steps were not such as to cause modesty to be in question. Also, on
occasion Camargo discarded heeled slippers that enabled dancers to increase their elevation. All told, she greatly advanced the cause of ballet
technique for women with her brilliant cabrioles, pirouettes, entrechats,
and the general brio of her performances. She danced duets with Michel
Blondi, David Dumoulin, and others, although she shone particularly in
the solo pas, such as the tambourin. Camargo was beautifully painted by
such outstanding artists as Nicolas Lancret and Maurice de la Tour.

Even before *Le Ballet Comique de la Reine Louise* and Arbeau's revealing manual, *Orchésographie,* court ballets had been divided into figured dances and free dances. The latter included comic numbers, frequently with many jumps, and serious numbers with gliding steps predominating. With the emergence of Camargo and her light, rapid steps, the *haute danse* could rival the *danse à terre* or *basse danse* in serious and noble ballets. This would have an effect on the music, of course. Until the appearance of professional dancers and theatres created specifically for lyric performances, with a designated place for the orchestra, the productions had been staged at one end of a large hall. The audience was seated around the sides on raised platforms while the monarch or patron and his party sat on the floor at the opposite end from the main performers. During Lully's time the ballets were performed in theatres, but the action generally remained horizontal, until a place for the orchestra next to the stage, and somewhat sunken, was finally established. In the period between Lully and Noverre, the technique of professional dancers gradually developed until leaps and jumps to the more rapid music of the new composers began to give increasing variety to the dance. We have noted that in his book, *Le Maître à Danser* (1725), Pierre Rameau credited the codification of the five basic foot positions used in all ballet to Beauchamps, although they may possibly have existed somewhat earlier. In any event, a half century of use by professionals led to a progressive strengthening of technique. Camargo was one of the first to use the ninety-degree turnout (later to be extended by Blasis and others). All this helped make the haute danse used more frequently, and eventually all choreographers and musicians became influenced by dancers' progress. Camargo was able to show her brilliant technique in numerous ballets with music by Rameau, Campra, and Lully, and their lesser followers. Among the ballets were *Ajax, Les Amours Déguisés, Les Amours des Dieux, Roland, Danse des Démons, Les Fêtes Grecques, Les Fêtes Venitiennes, Pirame et Thisbé.* Camargo's career was spectacular, and her personal life was tempestuous, so much so that one could be tempted to ask whether l'Abbé Prévost had a knowledge of her life and loves when he wrote his story of Manon.

While a number of the steps and positions basic to theatrical dancing have their origin in spectacles of the fourteenth to the sixteenth centuries, many more were created during and after the long reign of France's Louis XIV as first male, then female, dancers became professionals, and the Académie de Danse codified the important steps. Gradually ballet became an international performing art with its own special traditions. Incidentally, L'Académie de Danse, important in the seventeenth and eighteenth centuries, has not survived to this day, as has the Académie de Musique; however, both music and dance are today housed in the Palais Garnier, home of the Paris Opéra, and repository of a great tradition.

Marie Sallé, whose favorite dance was the gentle musette she made so expressive, was Camargo's great rival and colleague (ballet often prospers and progresses on rivalry). Camargo's artistry greatly advanced technique, and Sallé's broadened dramatic expression in the performing arts. Also a pupil of Françoise Prévost, as well as of Balon and Blondi, Sallé made her debut at the Paris Opéra in Campra's *Les Fêtes Venitiennes* in 1721, later dancing in many works of Rameau, Destouches, and Rebel. Among the numerous French ballets in which she appeared were *La Princesse de Carisme, Un matelot français et sa femme, Un berger et une bergère, Les Deux Pierrots, Les Amours des Dieux, Le Masque Nuptiale, Bacchus et Ariane, L'Europe Galante, Les Caractères de l'Amour,* and such works of Rameau as "L'Acte des fleurs" from *Les Indes Galantes* and *Les Fêtes d'Hébé* (a typical Rameau orchestration called for two flutes and *piccolos,* three oboes, two bassoons, *musettes, horns,* trumpets, percussion, continuo, and strings).

Sallé's partners included members of her own family, David Dumoulin, M. Malter, and at the end of her career, the young Gaetan Vestris. (Gaetan was the founder of the Vestris dancing dynasty, and his son Augustin danced with young Marie Taglioni almost a century later.) Certainly, the dance is ephemeral, but its history involves continuous development of école, and also passing the mantle of various types and various roles from interpreter to interpreter. Sallé, whose morals apparently were as strict as Camargo's definitely were not, was a friend and collaborator of a number of important figures in France and England, including Voltaire, Gay, Pope, and Garrick.

In addition to performing splendidly in the new works of Handel and Rameau, in London she also created a most unusual ballet, *Pygmalion.* Instead of appearing in the usual heavy, hooped skirts of the court costume she appeared in a simple draped muslin costume. Using a score by J. J. Mouret, Sallé repeated her London success in Paris. Her expressive dancing had no precedent, but it created one for Noverre, Duncan, Graham, and many more.

Over a period of more than twenty years, Camargo and Sallé each spent more than nine years as members of the Paris Opéra Ballet. Records show that they appeared together regularly only in 1727 and 1728; thereafter, when one was dancing there the other retired temporarily or was on tour. In company with Mademoiselle Petit, they were applauded together in an effective pas de trois from Gervais' opera, *Hypermnestre,* in which the charm and gaiety of Camargo could be compared directly with the expression and dramatic veracity of Sallé.

The Impact of Noverre

About the middle of the eighteenth century, historical and social documentation becomes more plentiful and more reliable, and this makes it easier for us to draw logical conclusions in artistic matters as we also become more selective in our presentation.

The life of Jean-Georges Noverre (1727–1809) was long and productive, particularly for the future of ballet as an independent form of artistic expression, which he not only foresaw but to a very large extent brought about. He influenced every choreographer since his own time, both directly and through his devoted pupils and disciples. His chronology matches that of Franz Joseph Haydn and two distinguished Frenchmen, the painter Fragonard and the dramatist Beaumarchais. Derek Lynham's excellent monograph (see Bibliography) tells us much about Noverre's activity in France, Austria, Germany, Italy, and England once he left his native Switzerland for Paris, where he became a leading pupil of Dupré as well as a friend of the progressive ballerina Sallé. Noverre's excellence as a dancer was first recognized in 1750 in Lyon, where he appeared as Camargo's partner in *Les Chasseurs et les Vendangeurs*. His most productive periods were as follows: 1760–1766 in Stuttgart at the enlightened court of Karl Eugene, the artistic Duke of Wurtemberg; 1767–1776 at the Viennese court; and 1776–1781 at the Paris Opéra.

From his first ballet to his last, 1751 to 1793, the road was not easy for Noverre. He was friendly with many dancers, both those with impressive techniques and those who emphasized expressivity. He collaborated with important composers, such as Gluck (1714–1787), Mozart (1756–1791), Jommelli (1714–1774), and Rodolphe (1730–1812), Starzer (1726–1787), Toeschi (1724–1788), Aspelmayr (1728–1786), and many more. He worked with gifted French decorators such as Louis Boquet and François Boucher, and the brilliant machinist Jerome Servandoni (1695–1766), and with dramatists and literary figures such as David Garrick (1717–1779) and Voltaire (1694–1778), as well as nobility in several countries. His outspoken comments and writings made him bitter enemies, however, and despite the support of a number of cultural figures his career did not proceed at all smoothly.

I have chosen to devote the central pages of this discussion of the classical century to Noverre not only because he was the single most

Jean Georges Noverre. From a print by Pierre Narcisse Guérin. *(Courtesy of the Harvard Theatre Collection)*

significant figure in the history of dance in his time, but because he was one of a handful of creative geniuses in the entire history of theatrical dancing to have finished his course and left his imperishable legacy. But, even accepting the "great man theory of history," and the premise that "choreographers are born, not made," one can create only when proceeding from the achievements of someone who has come before. Noverre was a truly original creator, but he had predecessors in the persons of Hilverding van Weven (1710–1768) and Jean-Baptiste de Hesse (1705–1769), and a slightly older colleague whose artistic ideals were also progressive, Gasparo Angiolini (1723–1796).

In our discussion of developments in the lyric theatre we have focused mostly on achievements by major figures in major halls or noble courts—emphasizing the accomplishments of the "establishment." As any chronicle that does not take into account all genuine accomplishments is unduly limited, we will attempt to give them all appropriate credit wherever they may be presented, despite difficulties in securing full documentation. In the case of Marie Sallé, some of her activity was in the major halls in collaboration with such figures as Rameau and Handel. However, her unusual *Pygmalion* (1734) was performed in smaller theatres. In Paris it was shown at the Théâtre Italien which, along with the Comédie-Française, often presented unusual dance spectacles. De Hesse was active as a dancer and choreographer at the Théâtre Italien, frequently collaborating with the Italian composer Vincenzo Manfredini (1737–1799), who incidentally was in Russia composing for the lyric theatre at the same time that Hilverding was there. (Vincenzo's father, Francesco Manfredini (1685–1748) was an important Bolognese composer of the Baroque Era.) Hilverding was trained in Paris under Beauchamps's nephew, Michel Blondi. He returned to his native Vienna, where he became court ballet master, choreographing works to music by Ignaz Holzbauer (1711–1783) and J. A. Hasse (1699–1783). He was also active in Stuttgart, where he experimented with the ballet d'action (story ballet, as opposed to the divertissements favored by many of Beauchamps's successors), the genre in which Noverre was to achieve so brilliantly. Among Hilverding's many ballets were a *Pigmalion,* with music by Josef Starzer; *Britannicus,* after Racine, which he mounted at Vienna's Kärntnerthor Theatre; *Alzire,* after Voltaire; *Idomeneo,* after Crébillon; *Amour et Psyché,* with music by Vincenzo Manfredini; and his own version of Rameau's *Le Turc Généreux,* which in the eighteenth century, was a very popular theme and the subject of works by Gluck, Mozart, and others. In 1759 Hilverding went to Saint Petersburg as ballet master, and in a few years he raised the standards of

Russian ballet by introducing such steps as the pirouette and the entrechat. When in 1766 Hilverding returned to Vienna, Angiolini took his place in Russia.[1]

Angiolini was an Italian dancer, choreographer, and composer who came to the Viennese court in 1757. Four years later he choreographed the first "dance drama," Gluck's *Don Juan,* and continued with several other important works along the same lines, including Gluck's *Semiramide* (1765). *Don Juan,* a truly inspiring ballet in three scenes, has thirty-one numbers. The first scene is at the home of the Commander, whom Don Juan kills when he is surprised during the seduction of the Commander's daughter. The second scene is the banquet at Don Juan's mansion; the third is the cemetery scene, from which Don Juan goes to Hell. Gluck's music is extremely varied and expressive throughout. In scene one there is one set piece: the siciliano serenade of the Don; in scene two there are five set pieces; in scene three there are two. All are used dramatically. The music is sixty-five percent in duple time and is predominantly fast. The main tonalities are D and A major, but there are four sections in minor tonalities. In this hour-long ballet, Gluck called for two flutes, two oboes, two bassoons, two horns, harpsichord, and strings, typical orchestration for his works.

Among Angiolini's other important ballets were *Pigmalion,* with music by Steinbock; *Le Diable à Quatre,* for which Angiolini composed the music himself; and *La Constance recompensée,* with music by Vincenzo Manfredini. Angiolini felt strongly that if a ballet was well choreographed it should not be necessary to give the story in a printed program, as was and generally, still is the custom. In the changing game of musical (or choreographic) chairs, when Angiolini left Vienna for Russia in 1766, Noverre was called to the Hapsburg capital where he produced a number of new ballets and repeated some of his Stuttgart successes.

Three years after his first ballet, in Lyon, in 1754 Noverre made his initial impression on Parisian audiences with *Les Fêtes Chinoises* (Rameau-Boquet), at the Opéra Comique. Chinoiseries had been popular in the arts ever since Marco Polo went from Venice to make contact with the Far East in the thirteenth century. The tradition of unified court ballet created by Lully had metamorphosed into a suite of conventional, if charming, dances (such as *Les Caractères de l'Amour*) often selected primarily to display the virtuosity of the leading dancers, at times performed to miscellaneous airs hastily strung together. Noverre affirmed and expanded Lully's principles of unity in design and logic in the progression of each work, even divertissements. He insisted that movements should be related to the tempo and texture of the music, not that he wished to return to the tunes or harmony of Lully, but rather that appropriate music should be used, whether the tunes were new or old, and new ballets should forsake divertissement for display only. Many of Noverre's ballets were reworkings of well known themes, such as the classic *Horace* (Corneille), or *Pygmalion*, and many were based on newer, more human subjects.

Noverre told choreographers to abandon entrechats, cabrioles, and complicated steps, and turn for inspiration to nature, which could be understood by everyone who saw the ballet. This was a move several had urged before him, but in which they had not been successful. Noverre followed some of the ideas of Sallé, and he made progress in his campaign to achieve more appropriate historical costuming, not merely decoration. This led him to banish masks, wigs, hoops, and other costume accessories, except where appropriate. Like England's great actor, David Garrick, Noverre advocated more effective makeup. In France Gaetan Vestris was the first man to abandon the indiscriminate wearing of the face mask, in 1773, and Maximilien Gardel followed suit shortly thereafter. The sixteenth and seventeenth century practice for ballerinas to wear masks had already been abandoned by Françoise Prévost.

In his *Lettres sur la Danse* (1760) Noverre noted that "A well-composed ballet must be expressive in all its detail and speak to the soul through the eyes." When the movements of the dance are not properly directed, he said one could admire the skill of the dancer, but remain unmoved. "Dancing is possessed of all the advantages of a beautiful language, yet it is not sufficient to know the alphabet alone." The ideas and precepts in his letters are as true today as they were when they were first published. In these letters Noverre explained thoroughly his method of creating ballets, noting that technique for technique's sake was not an end in itself, this in spite of the fact that he was on excellent terms with the finest technicians of the century, from Camargo to Vestris.

In preparing the creation of a ballet, Noverre took subjects from mythology, history, or his own imagination and always selected ideas that would please or inspire. He believed the theme should offer opportunities for dancing and also have some dramatic interest. Once he had conceived his libretto, he studied the gestures, movements, and expressions that could reveal and render best the appropriate passions and sentiments. Next, he explained to his musical collaborator the details of his plan, asking for music adapted to each situation and each feeling. Instead of providing steps to music, Noverre choreographed the dramatic action, and then asked the composer to write music suitable to each phrase and thought, just as Petipa was to do a century later.

"Thus, I explained to Gluck the characteristics of the ballet of the savages in *Iphigénie in Tauride:* the steps, the gestures, the attitudes and expressions of the different characters, which I outlined to him, giving this celebrated composer the theme for that fine piece of music." Gluck in his lyric theatre used such set forms as the gavotte, minuet, fandango, forlana, and chaconne. He also used a number of free forms, which Noverre choreographed.

Disdaining the constant use of symmetrical formations that had been so popular for the corps de ballet in every era (and which in our time fascinated the director Busby Berkley), Noverre sought originality and spontaneity in the figures of the ensemble, which in some ballets he stressed above the importance of the soloists. He insisted that the choreographer must give each character, each dancer, a different, complementary action, so that they all would contribute to the same end by means of different impact.

Noverre wrote that all choreographers should study *music,* to make the movements and the music expressively attuned; *art,* to cultivate a harmonious sense of color, line, and proportion; *history, literature, and nature,* to discover better subjects, *machinery,* to direct the construction of scenic effects, and *anatomy,* to correct the faults of students. Choreographers should observe all natural forms of movement and make use of them as appropriate, not merely as novelty or variety without logical reason. Noverre's competence in choosing the colors of costumes to give harmony yet contrast, and also in the graded placement of dancers of the ensemble, rather than letting them arrange themselves, was worthy of Lully's before him and Fokine's in our own day. Noverre made a curious reference to the five positions of the feet, saying it was well to know them, and better yet to forget them in creating roles that were totally consistent with characterization. How well he followed his own advice is evidenced by Baron Grimm's recollection that the country dance that concluded *Les Ruses de l'Amour* was lively and brilliant, offering a rural, voluptuous picture as rich as Teniers, and as pleasant as Boucher. Elsewhere, Grimm noted that "Even the best friends of the Gardel family [Noverre's bitter rivals] were forced to admit that Noverre is a man of genius." In all of Noverre's ballets about which we have proper documentation, it is clear that his creative artistic sense was thoroughly supported by professionalism on every level—dancing, drama, music, decor.

Although reportedly Noverre choreographed more than one hundred and fifty ballets short and long in the years 1751–1793, we can only identify about one hundred and twenty-five of them. Some of these one hundred and twenty-five appear to be revivals of his own works, and in a few cases revisions of the works of others. Also, a number of his collaborators in the various works are not known. Among the ballets about which we have some information, about half take their themes from Greek mythology, however, there are a number of more modern works, both noble and comic, many divertissements, and others whose inspiration comes from great literature such as *Don Quixote*. A list of his ballets is to be found in Derek Lynham's biography (see Bibliography). In spite of the fact that he did not concentrate on new forms of the dance or of music, Noverre's use of what was available (like works of Mozart) revealed his remarkable powers of concentrated artistic expression, and his ideas of unity and variety in all kinds of ballets were impressive. Aside from those already mentioned, Noverre's influence on Vigano, Blasis, Didelot, Taglioni, Le Pic, Saint-Léon, Perrot, Bournonville, Petipa, and almost every choreographer since his time was direct or indirect, through his dance-ballet-mime continuum.

Only in the years he was at Stuttgart, 1760–1766, did Noverre probably have the resources at his disposal that enabled him to produce ballets in a manner true to his creative vision. (Despite Jommelli's more elevated position in the Stuttgart hierarchy, Noverre's artistic integrity was genuinely respected.) He believed *Medée et Jason* was perhaps his masterpiece, and after creating it in 1763 he later revived it in a number of capitals. In this ballet of nine scenes and sixteen numbers, the composer J. J. Rodolphe (1730–1812) called for the conventional orchestration of two flutes, two oboes, two horns, two trumpets, timpani, and strings. The main tonalities are F and B flat major, though there is considerable variety and appropriate use of minor keys. Most tempos are moderate. The rhythms are equally divided between duple and triple; there are only three set forms. The imaginative music is varied in form, tonality, tempo, harmony, and texture, fitting the lurid classic story from Euripides of how Medea, the heartbroken enchantress abandoned by Jason for whom she had dutifully and lovingly sacrificed herself, gets demoniacal revenge by killing the daughter of King Creon (her new rival for Jason's affections) and also by killing her own children by Jason.

Noverre's ballet *Les Petits Riens* was a thirty-minute divertissement in three episodes that he mounted in three different European capitals. The action is as follows: in the first scene Cupid is caught in a net and put into a

Scene from Noverre's *Jason et Medée* (Mlle. Nency, M. Vestris, Mlle. Toscany, c. 1780). From a print by John Boydell. *(Courtesy of the Harvard Theatre Collection)*

Madeleine Guimard in *Les Petits Riens*.

cage (in the Paris production of 1778 La Guimard and Auguste Vestris were extremely graceful); the second scene presents a game of blindman's bluff (in Paris the principal part was danced brilliantly by Noverre's pupil and successor, Jean Dauberval); in the final scene the mischievous Cupid introduces two shepherdesses (Mlles. Guimard and Allard) to a "shepherd," really a third shepherdess in disguise (Mlle. Asselin). The two women are enamored of the "shepherd," who to enlighten them, uncovers her breasts (the choreography of this section was particularly appreciated). The *Journal de Paris* of June 12, 1778 assures us that the scene was made very piquant by the intelligence and the grace of the three famous dancers. There was hearty applause and demands for an encore at the moment when Mlle. Asselin undeceived the two ballerinas, though according to a report by Baron Grimm, a part of the audience was not amused by the questionable dénouement.

Noverre's *Les Petits Riens* had first been performed in 1768 in Vienna to music variously ascribed to Gluck and Aspelmayr. In 1781 Noverre revived it in London with music by F. H. Barthelémon (1741–1808) (a French theatrical composer, also active as a church musician in England). For several reasons, however, we are most interested in the Paris version (performed on a double bill with Piccinni's *Le Finte Gemelle*), in which about two-thirds of the music is by Mozart. Mozart and Noverre had met in 1771 in Italy, where they collaborated on Mozart's *Ascanio,* and perhaps other projects, and they had renewed acquaintance in Vienna in 1773.

When they met again in Paris, Mozart (introduced to nobility by his influential friend Baron Grimm) was hopeful of working on major commissions but, alas, this was not to be. Only a few weeks after his brief moment in the sun as a result of Noverre's production of *Les Petits Riens* (K. Anhang 10) with his music at the Paris Opéra in June of 1778, Mozart's mother died. Shortly after that, he began his slow, debilitating return to Salzburg, and another four years of a life that, more and more, he came to feel was not a life at all.

Mozart's extant music for Noverre's *Les Petits Riens* shows a masterful overture and fifteen carefully planned numbers, including an elaborate German dance. In a letter to his father Mozart notes that six more numbers were needed for the ballet. (There is also an extra gavotte, K. 300, which may have been intended for, or even included in some performances of the ballet.) In the Mozart Neue Ausgabe, II, 6, 2 (Kassel, 1963), Harald Heckmann discusses the score and what parts of the ballet were performed to music by Mozart. He indicates that after Mozart's extended sonata form overture was played, six numbers (some by anonymous composers) made up the music for scene one—allegro, minuet, allegro, andantino, agité, minuet. It is believed most of the six numbers for scene two were by Mozart—largo, vivo, andantino, allegro, larghetto, gavotte. For scene three, the ballet probably used six numbers by Mozart—adagio, andantino, gavotte, pantomime, passepied, gavotte—then an andante, and finally a closing gigue (the last two numbers composed by other musicians). The central tonality is C major, and the primary rhythm is duple. Mozart's score is gracious and piquant throughout in a way that is ideally suitable for the subject. His orchestra calls for two flutes (doubling with piccolo), two oboes, *two clarinets,* two bassoons, two horns, two trumpets, timpani, and strings. Habitually, Mozart used clarinets in works which meant a lot to him personally. Their inclusion here indicates to listeners his own deep involvement with the theme.

It was during the lifetime of Noverre, and to a significant degree through his ballets and writings, that the ballet d'action became a truly independent art form, no longer including singing as a quasi-integral part of its structure. At the same time opera, which usually had involved dance as part of its structure, began to treat subjects that no longer demanded ballet. This is not to say that ballet and opera were separated henceforth, but rather that their characteristic structures were no longer inextricably intertwined. Noverre's achievement in this artistic metamorphosis of lyric theatre was remarkable.

A Redefinition with the Approach of the Nineteenth Century: The Pre-Romantic Period at the Time of the French Revolution

In our consideration of the sister arts dance and music, we have noted that in medieval and Renaissance times the innovative dance and mime tended to dominate the repetitious music that accompanied it. In Baroque times under Lully and his colleagues, music became a leading element in dance spectacles, the forms became more varied and more complex. In the Classical Age there was at first a regression in music and dance, if not decor. The ideals of Noverre penetrated slowly and had great trouble flourishing in hostile atmospheres. But their influence became ever greater, and the active presence in the theatre of such musical giants as Rameau, Handel, and Gluck did provide parallel inspiration and did lead to change.

Inevitably, the coming of the French Revolution and the turbulent Napoleonic Era was responsible for much that was new in European art. This art was already announced by Goethe and the pre-romantics in the German literary Sturm und Drang movement, expressing a freer, though tormented and involved society, just as such social thinkers as Rousseau, Voltaire, and Diderot led the French Enlightenment. It took more than half a century before the full impact of Romanticism brought the Classical Age to an end in the theatre, yet there was enormous theatrical activity throughout the unruly period. In music Beethoven contributed to the new aesthetic, namely that man was to be master of his destiny, at least in part. The lifetime of Ludwig van Beethoven (1770–1827) saw a musical revolution of the magnitude of that caused by Jean-Baptiste Lully with the development of new forms, procedures, and sonorities. At first this revolution was evidenced in the emergence of instrumental music as a genre of its own, and the full application to lyric theatre was recognized only gradually. Among the many composers active in the lyric theatre during this period of transition were Grétry, Méhul, Cherubini, Spontini, and Rossini. We will of course consider how musicians of the Romantic Age reacted to Beethoven and his participation in the musical revolution from Classic to Romantic. Here, however, we are concerned with another period of transition.

The story of theatrical dance for the immediate time after the retirement of Jean-Georges Noverre (as the ancien régime gave way to the Revolution and then the Napoleonic empire) has three main threads: traditional, comic, and noble. All the main choreographers of this period had been influenced by Noverre: the two Vestris, who were conservatives; the middle-of-the-roaders including Dauberval and Pierre Gardel; and the lone experimenter, Vigano. None of them, however, went beyond dance as a profession, as Noverre so clearly did. Like Lully and Wagner he saw music as more than an art, as a life.

The traditional strain was maintained in France by the Italian Gaetan Vestris (1729–1808), who was a great dancer both with and separate from Noverre. Although not a good choreographer, when he saw what Noverre was doing in Stuttgart in the 1760s, he readily accepted the new aesthetic and served the art with all his great technique. Members of his family continued to perform brilliantly and uninterruptedly down to the Romantic Age. Gaetan's son, Auguste (1760–1842), was an even more remarkable dancer than his father, and in his last appearance at the Paris Opéra he partnered young Marie Taglioni.

At least partially foreshadowed by Noverre, the popular new comedy-ballet was characterized by the works of Jean Dauberval (1742–1806) and Pierre Gardel (1758–1840). In 1786 Dauberval choreographed *La Fille Mal Gardée,* a famous ballet in two acts that has remained in the repertoire ever since despite the fact that the music was lost at least twice. It is a rustic story, a balletic version of a painting by Jean-Baptiste Greuze (also the subject of an earlier opéra comique, and based on a subject even used by Lully) about everyday happenings: a mother wishes her daughter to marry "properly" the son of a village official, without reckoning on the will of her ingenious daughter and the daughter's winsome if impecunious young swain, who prevail despite the mother's opposition. The choreography was revised in the 1820s by Jean Aumer, and it has been re-revised several times since; what we see today is not in any sense authentic, but it is still a charming period piece. And, the music is a pastiche, which at one time or another included numbers by Hérold, Hertel, Delibes, Donizetti, Minkus, Pugni, and Drigo. Pierre Gardel, (*La Dansomanie,* Méhul, 1800) and his older brother Maximilien controlled productions at the Paris Opéra for about four decades. Although they were not particularly outstanding choreographers and were bitter enemies of Noverre, they were excellent dancers, musicians, and administrators.

Noverre's noble tradition, modified, was carried on by the Italian choreographer and composer Salvatore Vigano (1769–1821), whose more than forty ballets included *The Creatures of Prometheus,* with music by Beethoven (1801); as well as *Richard Coeur de Lion, Didone, Il Noce di Benevento, Otello, I Titani,* with music by Weigl, himself, Süssmayr, Rossini, Haydn, and others.

In the course of our discussion of important figures in theatrical dancing we have seen that even when persons were not French-born, in most instances the interesting developments in which they participated took place in France or caused a significant reaction on the French lyric scene. The case of Vigano is different, for not only was he an Italian, his great successes took place in Vienna and Milan.

Vigano was a most imaginative dancer, with a beautiful ballerina wife who rewarded her admirers, much to her husband's discomfiture. Vigano's Italian ballets were tastefully decorated by the gifted designer, Alessandro Sanquirico (1777–1849). His work, which Stendahl compared to that of Shakespeare and other great artists of the past, definitely profited from the aesthetics of the French Revolution. He embraced grandiosity in ideas and in actuality, often building his large spectacle ballets on the themes of successful operas. His control over all aspects of the productions recalls Lully and Noverre. He gave each dancer individual character, instead of using the corps de ballet for "military" formations.

Vigano's *Prometheus,* premiered in 1801 in Vienna and revived several times, is an extremely effective hour-long ballet in two scenes. It is based on mythology, but the character and great strength of Beethoven's music helps make the story one that even today moves audiences—seeing Prometheus's animation of two statues, their conquering of death and then reception of immortality as granted by the gods. Beethoven's orchestra here is conventional for his time, but he uses it expressively: two flutes, two oboes, two clarinets, two bassoons, two horns, two trumpets, timpani, *harp,* and strings. Uncharacteristically for ballet, the overture is in sonata form, as is one number in scene II. The finale is the famous Eroica theme in E flat major, once more with variations. Thirteen of the fifteen other numbers (short or long) are in duple rhythm, two are in triple. The main tonalities are C, F, D, E flat, B Flat, and G major in that order of frequency. There are really no set dance forms, although the nuptial dances feature a quasi-minuet. Already noted are the two numbers in sonata form (exposition–development–recapitulation); several are variations (A–A'–A''); several are simple rondo (ABA); and several are through-composed.[2] The tempos are evenly divided between fast, moderate, and slow. There is a certain amount of moving melodrama, foreshadowing Beethoven's unique opera, *Fidelio.* There is a storm, which often has been an effective part of lyric theatre productions and was used by Lully, Gluck, and Rossini among others. This work of Beethoven and Vigano forms a fitting conclusion to our discussion of the Classical Age, for although it is neoclassic, its treatment of a classic theme was timeless.

As a postscript to our discussion of Vigano, let us mention his Italian disciple, the choreographer, dancer, teacher, and theoretician Carlo Blasis (1797–1878) who was active in Paris, Milan, Saint Petersburg, and many other cities. His *Treatise on the Dance* (1820) and *The Code of Terpsichore* (1830) form a basis for much of our modern classical ballet training. Taught under the heritage of Vigano, the ideas of Blasis influenced a number of developments in nineteenth-century ballet, most particularly through the great Italian dancers who went to Russia, along with Bournonville's pupil Johansson, and who with Petipa and Legat were responsible for the fine Russian school that was established. Incidentally, they forced Petipa to feature technique for technique's sake somewhat more than was his basic intention. And for another Frenchman, Charles Didelot, whose concern with technique and with production helped make way for The Romantic Age, let us turn to the next chapter.

5

The Nineteenth Century

In this chapter we will be discussing the choreographers and musicians who created three of the great ballets of all time: *Giselle, Coppélia,* and *The Sleeping Beauty*. In the nineteenth century the progressive freeing of musical forms and dramatic structures and visual and decorative romanticism was paralleled by great changes in dance steps. The beginnings of modern technique came as danseuses performed regularly on their toes: first to indicate they were supernatural creatures, and later as standard practice in the majority of ballets. Following Beethoven's expansion of all forms of music, such composers as Daniel François Esprit Auber (1782–1871), Adolphe Adam (1803–1856), Cesare Pugni (1805–1870), and Friedrich Burgmüller (1806–1874) began to compose longer, free-flowing music for the new dance phrases imagined by the choreographers of the grand, realistic, mysterious Romantic ballets. (It is my personal regret that Franz Schubert never composed for the ballet; although he composed a number of operas, none of them was successful.)

In our consideration of music and dance in the nineteenth century, as we follow important developments in Denmark and Russia as well as France, I have chosen to discuss works of seven choreographers—one Italian and the remainder Frenchmen—all active and important in France at one time or another. Six of the seven were involved in one way or another in the phenomenal development of Russian ballet. The combination of French rationality and Italian virtuosity together with rapidly developing Russian involvement in and infinite concentration on the ballet produced the school that made Russia the purveyor of ballet to the world in the twentieth century. Meanwhile, the Franco-Danish choreographer Bournonville learned his craft mostly in the French capital, then returned

to Copenhagen to become a wonderfully creative curator of eighteenth-
and nineteenth-century styles; in Denmark he purified the Romantic style
while maintaining early ballets of Galeotti in the repertoire he danced and
produced.

Musically, the nineteenth century began with the far-reaching and very
personal achievements of Beethoven, who touched all music, vocal and
instrumental, solo and ensemble, as he influenced all musicians. Yet,
although he composed ländler for many court balls, wrote an opera (with
no ballet), and composed the vigorous *Prometheus* ballet, he did not
generally compose in the various set dance forms. These continued to
expand during the nineteenth century, as a number of national dances were
introduced into ballets with ethnic themes, and period dances were
continued where they were appropriate.

Didelot and *Flore et Zéphyre*

A most important forerunner in the inception of the Romantic ballet was
the choreographer Charles Louis Didelot (1767–1836), son of a
Frenchman who was premier danseur at the Royal Swedish Theatre. After
training with his father in Stockholm, he was sent to Paris for further
study with Noverre, Auguste Vestris, Dauberval, and Lany. In the 1780s
and 1790s he traveled to London with Noverre, where he appeared in a
number of ballets by Noverre, partnering Madeleine Guimard and others.
In London he produced several of his early ballets, *La Bonté du Seigneur* and
L'Embarquement pour Cythère (Venus' Island), and back in Sweden he produced *Freya*. In 1790 he made his debut at the Paris Opéra, again
partnering Mlle. Guimard. He performed in a number of new ballets,
including one with music by Cherubini. Didelot applied the dramatic
principles of Noverre to his own many and varied ballets, both as to the
choreography and to the direction of the other elements, which he
correctly noted had to be unified within the general theme. For example,
Didelot insisted on appropriate costumes, and in one of his early ballets,
Arianne et Bacchus, dressed his dancers in flesh-colored tights (something
he may have learned from his appearance as Zéphyr in Langlé's opera
Corisandre in 1791, a version of the Amadis story). As he was a good
musician, he saw to it that the music was appropriate to the theme he had
chosen (generally following the standards of pre-Romantic composers).
The themes of his ballets varied from classic to modern, European to
exotic, noble to comic.

Charles Didelot, in costume for his ballet, *Flore et Zéphyre*. (*Courtesy of the Harvard Theatre Collection*)

In London in 1796, with his wife Rose and himself in the title roles, Didelot produced an aerial ballet for the first time; it was to become one of his greatest claims to fame. *Flore et Zéphyre* (with decors by Liparotti) was set to msic by Cesare Bossi (1770–1830?), although later he revived it with music by F. M. Venua (1790–1850?). Noted as the first ballet in which wires were used to help simulate dancers in aerial flight, *Flore et Zéphyre* was also mounted in Paris (1815) and in Saint Petersburg (1808). For the Russian production the composer was Cattarino Cavos (1776–1840), a prolific Italian composer of opera and ballet who was Pugni's predecessor as Imperial Ballet Composer, a title that later passed to Minkus, and finally to Drigo. The attraction of aerial flight proved to be an indispensable element in the Romantic ballets of Taglioni and Coralli, and later opera also used aerial effects and techniques in many fantastic scenes.

The story of Didelot's effective one-act ballet has the airborne god Zephyrus request that Cupid enflame the heart of the nymph Chloris (Flore) with the same burning love for him that he has for her. Cupid agrees, but knowing that Zephyrus has the reputation for being a dallier, requires Zephyrus to write his oath of constancy to Flore on the wall of the temple. When this has been done, and when Flore has shown that she too can fly by temporarily borrowing Zephyrus' wings, all the shepherdesses and shepherds congratulate the amorous pair, who now express their delirious pleasure in a pas de deux, partly in the air. The audiences of the time marveled at the illusion of flying since the wires were invisible, and the original English production was revived frequently, and even produced as a vehicle for Marie Taglioni's London debut in 1830.

Didelot's other ballets at this time were not successful, and he went to Russia for a decade. Returning to London, he produced his *La Reine de Golconde* in 1812, and then *Corisandre* in Paris. What he wanted above all, however, was to have Paris see his *Flore et Zéphyre,* and to receive an appointment at the Paris Opéra. Finally, he was permitted to mount the ballet at his own expense; but though the work was well received, Pierre Gardel, the resident choreographer, succeeded in blocking his appointment at the Opéra, just as he and his brother Maximilien had created insurmountable difficulties for Noverre earlier.

During Didelot's first visit to Russia he had been extremely concerned with improving the quality of the dancing, although he had introduced several of his own ballets. Most of these were based on classical themes, such as *Cupid et Psyché,* for which Joseph Mazzinghi (1765–1844) composed the score. In Didelot's second Russian period, which lasted until his death, he choreographed many more ballets and mounted revivals. In the eleven years of his activity he created about two ballets a year, including his epoch-making *Flore et Zéphyre*, a total of more than one hundred.

Throughout the history of lyric theatre, certain titles and variations thereof are repeatedly encountered. Most often these refer to new productions, but in some cases choreographers who may have previously danced in a certain ballet merely revised the original. In this discussion we will try to differentiate between new works and revivals.

Among the many interesting and varied ballets produced by Didelot in his second Russian period there were both noble and comic works: *The Young Dairymaid; Hunting Adventures* (which was inspired by a Teniers oil painting hanging in the Hermitage Palace); *Raoul de Crequis*, a story of the Crusades, with music by Cavos; the Chinese ballet *Hensi et Tao* with music by Cesare Bossi; the Peruvian ballet *Cora et Alonzo; Alceste*, in which the Demon scene was notably ferocious; *Phaedra et Hippolyte*, the Oedipus story adapted from Racine; *The Prisoner of the Caucasus*, after Pushkin; and *La Capanna Ungherse*, music by F. Benois. Most of the music of Didelot's ballets was practical but not very original. The orchestration was generally pre-Beethoven in size: two flutes, two oboes, two clarinets, two bassoons, two horns, two trumpets, percussion, and strings.

Filippo Taglioni and *La Sylphide*

For many years in theatrical dancing all roads led to Paris, although relatively little happened after the enforced retirement of Noverre, in part due to the political uncertainty between 1789 and 1815. The Milanese Filippo (Philippe) Taglioni (1778–1871) secured excellent training in Paris as a young man, where he made his debut in 1799. He then spent most of the next two decades as a dancer and choreographer in Stockholm, where he raised a family. Filippo Taglioni represented the second of four generations of illustrious dancers whose activity was of prime importance for the Romantic Age. In the 1820s Filippo began three decades of intermittent traveling, producing his forty-one ballets in all the capitals of Europe, including Russia. About 1829 he returned to Paris where such composers as Cherubini, Rossini, and Meyerbeer were bringing elements of Beethoven's musical revolution into the lyric theatre; in drama the revolution of Victor Hugo was about to explode.

It was the combination of the musical and literary revolutions that enabled ballet to recognize many ideals of Noverre about the ballet d'action (plot), thus prevailing over those who believed ballet's primary purpose was divertissement. Thanks also to the advances in performance technique and to production facilities, ballet in the Romantic Age established its place in the mystique of the mysterious.

Taglioni brought together a number of new ballet ideas and achieved them very effectively, usually with the collaboration of his gifted children, Marie and Paul, and the offspring of different members of his large family. In general he was fortunate in his good relations with numerous theatre directors and with the many composers with whom he collaborated. He choreographed a number of ballets composed by Auber, Adam, and others, and he arranged the dances in many operas by Meyerbeer, Halévy, and Auber. In addition to *La Sylphide,* his most important ballets were Auber's *Le Dieu et la Bayadère,* Adam's *La Fille du Danube, La Gitana* (Auber-Schmidt), and *Nathalie ou la Laitière Suisse* (Gyrowetz-Caraffa).

Probably a ballerina with all the qualities of Marie Taglioni would have made her mark even without a brilliant father, for with her ethereal style she became an emblem of the Romantic Age almost overnight. She was far from the first danseuse to rise on her toes. The technique, known in Didelot's youth, had been encountered ever more frequently in the previous four decades, but Taglioni's apparent effortlessness made it appear easy, natural, or even supernatural. Her ability to dance on her toes in the many new ballets her father created helped make her the center of a cult. To this day most ballerinas, and many who affect the art, even continue to part their hair much as she did. As the original choreographer of *La Sylphide,* Filippo Taglioni created a work that with *Giselle* and *Pas de Quatre* represents Romanticism perfectly. Also, it gave Marie Taglioni everlasting fame: in her Sylphide costume with the little delicate wings at the back, she was depicted in innumerable celebrated lithographs.

The production of the poetic *La Sylphide* was the result of two circumstances. The first was the extraordinary success of the haunting and lascivious ballet des nonnes from act III of Meyerbeer's *Robert le Diable,* in which the spirits joined in a bacchanal. Filippo Taglioni was the choreographer and Marie was the leading dancer. The second circumstance was that Dr. L. D. Véron, the new director of the Paris Opéra, was excited about the libretto that Adolphe Nourrit, the great French tenor who starred in Meyerbeer's opera, had derived from *Trilby,* a tale by Charles Nodier.

Dr. Véron engaged the French musician Jean Madeleine Schneitzhöffer (1785–1852) to compose the score. Schneitzhöffer was the composer of a symphony and five ballets, some of them for the Paris Opéra, but in many ways *La Sylphide* was his masterpiece. The first performance of *La Sylphide,*

LA SYLPHIDE

DIRECTION RUE D'HANOVRE, 17.

Marie Taglioni, in the Filippo Taglioni production of *La Sylphide*. *(Courtesy of the Collection of Lily and Baird Hastings)*

with decors by Ciceri and costumes by Lormier, took place December 3, 1832. The cast was excellent, and Marie Taglioni's success immediately earned her the "title" of "ethereal ballerina of her time." (A few years later she had to defend her supremacy against Fanny Elssler, who was rather down to earth, in art and in business dealings; careful planning enabled Taglioni to keep her crown intact until her retirement.)

This two-act ballet, lasting about eighty minutes, opens in a large Scottish farmhouse. The dreaming James Reuben is dozing fitfully in an ample wing chair on the morning of his wedding to a charming neighbor, Effie. He is troubled by the visit of a floating, supernatural Sylphide who declares her love for him and dances with him at dawn, finally disappearing up the chimney. When the wedding guests begin to arrive, everything seems to appear normal to James. His friend Gurn, however, who is hopelessly in love with Effie, witnesses James's bewitchment during a second expressive visit of La Sylphide. The repulsive fortune-teller, Madge, predicts James's desertion of Effie, and is angrily turned out of the house by James. The wedding celebration next features the presentation of the tartans, and highland reels. Just as James is about to place the ring on Effie's finger, La Sylphide snatches it away and coldly entices James to follow her out of his house into the forest. Effie is left fainting from disappointment, with James's mother, Gurn, the bridesmaids and the guests at her side.

Act II begins with a witches' dance in moonlit woods led by sinister Madge, who had placed a curse on James. As a new dawn breaks James appears, searching for his thereal love. La Sylphide appears from the sky on wires, joined by her twelve sisters who also float in. This scene of multiple flying was a source of wonderment. (How much more exciting the ballet might have been had not the witches' flying wires been preempted by the Opéra manager to serve in a demon scene of the now forgotten opera by Halévy and Gide, *La Tentation*.) Tenderly, James and La Sylphide now dance together, but though affectionate, she is fragile, imponderable, and evasive, and he can never hold her for long. Catching sight of Madge, James apologizes for his threatening temper the previous day, and he asks the witch for help. Madge gives James a scarf that she has treated with poison to make La Sylphide's wings fall off, so she will not be able to fly away from him. When next La Sylphide floats in, James lovingly captures her with the bewitched scarf, but his pleasure is shortlived. The scarf causes the wings to fall off and its poison to invade the body of the noble Sylphide. She dies forgiving her grieving lover. The Sylphides come to carry their sister away through the sky. In the distance we see the happy wedding procession of Effie and Gurn. James is heartbroken; he has sacrificed the attainable for the unattainable, and he now has neither.

There have been many descriptions of Taglioni, her dancing, her acting, her delicate, filmy costume, and her character. Here we are primarily concerned with the work itself, more than the interpretation. It is clear, however, that without Taglioni's extraordinary toe work and dramatic ability to make the story believable, combined with the creative work of Taglioni père and his collaborators, the ballet might not have achieved the great success it did.

Act I begins with an overture, followed by seven sections: 1. James and La Sylphide; 2. The entrance of Effie; 3. Effie's friends—a. Pas de deux; b. Pas de quatre; 4. The fortune-telling scene; Effie tries to calm James, then leaves to prepare for the wedding; 5. James and La Sylphide (observed by Gurn); 6. The betrothal dances, including solos for Effie, James, and La Sylphide; 7. The wedding ceremony, flight, and finale, ending on an ominous note.

Act II also has seven sections: 1. The dance of Madge and the Witches; 2. The entry of James; 3. The arrival of La Sylphide, then the pas de deux, accompanied by strings; 4. The dance of the Sylphides, pas de trois and ensemble; 5. Madge gives James the scarf; 6. The scarf pas de deux, the death of La Sylphide, and the funeral in the sky; 7. The sad finale, with James alone.

The music, some of which is in binary form, is almost a suite of dances, rather than a more unified score as is found in *Giselle*. Schneitzhöffer's varied music, which is by turns playful, graceful, and inexorable but never particularly mysterious, is largely duple in time, fast or moderate, in the sharp keys; however, various influences seem obvious, namely, Boieldieu, Pauline Duchambge, Süssmayr, and Paganini. Schneitzhöffer makes frequent use of the ABA form, and his effective instrumentation often resembles Schubert's, with the addition of a tuba and a harp. His orchestra calls for two flutes, two oboes, two clarinets, two bassoons, two horns, two trumpets, two trombones, *tuba,* percussion, *harp,* and strings.

Adam and the Creation of *Giselle*

No matter how objective one may try to be, the best one can do is always to make clear the criteria for drawing conclusions, and then aid others to come to their own appreciation. As we discuss relevant considerations about *Giselle,* we are well aware how many readers already have thoughts

Carlotta Grisi as Giselle. *(Courtesy of the Harvard Theatre Collection)*

on this subject: this Romantic work can probably be interpreted in several ways; besides, very likely it was said before.

Any way one approaches it, *Giselle* involves the Romantic Age, the Paris Opéra, Jean Coralli, Adolphe Adam, Carlotta Grisi, Jules Perrot, Saint Georges, Gautier, Heine, and Léon Pillet. Each made an important contribution to the original, which is now as much of a classic as *Hamlet*. (The historical background of each participant is fascinating. For those seeking detailed information, the best place to start is with the writings of Cyril W. Beaumont; see Bibliography.) More than one hundred and forty years have elapsed since the first performance of the eighty minute *Giselle* on June 28, 1841 (preceded by act III of Rossini's *Moïse*), when it was hailed as the greatest ballet triumph since that other pioneering mysterious work, *La Sylphide*. Many, many artists have sincerely contributed to the evolution of *Giselle,* and what we have now in the form and shape of its choreography must only be in general relation to what was created in 1841; but we do have the authentic music, and we can proceed from there.

Adolphe Adam (1803–1856) has not really been appreciated for the important lyric composer he was. He wrote almost sixty works for the stage, about thirteen of them on a very high level indeed. Perhaps his compositions for piano are not as distinguished as those of his father, but his celebrated "Minuit, Chrétiens," which was sung for the first time in the Church of Roquemaure (near Avignon), has moved more listeners than even his best ballets or operas.

If historically Lully was on the evidence the greatest composer of a body of dance music, rivalled possibly only by Stravinsky, then immediately on the next level come such composers as Gluck, Adam, Delibes, and Tchaikovsky, to mention them chronologically. Earlier we noted Handel's and Mozart's and Beethoven's preeminent contributions, regretting only that they had written relatively little for the dance.

Although not of outstanding merit in itself, the music used by Taglioni had generally served its purpose well; we can only regret that Auber's ballet music was not on the level of that in his operatic works. Now Adam did not have the problem of straddling the Classical and Romantic Ages (as did Auber), and five of the thirteen ballets he wrote for the choreographers (Coralli, Perrot, Taglioni, Deshayes, Guerra, Albert, and Mazilier) are excellent. One, *Giselle,* is unique. Leaving behind the style of Grétry and his contemporaries, Adam's music generally benefitted from the Méhul-Rossini-Weber expansive and melodic adaptation to the lyric stage of Beethoven's revolution. Adam's romantic scores for ballets and operas are original, rhythmic, graceful, melodic, well harmonized, and well constructed, often somewhat in the vein of Cherubini, Bellini, and even Donizetti. Perhaps they are a bit lacking in the genius of orchestration found in a later French generation of composers: Delibes, Gounod, Bizet. Too frequently speed of composition forced Adam to resort to formulas without modification. The instrumentation of his works often was as follows: two each of flutes, oboes, clarinets, bassoons, *four horns,* three trumpets, three trombones and tuba, percussion, harp, and strings. In any event Adam's orchestration was fuller and more varied than that of Schneitzhöffer.

In *Giselle* Adam used five leitmotifs, each of which indicated the mood of the particular scene, and each of which was faithfully mirrored in the choreography. Motivation, movement, and music were thus given psychological and dramatic unity. Adam had an excellent sense of form, both within a dance and within an act, knowing when to use village dances and symphonic fragments appropriately, all within the dramatic frame. The story of *Giselle* tells of a fragile and lovely peasant girl in love with life, with dancing, and with Albrecht, a noble whose family connections force an arranged marriage on him; Giselle dies heartbroken from the shock of her suitor's deceit, but in the second act her repentant and mourning lover meets her at midnight, and forgiving she manages to save his life before she vanishes forever, as a Wili, one of a group of girls who have died before their wedding day, and assemble to dance every evening in a bewitched forest, under the spell of their vampire leader.

I have begun this discussion of *Giselle* with emphasis on the musician for good and sufficient reasons, the main one being that he is the one of the eight collaborators on this great ballet whose individual contribution can best be evaluated. The theme of the ballet was derived from a work by the beloved German romantic poet Heinrich Heine. It was envisaged as a ballet by the highly sensitive French litterateur Théophile Gautier, who then called in his friend Vernoy de Saint-Georges to help him work out dramatic action in act I which would fit effectively with his idea for the eerie second act. The director of the Paris Opéra replacing Dr. Véron was Léon Pillet, who had been so satisfied with Carlotta Grisi's successful debut that he was planning *La Jolie Fille de Gand* (music by Adam) as a premiere for her. Enthused by Gautier, Adam persuaded Pillet that *Giselle* should be produced first, and Pillet in turn convinced Albert, the choreographer of *La Jolie Fille de Gand* to postpone his work. This leaves us with the young ballerina, Carlotta Grisi (1819–1899), her brilliant choreographer husband, Jules Perrot (1810–1892), and the resident choreographer, Jean Coralli.[2] Presumably Grisi was agreeable to appearing in two premieres in succession. Perrot was enthusiastic about the project, and he may well have felt that if he could arrange her solos he could present her better, and perhaps obtain an appointment for himself as choreographer. And certainly Coralli, choreographer at the Paris Opéra from 1831 to 1848, did not want to be passed over. Thus for *Giselle,* the arrangement appears to have been that Perrot would choreograph Grisi's solos and Coralli would produce the ballet and receive official credit. Everything worked out. Yet it is difficult to believe that a committee could produce such a masterpiece. Who was actually the leader? was it Léon Pillet, or charming Carlotta Grisi, or, most probably, the "old professional" Adolphe Adam.

Of Italian extraction, Jean Coralli (1779–1854) was born in Paris and trained there. Although his first ballets and most of his dancing took place in other cities, Vienna, Milan, Lisbon, and Marseille, the important part of his career was while he was ballet master at the Paris Opéra from 1831 to 1848, under several administrations during the reign of citizen King Louis-Philippe. Coralli's first ballet was *L'Orgie* (1831); presently this was followed by Fanny Elssler's first success, in which she danced her famous cachucha: Gide's *Le Diable Boiteux* (1836); and later Burgmüller's *La Peri* (1843), starring airborne Carlotta Grisi. Other ballets for which Adolphe Adam provided scintillating scores included *La Tarentule* (1839), in which Elssler danced the tarantella; *Le Diable à Quatre,* starring Grisi; *Le Corsaire* starring Rosati; and the previously mentioned *La Jolie Fille de Gand.*

In act I of *Giselle* the eleven numbers of the score are predominantly fast and gay. The rhythm is mainly duple. The act begins with a brief, unsettled overture in C major, and uses the following tonalities G, D, A, F, E, B flat, A flat, and ends in e minor. The set pieces include two waltzes, a galop, a march, and a loure. The second act tempos are divided evenly among fast, moderate, and slow. It begins in D and ends in F major; in between Adam uses D major and d minor, E flat and c minor, C major, G major, g minor, B major, B flat, and A flat; the use of minor tonalities is definitely related to the sad outcome of events. The set pieces include two waltzes, a fugue, and snippets of other forms—in all nine numbers. In addition to these extremely well coordinated numbers, several numbers by Minkus and Burgmüller are often interpolated, but they are not indispensable to the action, and in fact often hold it up unnecessarily.

Following Grisi's great success in the title role, within the next ten years *Giselle* was performed in London and a number of cities in Europe and America by Marie Taglioni, Fanny Elssler, Lucille Grahn, Elena Andreyanova, and countless others. It is important to note that in Romantic ballet new styles and techniques were used to advance the story and mood. In *Giselle* the solos and the ensembles in both acts were totally involved in the overall development of the main theme—Giselle's love of dance, and of Albrecht. The various "colors of the Romantic Age," as Cyril W. Beaumont called them, geographical, historical, supernatural, and technical, all contributed to the story and to its successful presentation.

Perrot and Pugni

So far, in dealing with developments in the first half of the nineteenth century, we have discussed the changes in technique and aesthetic that Didelot and Taglioni brought about by combining the liberating ideas of Noverre and the technical advances of the Romantic aura that enveloped the lyric theatre in the 1830s. We have seen this Romantic Age in full bloom in music and dance in *Giselle* (1841).

After 1841 there was approximately a decade of full Romanticism in France and England before the stirring of yet another influence on lyric theatre, the Wagnerian wave. In this decade, among the outstanding figures were the great French dancer and choreographer Jules Perrot and the prolific Milanese musician Cesare Pugni (1802–1870). As we have seen, Perrot contributed to *Giselle* through the dances for his wife, Carlotta Grisi.

Cesare Pugni, whose work has been rather underestimated for a century, composed some three hundred ballets for Perrot, Saint-Léon, Paul Taglioni, Marius Petipa, and many others. Also beginning in 1823 he composed about ten operas, forty masses, assorted chamber works, and other pieces. After some years in Italy he went to France and then to London, where he was the main ballet composer for over a decade at the King's Theatre. He then traveled to Russia, where he became the official ballet composer to the Imperial Theatres during the last third of his life. Given the fact that he produced three hundred ballets in his lifetime, we can appreciate that he composed about six ballets a year, new, adapted, or revised. We have already noted that numerous French and Italian composers were attached to the Russian court in the seventeenth and eighteenth centuries. The nineteenth century also produced its chain, including Cavos, Pugni (followed by the Viennese, Minkus), and finally Drigo. Before we discuss several of the seventeen or more collaborations of Perrot and Pugni, let us set the stage with a few words about Perrot, the choreographer of more than fifty ballets, many set to music by Adam, Bajetti, Costa, Panizza.

Perrot had an incredible technique that he first developed in his early career as an acrobat. But he had other ambitions, and by dint of great effort in his studies with Auguste Vestris, he was called to make his debut in ballet at London's King's Theatre in 1830, a few months before he made his debut at the Paris Opéra. Both debuts were received enthusiastically. Probably even more than Arthur Saint-Léon and Lucien Petipa, Perrot represented nineteenth-century male dancing at its best, both dramatically and technically. He partnered and choreographed ballets for Marie Taglioni, Fanny Elssler, Carlotta Grisi, Fanny Cerito, and Lucille Grahn. He produced his ballets in France, England, Italy, Germany, and Russia. His choreography broadened psychological realism, telling a story through dancing, and not separating mime and dance as Noverre had sometimes done. He integrated movement and music, mime and story, poetry and vision perhaps better than anyone since Noverre. Although both Vigano and Didelot (important transitional figures in choreography) had continued Noverre's ideals of unification, they did not have the extraordinary technical dancers to work with that Perrot had. This is not to say that Perrot's ballets were better because of the technique of the dancers, any more than one can say music composed for piano is better than music composed for harpsichord. The times were different, however, and techniques were improved; but ideas, whether Plato's or Einstein's, remain ideas. Thus in addition to taking advantage of the excellent techniques of the dancers, Perrot was temperamentally and intellectually able to take into account the changing rationale of the Romantic Age and translate it into good theatre.

We have chosen to discuss first *Esmeralda,* a ninety-minute, three-act ballet based on Victor Hugo's novel, *Notre Dame de Paris* which was first performed March 9, 1844, in London. Although several ballets and operas on this subject were produced, this is the only one to survive to this day, through a revision in Russia. The first scene dramatically presents all the characters—the king of the beggars, the gypsy dancer Esmeralda, the impecunious poet she saves by "marrying," the demented priest, the hunchback bell-ringer of Notre Dame, and the noble captain who rescues Esmeralda. The next scene is devoted to the priest's second attempt to seduce the attractive dancer, but again she escapes. In the third scene the noble captain forsakes his official fiancée at their betrothal celebration to follow Esmeralda. The tender and impassioned rendezvous of the lovers in the next scene is interrupted by the determined priest, who overpowers the captain. In the final scene Esmeralda is at last saved from the gallows by the combined forces of the poet, the captain, and the crowd, while the hunchback kills the priest.

Perrot was a master at providing different moods for different characters, depending on their station, circumstances, and emotions, and Pugni's music for this ballet was most appropriate. While it would be inaccurate to state that Pugni (any more than Minkus) had the mastery of Adam, to say nothing of that of Beethoven, Mozart, or Handel, it would also be unfair to dismiss this music. From every point of view it was one of their best collaborations, and the fact that there were at least sixteen others shows that these artists could work well together. In *Esmeralda* Pugni was varied as the first scene unfolded, then dramatic in the second scene, festive in the third (until the dénouement called for a change of pace), passionate in the fourth, and finally pathetic, stormy, and triumphant in the end.

Pugni's set pieces include several waltzes, polkas, galops, saltarellos, and marches, very effective mazurkas, and several free forms he created, including the "truandise." His tempos were rather evenly divided among fast, moderate, and slow. His tonalities were quite varied, usually coming back to home key for unity. His rhythms were more duple than triple.

Pas de Quatre can be considered the touchstone in the collaborations of Perrot and Pugni both because it is a beautiful ballet in itself and because it was a milestone in ballet history. It was the first time a "pure" Romantic ballet was created, that is, an abstract ballet without a story, created for the experience of presenting four of the greatest ballerinas alive in one performance: Taglioni, Grisi, Cerito, and Grahn. Enterprising balletomanes could have seen any of these ballerinas dancing in *Giselle* or *La Sylphide*, but what an idea it was to bring them together on one stage in the same ballet. Performed only three times and revived for two later performances, *Pas de Quatre* (unforgettably depicted by Chalon) made history and created precedent. Enterprising succeeding managers have tried to revive the idea several times. In 1948 the Ballet Russe de Monte Carlo presented *Pas de Quatre* with a cast headed by Alicia Markova as Taglioni and Alexandra Danilova as Cerito; if only Galina Ulanova and Margot Fonteyn had danced Grisi and Grahn.

In 1845 the harassed but determined Benjamin Lumley described the trials of preparing, managing, and presenting the July 12 premiere in London, the lengths to which Perrot went to enable each danseuse to shine in her particular style "to the last stretch of perfection," and how the order of solos was determined to accomplish a triumph. After a prelude in D major in duple time, the twelve-minute ballet begins with the entry of the four ballerinas, hand in hand. To Pugni's gracefully langourous music they form a series of poses, always with Taglioni in the center, and engage in

Taglioni, Grisi, Cerito, Grahn in *Pas de Quatre*. (*Courtesy of the Harvard Theatre Collection*)

various courtesies as the tempo increases and the tonality changes to G major.

Lucille Grahn stepped forward with a tantalizing, brief variation, followed by an equally brief duet by Grisi and Cerito, and the introduction concluded as Taglioni crossed the stage with her famous apparently effortless leaps. The main allegro variation of Grahn is a very graceful waltz in D major, which increases slowly in speed and controlled brilliance as the dancer adds variations in her circle of rapid steps, turns, and hops. Then she bows as she introduces her colleague. The andante variation of Grisi, once again in G major, is piquant and coquettish, in duple time. According to her great admirer, Théophile Gautier, "Each one of her poses, each one of her dainty or virtuoso movements is stamped with the seal of originality." This is followed by a brief, gracious duet of Taglioni and Grahn, andantino in E flat, in duple time, ending on a delicious trill. The andante variation with Cerito performing a diagonal series of revolving bounds, turns, and leaps is in the unusual tonality of B major, in duple time. Taglioni's consummate variation, allegro in G major in duple time, is replete with her amazing flights and leaps, and also her unique arabesque characterizing the immortal Sylphide. The coda for the four ballerinas first gives each dancer one more occasion for brilliant display, and then the andante theme of the introduction returns, D major in duple time, as the dancers hand in hand perform a series of échappés and finally graciously assume the celebrated pose we know from the lovely Chalon lithograph. Although there is a kind of festive competition in *Pas de Quatre,* it remains probably the earliest ballet devoted to dance in the abstract.

In another of the Perrot-Pugni collaborations, *Eoline* (London, 1845), a pastoral ballet on a classical theme, Pugni's rhythms were more evenly divided between duple and triple time, and the tempos are more consistently moderate. Pugni's effective but conservative orchestrations were quite representative of what he learned in school: woodwinds in twos, brass generally in twos and threes, percussion, an occasional harp, and strings.

Delibes and *Coppélia*

The immediate effects of the French Revolution on the arts were largely absorbed after two decades of the Romantic Age in Paris, London, and elsewhere with such wonderful dancers as Taglioni, Elssler, Grisi, Cerito, and Grahn performing in *La Sylphide, Giselle* and other ballets, inspired by

Lucille Grahn in the Bournonville production of *La Sylphide*. (*Courtesy of the Harvard Theatre Collection*)

the figures we have already discussed. The new political wave of nationalism plus the artistic changes aggressively propounded by Berlioz, Liszt, and Wagner increasingly influenced the lyric theatre.

The next masterpiece of ballet was *Coppélia,* first performed on May 25, 1870, at the Paris Opéra. For over a decade prior to that premiere very little that was important happened in ballet except for revivals. The choreographer of *Coppélia,* Arthur Saint-Léon (ca. 1815–1870), sometime husband of the ebullient ballerina Fanny Cerito, was an important dancer as well as the choreographer of about fifty ballets. He invented a system of notating dances, which, while accurate enough, is no less laborious to use than the many other systems that have been conceived. Saint-Léon, also a violinist and a composer, was active in all the major European capitals. In 1860 he replaced Perrot as the leading choreographer in Saint Petersburg, but after a few years he returned to France to finish his career where he had begun, at the Paris Opéra.

Léo Delibes (1836–1891) was an important French composer of operas and ballets, as well as being active in other musical fields. He was nowhere near as prolific as his teacher, Adolphe Adam, but his score of *Coppélia* contains music which is undeniably more distinguished than most ballet scores of his time.

The story of the production of *Coppélia* and its reception has been excellently recounted in Cyril W. Beaumont's *Complete Book of Ballets.* Suffice to say that Saint-Léon, himself a trained musician, certainly understood Delibes's attractive score very well. The choreographer has provided an outstanding sequence of movements, some of which is said to have been invented by Léon Mérante. How much of Saint-Léon's original choreography for *Coppélia* has resisted the passing of time and the numerous revivals and revisions (principally Russian) who can say, any more than how much of the even older *Giselle* is faithful to its original production.

Adapted by Charles Nuitter from an "autobiographical" story by the German author-composer E. T. A. Hoffmann, *Coppélia* is a joyous ninety minute ballet in three acts. Swanhilda and Frantz are village sweethearts, but their mysterious neighbor, Dr. Coppelius, has a "daughter," Coppélia, by whom Frantz is fascinated. In act II, in Dr. Coppelius's absence, Swanhilda and her girl friends enter his house to find Coppélia is only a remarkable mechanical doll among a roomful of others. When Frantz also comes to investigate, Dr. Coppelius has returned, and after drugging Frantz he attempts to give Coppélia, now impersonated by Swanhilda, the young man's soul. Coppélia apparently comes to life. After several attractive character dances, the impish Coppélia-Swanhilda drops her pretense, and she and Frantz escape together. In the third act all is set right at the festival of the bells, while Dr. Coppelius is compensated for the mischievous damage Swanhilda and her friends did to his dolls. Then comes a glorious divertissement, with Dawn, Prayer, Work, Hymen, Discord, and War all integrated into the joyous finale.

By the late 1860s when Delibes composed the thirty-one numbers for *Coppélia* he had already proved his skill with *La Source,* in which his part of this ballet was far more appreciated than the portion composed by Ludwig Minkus. Following the predominantly sunny disposition of *Coppélia,* Delibes used a minor tonality only once. (Readers will recall that generally composers use minor tonalities to suggest stress and sadness, and major keys to suggest determination and joyous, positive feelings.) In acts I and II Delibes favored sharp keys; in act III he turned more to the flat keys. After the prelude in D major, which opens quizzically, mysteriously, continues ominously, then closes gloriously with the mazurka, Delibes begins the ballet with the dramatically lilting valse lente for Swanhilda in E flat and closes with the festive final galop, also in E flat. Although act I is amost equally divided between duple and triple time, acts II and III are heavily weighted in favor of duple time. As regards tempo, act I is mostly moderate, act II is faster, and act III is fast to moderate. Despite the fact that at the time Delibes was accused of being too "symphonic," he never once in *Coppélia* used the symphonists' favorite form, the sonata form. He does use the ABA form quite frequently (at least a quarter of the time). His set pieces include that opening valse and also two others, and one each of the following: mazurka, csardas, variations, bolero, gigue, marche, and galop.

The principal reasons I believe *Coppélia* is a masterpiece are Delibes's extraordinary gifts for melody, his provocative yet refined harmony, and his unusually keen sense of orchestration. His instrumentation, two flutes, two oboes, two clarinets, two bassoons, four horns, four trumpets, three trombones and tuba, percussion, harp, and strings was not particularly original, but the way he varied his use of the instruments was.

We know that Tchaikovsky and Stravinsky were both very partial to the music of Delibes (including *Sylvia* and *Coppélia*). No doubt, major reasons for their enthusiasm were Delibes's fine sense of form and his acute ear. The infectious gaiety of his music makes the fairy tale story of *Coppélia,* with its eternal dilemma of "greener grass on the other side of the fence" and its obvious, rational conclusion memorable and irresistible, even though some of the dramatic veracity was removed because originally there was no male variation. That was principally due to the decline of male virtuosity in Western Europe once Jules Perrot, Lucien Petipa, and Saint-Léon no longer took leading roles.

In general, the elegant and vivacious score for *Coppélia* characteristically points up the action at every turn in the way the Adam, Tchaikovsky, and Stravinsky ballets do. *Coppélia* is not a grand ballet, any more than Mozart's *The Marriage of Figaro* is like Wagner, but it very definitely has an important place in the aesthetic picture as one of the most significant ballets of the nineteenth century.

Coppélia is important for itself, however, and not just as a period piece or as a vehicle. (Let it not be imagined that any of the ballets we discuss are merely vehicles.) Its successive numbers are appropriate and the scenes have dramatic validity as they are in turn ceremonious, sweeping, delicate, lyrical, piquant, ebullient, and finally winning in the culminating galop. The heroine, like Susanna in *The Marriage of Figaro,* gets her proud, beloved man without fighting, pushing, or scheming, but with charm, wit, intelligence, character, and persuasion, and with victorious energy—brilliant and marvellous, all within a frame.

Bournonville and the Danish Tradition

The origin of ballet in Denmark, which can be traced to court balls in the sixteenth and seventeenth centuries, began in earnest when pupils of Beauchamps and Balon came to Copenhagen to direct the teaching and to produce performances in the early eighteenth century. Their many French and Italian successors included M. des Larches, Antonio Como, J. B. Martin, Innocenzo Gambuzzi, and finally Vincenzo Galeotti (1733–1816), who had been a pupil of Angiolini and Noverre. Galeotti's numerous ballets included *Dido* (1777), *Lagertha* (1801), which was apparently the first Danish ballet based on a Nordic theme, *Romeo and Juliet* (1811), and most particularly the ballet that has the longest continuous performing history, *The Whims of Cupid and the Balletmaster* (1786). In this amusing work to music by Jens Lolle, seven blindfolded couples and a group of six blackamoors enter the tunnel of love, and through the whims of Cupid they emerge quite ill-assorted: a peasant with a noble, a prim lady with a most eager lad, and so on. When Galeotti died his place was taken temporarily by several dancers, including the French-born Antoine de Bournonville. Following a brief interregnum, his son, August Bournonville (1805–1879), who had been a member of the company in his youth, was recalled from Paris where he was studying with Auguste Vestris and performing at the Paris Opéra. A violinist as well as a brilliant young dancer and disciple of the ideas of Noverre, Bournonville was ballet master in Copenhagen from 1830 until 1877. He perpetuated what there was and what he knew of French style, and gradually he formed a Danish school that has resulted in the establishment of a wonderful living tradition. Additionally, he had a direct influence on traditions in other countries through his pupils Lucille Grahn in Germany, and Christian Johansson in Russia.

The style we see in the Royal Danish Ballet today certainly has changed some, but most probably far less than in most other countries and companies over the last hundred years. Partly this is due to Denmark's relative isolation, and partly to the understandable pride the Danes have taken in what they recognized as their own style. Following Bournonville's death, the ballet master Hans Beck undertook to keep fresh and alive the Bournonville repertoire and school of dancing. Beck died only in 1932, and since then others have taken up the duty of continuing the tradition.

We have already noted how the subject matter for ballets (as for operas) was changing and how nineteenth century interest in heroic and tragic themes or elegant ones began to give way to drama, increasingly frank burlesque, and occasionally nationalistic themes. Also increasingly in vogue were romantic subjects featuring idyllic or supernatural happenings, ballets such as *La Sylphide* or *Giselle,* and also ballets featuring varied character and national dances. For example, Fanny Elssler introduced the cachucha, and her energy provided a special dimension in many of the ballets in which she appeared, even if the music or some of the other elements were not particularly original.

Before we consider Bournonville's production of *La Sylphide,* which with *Napoli* was probably his most enduring work, we should introduce ourselves to a variety of the choreographer's many ballets. Despite his apparent isolation in a small northern country he actually was a frequent traveler and an artist with unlimited curiosity whose works reflect his amazing range of interests. Using the excellent foundations of his predecessors, Bournonville choreographed thirty-six major ballets according to his own meticulous count, but with his many revisions, revivals, and occasional works he produced more than one hundred. The names of his important ballets will have to suffice here; readers who desire more information are referred to the Bibliography. In addition to pure divertissements, Bournonville choreographed ballets on Hellenic themes, travels, and Danish history, and folk tales. Besides waltzes, his favorite set forms included the galop, tarantella, seguidilla, bolero and other Spanish dances, slovanka, hornpipe, polka, polacca, polonaise, as well as Indian,

Margot Lander and Børge Ralov in the final scene from the Royal Danish Ballet production of *Napoli*. (*Courtesy of the Collection of Lily and Baird Hastings*)

Eskimo, South Sea, South American and other ethnic dances, for all of which and more he found place in his varied works.

The following Bournonville ballets except *Valdemar* and *The Toreador* are still performed by the Royal Danish Ballet (and four of them are performed by a number of companies):

1835	*Valdemar,* 4 acts (music by J. H. Frølich, 1806–1860)
1836	*La Sylphide,* 2 acts (music by H. S. Løvenskjold, 1815–1870)
1840	*The Toreador,* 2 acts (music by Edvard Helsted, 1816–1900)
1842	*Napoli,* 3 acts (music by H. S. Paulli, 1810–1891; Helsted; N. W. Gade, 1817–1890; H. C. Lumbye, 1810–1874)
1849	*Konservatoriet,* 2 acts (Paulli) *Kermesse in Bruges, or The Three Gifts,* 4 acts (Paulli)
1854	*A Folk Tale,* 3 acts (music by Gade and J. P. E. Hartmann, 1805–1900)
1858	*Flower Festival in Genzano,* 1 act (Helsted-Gade)
1860	*Far from Denmark,* 2 acts (music by J. P. Glaeser, ca. 1798–1860, Lumbye, and others)
1871	*The Life Guards,* 1 act (music by P. Holm, ca. 1840–1900; J. B. E. Dupuy, 1775–1825; Lumbye)
1875	*From Siberia to Moscow,* 2 acts (music by C. C. Møller, ca. 1840–1900)

There are two interesting points to be made about the eleven ballets that are listed: first, the subjects, and second, the composers.

The subjects are: ancient Denmark, Scotland, Spain, Italy, ballet school, Belgium, a world tour, a battle campaign, and Russia. Every one is in some sense exotic, and in every one Bournonville was able to use folk dance or unusual color from a region or a profession that had appeal to the Danes. They love to travel, are cultured far beyond the resources of their proud little country, and have an extended history of their own that stretches back many centuries, far and wide. Even the ballet school offers a dramatic excuse for divertissement of which Bournonville made effective use. The choreographer's great respect for high art and for the French ideals of Noverre did not permit him to create ballets which were mere technical displays. He integrated the exotic into well-made dramatic works, of which the three-act *Napoli* is a particularly fine example. The dramatic first act takes place an evening in Naples by the Bay of Santa Lucia. The fantastic second act is set among the spirits in the Blue Grotto of Capri. The joyous third act has a festive setting at Monte Vergines, near Naples. Full of mime and varied dance, as the lovers are united, in the last act Bournonville makes use of numerous Italian folk dances: pas seuls, duets, trios, pas de six, and scintillating ensembles, concluding with an irresistible tarantella. In the other ten ballets listed above this is also frequently his manner of construction for dramatic and artistic unity and variety. Generally an optimist in all things, Bournonville's own particular favorite ballet was *A Folk Tale,* the ninety minute story of two girls who had been exchanged shortly after birth, one nasty brought up a lady, and one pleasant brought up a peasant—and of how good fortune prevailed.

In the eleven ballets listed, Bournonville choreographed scores by eleven different composers. Only five were composed by just one musician. The other six were musical collaborations of two or three composers, all carefully controlled by Bournonville, so that the style would be appropriate for the parts and for the whole. As a viewer I can state positively that Bournonville integrated theme, dance, and music to a remarkable extent.

Over the years the composers who were his trusted and close collaborators were Frølich, Løvenskjold, Gade, Paulli, and Lumbye. Gade, a student of Mendelssohn and a teacher of Carl Nielsen (whose work Martha Graham recently choreographed) is perhaps the nineteenth-century Danish composer whose music is best known beyond the ballet, though frequently Lumbye is referred to as the Danish Johann Strauss. In any event, how effective the music was of these half-dozen composers can easily be verified when we see the Bournonville ballets on which they collaborated.

Although Bournonville did not attend the premiere of *La Sylphide,* he did see and admire Marie Taglioni and Joseph Mazilier in Filippo Taglioni's production at the Paris Opéra. He decided to present this ballet in Denmark with his gifted student Lucille Grahn[3] and himself, and he commissioned Løvenskjold to compose a new score for this version. Careful comparison of the stories of the Taglioni and Bournonville ballets reveals that Bournonville made changes, which, however minor individually, definitely strengthened the dramatic line, and of course there were changes imposed by the different music. In act I Bournonville makes much more of the tender relation between La Sylphide and James Reuben. In act II the action is more unified, with a more important part for the revengeful Madge. The action is handled more as Noverre might have wished (or Fokine), rather than as a suite of dances.

Jean Schneitzhöffer was, as we have noted, a minor French composer of the time, yet in this ballet he showed what he might have become had his talent been developed through more works. Løvenskjold also was a minor composer, a student of Kuhlau and Weyse who was influenced by Schubert and Weber; in working under somewhat less pressure he produced the superior score. His orchestration for *La Sylphide* was for two flutes, two oboes, two clarinets, two bassoons, *four horns,* three trumpets, three trombones and tuba, percussion, harp, and strings. This orchestration was virtually identical with Schneitzhöffer's, but it was more imaginatively used. Although Løvenskjold did not develop his ideas as well as Adam in *Giselle,* he did use leitmotifs. Another important difference between the two versions of *La Sylphide* is Løvenskjold's effective use of minor tonality to heighten the drama at several crucial points in the action.

The four-minute overture to this version begins ominously moderato with a mysterious atmosphere in minor, in duple time (the entire ballet is mostly in duple time). There is a brief solo on the violoncello, and then an accelerando and a crashing fortissimo bring on a chilling effect. Following a brief episode lento, there is a scurrying allegro clearly revealing a Weberian influence, after which the overture concludes on a rousing climax. Act I is divided into seven sections: 1. Sleeping, James dreams of La Sylphide who appears before dawn and kisses him as we hear a brief violin solo; he wakes up; 2. James's fiancée, Effie, makes a vivacious entrance, accompanied by James's mother, the widow Reuben; James is distracted, and Effie scolds him; 3. Effie's friends arrive to congratulate her; 4. The sinister Madge comes to tell fortunes, predicting that Effie will marry James's friend Gurn, who also loves Effie, rather than James; James is very angry and bids her begone; Madge swears revenge; 5. During a quiet interlude while the others go to prepare for the wedding, James has a tender moment again with the soft, yet impish La Sylphide. Seeing them together, Gurn goes to call the others but by the time they arrive La Sylphide has disappeared up the chimney and no one will believe Gurn; 6. After another moment of quiet, the betrothal dances, Scottish reels and the like including a solo for James give pleasure to the entire group of villagers; 7. In the middle of the wedding ceremony La Sylphide returns, snatches the ring James had for Effie and disappears into the forest; James follows. When James's absence is noticed there is great consternation, and weeping Effie is comforted by Mother Reuben and Gurn.

Act II has nine sections: 1. A brief introduction begins quietly, then crescendos, and finally turns into the dance of Madge and the witches in triple time, as at midnight they plan the death of La Sylphide. Then night fades; 2. It is dawn again; birds twitter, and while a violoncello recalls the moment in the overture, the lovers meet; 3. There is a pas de deux with violin solo for the two lovers (all in duple time) reminiscent of Auber; 4. The sisters of La Sylphide arrive from the sky, and dance; 5. Dramatically, Gurn comes upon the hat of James for whom he had been searching, but he sees Madge who promises to help him win Effie's hand (all in duple time); 6. Tormented by the fact that he can never hold La Sylphide in his arms for long, James comes to Madge and begs her to help him. She gives him the poisoned scarf she was preparing the night before, saying that thus La Sylphide will be his (again in duple time); 7. There is a touching scene of love as James enfolds La Sylphide with the scarf, but then she is stricken and pleads for James's help. She vows eternal love and gives him her blessing before she dies (partly triple time); 8. The sisters come and carry La Sylphide toward heaven; 9. James sees the happy and jaunty wedding procession of Effie and Gurn (in duple time). Madge exults as he collapses and dies.

Comparing this version with the Taglioni *Sylphide* we can realize how the differences, though small, change the emphasis and improve the ballet. In the former version James does not die; he loses the tangible and does not achieve the intangible, and can regret his actions all his life. In the romantic and poetic Bournonville version there is a powerful, perhaps redeeming, love, not merely the weakness of one human being. One is left with the hope that James will be reunited with La Sylphide.

Virtuosity in Russia: Petipa Achieves Romantic Ideals

"Few spectators realize what it means to produce a *ballet,* even of one act. The selection of the theme, the music, the designs; the casting of the roles, the planning of the *choreography,* the making of the costumes, the painting of the scenery, the arrangements of the finances and then the million and one things that still have to be decided when everything seems accomplished."

I have begun this final section devoted to developments in the nineteenth century with the above quotation from *Complete Book of Ballets* by Cyril W. Beaumont in order to reinforce in the mind of the reader the elements that must be thoroughly coordinated in the lyric theatre if following the spectacle the audience is to depart thoroughly satisfied in every way. (If the italicized words "ballet" and "choreography" were replaced by "work" and "action" the quotation would apply to any theatrical production.)

It is particularly appropriate to discuss ballets of Petipa with this quotation in mind, for he had an extraordinary ability to create and organize within the framework of the conditions (both good and bad) in which he worked in sixty-three years in Russia. I do not intend that readers of this historical discussion should draw comparative value judgments concerning the ballets of Petipa (which I greatly admire, among many others) over other masterworks from the past or the present. It is not the purpose of this essay to enumerate the relative merits of, and ways in which such diverse masterworks as the *Play of Daniel, Everyman, The Last Supper, Hamlet, Messiah, The Marriage of Figaro, The Ninth Symphony, Parsifal, The Sleeping Beauty, Les Sylphides, Apollo* have charmed and moved audiences throughout the ages—art is too wide a kingdom to be parochial. One should, one must be ready to welcome masterworks of whatever kind, equally, even if some would welcome the allegorical and wonderful rendition of Perrault's fairy story, *The Sleeping Beauty,* a little more equally.

Marius Petipa (1822–1910) came from a family of excellent dancers, and received thorough training from his father as well as from Auguste Vestris. After dancing in Marseille, Brussels, Nantes, America, and briefly in Paris, he went to Russia in 1847 and remained there the rest of his life, except for at least one short return to the West. He married a young Russian dancer, and after her death married another. He was appointed ballet master in Saint Petersburg in 1862, and for over four decades he directed ballet in Russia. Building on the firm foundations of Didelot, Perrot, and others, he created the Russian dancer we have known, aided by the influx of a number of brilliant Italian dancers formed in the school of Blasis (Carlotta Brianza, Virginia Zucchi, Pierina Legnani, Enrico Cecchetti), by the Swedish pupil of August Bournonville, Christian Johansson, and by the Russian Lev Ivanov, who was assistant choreographer and ballet master in charge of some of Petipa's ballets. (Anyone directing the same organization for such a long time is bound to have opposition develop to his way of operation, and eventually this was a factor in the emergence of Fokine.)

Petipa choreographed or revived more than 100 ballets, many full evening works, to music by more than twenty composers, some of which are still remembered in their original Saint Petersburg or Moscow productions. While thirty of Petipa's successful ballets were mounted to scores by Pugni or Minkus, it was with the three late scores by Tchaikovsky that Petipa achieved his most perfect results.

Although many of us have seen only a handful of Petipa's greatest achievements, we can recognize the French influence on his ballets.

Despite the fact that France, the original "source-mother and father-home" of the ballet, produced *La Sylphide, Giselle,* and *Coppélia,* later in the century the focus of originality moved to Russia, where Petipa was developing the Franco-Russian school of dancers while he perpetuated many of the ideals of Noverre. (In Denmark, meanwhile, Bournonville was independently perpetuating many Noverre ideals.)

That Petipa was extremely musical, his varied ballets prove. Certainly each composer he collaborated with gave Petipa what he wanted and needed to achieve his romantic and classic masterpieces. The scores were and are very danceable, and if they are not all memorable to musicians, one should realize that ballet as an art form depends on fusion.

Cesare Pugni was probably the most prolific composer in ballet history. We have already noted that *Esmeralda* and *Pas de Quatre* were imaginative, expressive, and even fanciful with brio, drama, and passion.

Ludwig Minkus (1827–1917?) was born in Vienna. After performing as a violinist in various theatres he traveled to Moscow perhaps as early as 1847. In 1869 his long series of collaborations with Petipa began with the infectious, tuneful, and pseudo-Spanish *Don Quixote.* Quite a success in its time, *Don Quixote* has been revived and revised often. Probably on a higher plane is *La Bayadère* (1876). Both ballets and several other Petipa-Minkus collaborations contained beautiful, mysterious scenes for groups of youthful spirits, which enabled Petipa to show off the wonders of the ballet blanc corps de ballet (along the lines of *La Sylphide, Giselle, Swan Lake,* and the "Dance of the Snowflakes" scene from *Nutcracker*), something that sets them apart from the ballets with music by Pugni. We should remember that frequently Minkus inserted attractive closed or set dance forms—polkas, mazurkas, and above all tuneful waltzes—whether or not they were appropriate in the action from a dramatic point of view. Still, Petipa treated all his musical collaborators to his usual instructions, and he knew very well what to do with the music he received.

Above all, Petipa, an excellent dancer with wide experience, had many other qualities, notably persistence. He danced in the periods when Filippo Taglioni, Perrot, and Saint-Léon were leading choreographers, and he went to Russia to continue dancing. He observed the elements that made Russian ballets appealing, and he was ready when the call came to make his own. He was inventive and created brilliant dances for soloists, and he was varied and superbly architectural in his handling of groups. Within the frame in which he worked in Russia he was faithful to the ideals of Noverre just as Bournonville was within his.

In *Dance Index,* volume 6, numbers 5 and 6, Yury Slonimsky writes perceptively about Petipa's libretto plans:

Jean-Georges Noverre demanded two things of ballet music: a rhythmico-melodic outline for the dance and a pictorial illustration of the stage action. Music in ballet exists in connection with the action, it helps the action and is subjected to its development on the stage. The problem is not the interpretation of music as a certain dominant characteristic of the ballet, but of musical accompaniment in the service of choreography.

Petipa shared Noverre's viewpoint. Whoever the composer might be—a worthless dilettante or the highly respected Peter Tchaikovsky—Petipa, as the author of the ballet, did not intend to yield one bit of the preeminence of choreography. From this premise stems the order in which he developed the component parts of the ballet. The choreographic exposition was always created first. It embraced questions of choreographic form, stage text, musical characteristics. Then came the musical exposition, pre-indicated to a substantial degree by the choreography; and last of all the actual staging.

Those who assume that Petipa laid out the first musical plan only for Tchaikovsky are mistaken. From the 1860s to the end of his days, Petipa always worked with composers only according to a plan laid out by him beforehand. We find such plans in the documents of Glazunov, Pugni, Minkus, in short, of everybody who had worked with him. But the importance of a pattern is not the creation of a pattern, so much as the manner in which Petipa did it.

At the moment of outlining the plan, Petipa, not yet in possession of the music, was already preparing the stage material of the future ballet. He built it on music which did not exist, but he clearly heard in tempo, rhythm, character, and even instrumentation. His preoccupation with music for the dance numbers and action scenes unquestionably afforded the composer good ideas.

What astonishes and wins us over in *The Sleeping Beauty* is Tchaikovsky's impressionistic manner in developing the figure of the (evil) fairy Carabosse. And now it turns out that Petipa carefully and vividly thought out all movements in his musical plan for Tchaikovsky.

As a graphic illustration we shall cite here a few examples of Petipa's libretto plan for Tchaikovsky *(The Sleeping Beauty):* (Petipa wrote down all texts in French.) . . .

Suddenly Aurora notices the old woman who beats on her knitting needles a 2/4 measure. Gradually she changes to a very melodious waltz in 3/4, but then suddenly a rest. Aurora pricks her finger. Screams, pain. Blood streams—give 8 measures in 4/4, wide. She begins her dance—dizziness. . . . Complete horror—this is not a dance any longer. It is frenzy. As if bitten by a tarantula she keeps turning and then falls unexpectedly, out of breath. This must last from 24 to 32 measures. At the end there should be a tremolo of a few measures, as if of shouts of pain and sobs: "Father, Mother!"

And later, when everybody notices the old woman, she throws off her clothes. For this moment it is necessary that a chromatic scale sound in the entire orchestra. . . ." (In Kalmus edition score, Volume I, p. 202, et sequitur).

The superbly witty dance of the "two cats" was suggested to Tchaikovsky by Petipa not only by a descriptive phrase but by a very definite musical characteristic, "Repeated mewing, denoting caressing and clawing. For the end— clawing and screaming of the male cat. It should begin 3/4 amoroso and end in 3/4 with accelerated mewing." (In Kalmus edition score, volume III, p. 128.)

In 1862 Petipa inaugurated the frame he used with great success through eleven of his extravagant evening-long masterworks, refining and refocusing it as appropriate. This frame was logical monumentality, in contrast to melodrama, romanticism, or divertissement that had no dramatic reason. This apparently pleased the Russians for many years. It seemed to fit their ego and their lifestyle. The specific theme he chose for his first splendorous monument was Egypt, in the news for its archeological treasures since Napoleon and before. (The story of Petipa's *The Daughter of the Pharaoh,* which predates H. Rider Haggard's novel *She,* involves the dream of Lord Wilson "temporarily transported back to the wonders of ancient Egypt.") Four years later, after a trip to Paris, Petipa was inspired to add spectacular effects to *The Daughter of the Pharaoh* (music by Pugni)—a high waterfall, behind which, protected by glass and lit by electric batteries, the ballerina "took her bath."

Meanwhile, in 1865 with *The Traveling Dancer (The Little Mujik)* he secured another popular success, as Pugni's score included a number of Russian themes. The road was long for Petipa, but when successes became ever more frequent, and Saint-Léon finally left for good, Petipa was put in charge. *Le Roi Candaule* (1868) was another Petipa-Pugni extravaganza with an original libretto by the French writer Saint-Georges to which the musician contributed rhythmically dependable, booming music to accompany the massive grandeur with overpowering effects. (This at the expense of more sensitive dramatic quality we find in Pugni's music for earlier Perrot ballets—which were appropriately passionate rather than just loud. But just consider if you had to deliver up to six ballets a year. . .)

In the 1870s Petipa sought novelty in his *Trilby,* a ballet containing a bird cage of dancers; the traditionally gorgeous *Camargo; The Bandits* based on Cervantes; *The Butterfly,* with its ballet of vegetables and insects; *Roxana,* which had fine folk dances and the fantastic scene of the spirits; and above all, *La Bayadère.* Although we see it in the West as revised by Natalia Makarova and John Lanchberry, it is still very romantic drama and marvellous spectacle, with carefully varied solo and ensemble dances, the Bayadère's death dance, and above all the act in the kingdom of the shades.

In the 1880s and 1890s Petipa was forced to turn further from some of Noverre's ideals. Plot was no longer of decisive importance; virtuosity was stressed, but even in fairy tales Petipa leaned toward the elegance of the

French school to temper the virtuosic Italians. During this period the Russian court wanted above all "to be amused," and as a servant of royalty Petipa performed his duty.

For Tchaikovsky, *The Sleeping Beauty* was Perrault's fairy tale, a struggle of light versus dark. But for Petipa, *The Sleeping Beauty* was life. There was Aurora, heiress to the throne, in a fight for happiness, representing by allegory the love of the Russian people for their ruler. The opening march of the prologue introduces us to this world, and its special atmosphere. In act I there is the famous waltz and the rose adagio. In act II, the vision and the Lilac Fairy. In act III, the Bluebird and Princess Florine, and the sweeping ensembles. Throughout, the pantomime scenes are mixed with ingenious solos and ensembles. In the scenes for the corps de ballet every torso, head, and arm is set in identical movements (which is against the ideas of Vigano), working perfectly here because the gain in grandeur more than offsets the loss in dramatic effect. The harmonious lines are used for brilliant buildups, as apparently Petipa had an inexhaustible gift for combinations. Though Petipa's actual steps in character dances often resemble those of his classic numbers, they almost all reveal elements of individual style. His solo dances were naturally built on the special strengths of the dancers first cast to perform them. He liked to give a basic pas to each variation, thus indicating the basic character; the next variation would have another character and another pas. Music and movement were to fit hand in glove in this way. Note in *The Sleeping Beauty* the extraordinary series: Diamond, Gold, Silver, Saphire variations. This procedure was increasingly followed in Petipa's ballets, through the three-act *Raymonda* (music by Glazunov), which was one of his last successes. After 1899, when Telyakovsky replaced Vsevolojsky as director of the Imperial Theatres, Petipa had a difficult time, and in 1903 he resigned. Until his death in 1910, however, he kept hoping he would be called back to the post where he had presided over the flowering of a glorious repertoire and an incomparable company.

This section can only summarize the qualities and characteristics of the music that Pugni, Minkus, Tchaikovsky, Glazunov, and others composed for ballets for Petipa to choreograph. Pugni used the standard orchestra for his time (two each in the winds, four horns, three trumpets, three trombones and tuba, percussion, harp, strings); standard forms, some based on folk tunes; graceful, delightful melodies; varied tonalities with generally unified structure; rhythms were two-thirds duple and tempos on the fast side. Minkus used the standard orchestra and conventional forms, some based on folk tunes; but though his pseudo-Spanish material was

The Sleeping Princess (Beauty). Group includes Felia Doubrovska, Lubov Egorova, Bronislava Nijinska, Vera Nemtchinova, and artists of the Diaghilev production (1921). *(Courtesy of the Collection of Lily and Baird Hastings)*

momentarily exciting it was not used nearly as artistically as that of Chabrier, Bizet, or Rimsky-Korsakov; his waltzes were numerous and very effective; his melodies were more passionate than Pugni's; his tonalities were varied and had a unified structure; his rhythms were duple two-thirds of the time and the tempos were on the fast side.

Tchaikovsky used a more varied orchestra, with English horn, for example; his standard forms were judiciously chosen; his melody showed real contrast and conformed more to character involvement; his tonalities were chosen carefully; two-thirds of the rhythms were duple and tempos were generally fast. Having numerous procedures at his fingertips, in *The Sleeping Beauty* Tchaikovsky used each for its artistic effect, from fanfares and brilliant tours de force, to tender emotional moments, to sweeping romantic waltzes, to orchestra effects that focus on the drama—all under Petipa's master plan. From the beginning the music of Tchaikovsky portrayed the storm involved between good and evil, starting in the Carabosse-designated tonality of e minor in a nervous allegro tempo, then moving to the Lilac Fairy-linked tonality of E major in a calmer and assured andantino. There are noble strains of the march, and in each tableau a series of variations. In the prologue, following the bustling preparations for the ceremony, there are the dances of the six fairies. In act I the sweeping waltz is followed by the grandeur of the rose adagio at the presentation of Princess Aurora to her suitors at court. In act II the series of five set divertissement pieces fails to divert Prince Florimund; and this is followed by the enchanting poetry of the vision scene "duo." In the final act there is yet a more brilliant series of pas de deux and pas de trois, concluding with the apotheosis presided over faithfully by the now trium-phant Lilac Fairy. In the thirty numbers of *The Sleeping Beauty* Tchaikovsky favored duple time, and fast tempos, and in order of frequency the tonalities of C major, B flat, and F, though always with supple and appropriate variety, and with the contrast of good and evil largely pre-sented in the tonalities of E major and e minor.

In the Royal Ballet production the pomp and circumstance have been analyzed and crystalized so that the detailed musical description of charac-ters and action becomes more than a fable. It captures human nature at large better than many modern works, although the Stravinsky-Balanchine *Le Baiser de la Fée* comes to mind as at least one recent ballet, which, while starting out as a fairy tale, becomes much more than make-believe.

Glazunov, whose orchestra varied by only a few instruments from that of Tchaikovsky, used the standard forms with color but much less imagination than Tchaikovsky, and the same could be said of his melody and harmony. While much of Drigo's music is effective on first hearing, its musical value is a step below that of Glazunov, and far below that of Delibes or Adam.

In sum, Petipa employed tastefully almost every artistic technique then known. Following his libretto, music, and decoration outlines, he gave detailed direction to decorators, composers, and dancers. Obtaining excellent results in this way from Tchaikovsky, he tried the same system with others, but many were unable to cooperate as fully as Tchaikovsky. Nevertheless the results of Petipa's method were some of lyric theatre's genuine masterworks standing alongside those of Lully, Noverre, Coralli, Perrot, and Bournonville.

We are about to discuss great creators of the twentieth century with as much detachment as possible. What posterity will think of Fokine, Massine, Balanchine (all products of Petipa's system, and all flourishing under Diaghilev), and Ashton, Tudor, Graham, Cunningham, time will tell. Because of his influence on major modern choreographers, it is very possible that Stravinsky will be the name that lives (with Lully's) as a musician whose importance in theatrical dance of his time exceeded that of the ballet master.

6

The Twentieth Century:
Three Great Russians

Each era in the history of lyric theatre we have discussed has involved major developments or major figures in music and dance resulting in new perspectives and achievements. Toward the end of the Middle Ages, sparked by the *"renaissance of the 12th century,"* there was the emergence of the religious pageant, which led to the origin of theatrical dancing and opera. At the conclusion of the Renaissance proper the proscenium theatre developed, which led to the birth of the idea of artistic unity in court spectacle-entertainments. In Lully's time there was the impact of professionalism; Noverre's demonstrated concern with dramatic veracity in the ballet, followed by Beethoven's musical revolution. The Romantic Age and later saw the triumph of technique and illusion. In our own century the widening range of both music and dance has enriched the contributions of the artists involved and the enjoyment of the increasing numbers of spectators. The twentieth century's greatest figure in the music of theatrical dance has been Igor Stravinsky, whose involvement with modern choreographers we will consider in some detail. Because of the special relationship between Stravinsky and George Balanchine (both of whose work the author was privileged to follow closely), it seems appropriate to discuss the achievements of the choreographer largely in terms of his relationship with the composer.

Fokine and the New Ballet

Although certainly twentieth-century ballet could not be imagined without the masterworks of Michel Fokine (1880–1942), today his period

105

seems almost as far away to many ballet-goers as the periods of Lully, Noverre, or Petipa. The emphasis on Diaghilev and Stravinsky and the revolution in ballet beginning in 1909 is justified, but mentioning only those two is rather like talking about a two-legged tripod or a three-legged table. Without the participation of Michel Fokine the success of the undertaking would have been questionable.

Fokine produced nearly one hundred ballets between 1905 and his death in 1942, and any standard book on ballets presents the basic facts on his masterworks, which number at least a dozen. Cyril W. Beaumont, whose first-hand accounts of virtually the entire Diaghilev era are invaluable, appropriately observed that Fokine's *Les Sylphides* to music orchestrated from piano pieces of Frédéric Chopin is the most poetic ballet of this century, which in itself would place the choreographer alongside of Jean Coralli and Jules Perrot, the authors of *Giselle*. Similarly, Lincoln Kirstein has acutely stated that *Petrouchka* is Fokine's masterpiece—a standard for dance-drama of our time.

By the time Diaghilev began to form a company, Fokine had already proved his worth, and thus his selection by Diaghilev to be ballet master and choreographer of the new venture, his Ballets Russes, was extremely à propos. The others who were gathered around initially included a number of gifted Russian collaborators: Alexandre Benois, Léon Bakst, Nicolas Tcherepnine, and principally through Fokine, such stimulating young dancers as Anna Pavlova, Tamara Karsavina, Vera Fokina, Adolph Bolm, and Vaslav Nijinsky.

Fokine graduated from the Saint Petersburg School in 1898 and joined the Maryinsky Ballet as a valued soloist. He began his choreographic career about the time that Isadora Duncan first visited Russia. Although Fokine rejected Duncan's barefoot approach, he was ready for her free ideas, and they helped him in his own attempt to bring new life into the Petipa-regulated Russian Imperial Ballet. Petipa, who saw the new attitude developing, was magnanimous and encouraged the young Fokine. Fokine looked for something more than ballet by the numbers— ensemble, solo, pas de trois, etc.—something more than divertissement—waltz, galop, march, etc. In his return to the ideals of Noverre he emphasized logically constructed one-act ballets with a beginning, a middle, and an end. His music, decors, and costumes are always representative of the theme. His movements in relation to the music and in relation to the style and atmosphere are always appropriate, they seem to grow directly out of the musical impulse. As one watches one of his ballets, one never questions why did he not direct his dancers to do this or that, for the good reason that he has always chosen the right steps for the particular phrase. Yet in spite of this, many of Fokine's ballets have been forgotten or are so poorly performed that they seem dated.

Fokine applied principles we noted in Noverre and even in somewhat loosely constructed works such as *Les Elfes, Le Carnaval,* and *Scheherazade* he showed that divertissement should be coordinated with dramatic content.

Fokine's crucial contributions to the first five years of the Diaghilev company are detailed in a number of publications. Among his many important ballets in his seasons there are the elegant *Pavillon d'Armide* (Tcherepnine), the invigorating *Prince Igor* (Borodin), which he considered his masterpiece, the romantic *Carnaval* (Schumann), the deftly plastic *Daphnis et Chloé* (Ravel), and the poetic *Spectre de la Rose* (Weber). In later years he was not so prolific, but he choreographed such varied works as the delicate *Les Elfes* (Mendelssohn), the classic *Don Juan* (Gluck), the sinister *Paganini* (Rachmaninov), the charming *L'Epreuve d'Amour* (Mozart), and the moving *Lt. Kije* (Prokoviev). More often than not Fokine choreographed music that was already composed, and in fact not contemporary; however, his mastery of all forms and all styles was evident in virtually every ballet he created, and he made every movement seem to come directly from the music.

G. B. L. Wilson has summarized Fokine's contributions in his admirable *Dictionary of Ballet,* and in this discussion I will draw on his remarks. When Fokine began to choreograph, the Petipa era was drawing to a close. Petipa himself had tried very hard to heed the teachings of Noverre, but the requirements of the Russian court were such that most ballets were evening-long affairs with set formulas that were designed to show off the virtuosity of the dancers, principally the ballerina. Most numbers, whatever the subject, were danced on point, even if they were based on folk dance, and the costumes were often lavish variations of conventional ballet-dress.

In a letter to the *Times* (London), June 6, 1914, Fokine summarized the five principles he followed:

1. Not to form combinations of ready-made and established dance steps, but to create in each case a new form corresponding to the subject, the most expressive form possible for the representation of the period and the character of the nation represented.
2. Dancing and mimetic gestures have no meaning in a ballet unless they serve as an expression of its dramatic action, and they must not be used

as a mere divertissement or entertainment having no connection with the scheme of the whole ballet.

3. The new ballet admits the use of conventional gesture only where it is required by the style of the ballet, and in all other cases endeavors to replace gestures of the hands by mimetic gesture of the whole body. Man can and should be expressive from head to foot.

4. The new ballet advances from the expressiveness of the face to the expressiveness of the whole body and from the expressiveness of the individual body to the expressiveness of a group of bodies and the expressiveness of the combined dancing of a crowd.

5. The new ballet, refusing to be the slave either of music or of scenic decoration and recognizing the alliances of the arts only on conditions of complete equality, allows perfect freedom both to the scenic artist and to the musician. In contradistinction to the older ballet, it does not demand "ballet" music of the composer as an accompaniment to dancing, it accepts music of every kind, provided only that it is good and expressive. It does not demand of the scenic artist that he should array the ballerinas in short skirts and pink slippers. It does not impose specific "ballet" conditions on the composer or the decorative artist, but gives complete liberty to their creative power. (Cf. creative independence of Cunningham's collaborators.)

Just as Noverre had tried to introduce both plasticity and range of subject into ballet, so did Fokine. In ballets such as *Petrouchka* he demonstrated that ballet was by no means limited to what was frivolous or fantastic, and in dealing directly with complex emotions he showed the way for Tudor, Graham, and Jooss. In *Les Sylphides,* Fokine's abstract interpretation of Chopin's music led to the work of Massine, Balanchine, and many others. In doing this Fokine fit into the Diaghilev pattern of presenting three one-act ballets of generally contrasting mood and subject matter, with a technique and an approach suitable to each separate ballet.

Actually, *Les Sylphides* originated as a suite of Polish dances performed in varied national costumes; it was entitled *Chopiniana,* orchestrated by Glazunov, and performed in Saint Petersburg in March of 1908. In April of the same year Fokine revised the work, which was also reorchestrated (except for one number) by Maurice Keller, as a purely classical ballet blanc in the manner of the Romantic Age with nineteen women and one man. When Diaghilev produced the work in Paris on June 2, 1909, with scenery and costumes by Alexandre Benois, he renamed it *Les Sylphides.* It consists of an overture, ensemble, four variations, pas de deux, and closing

Andre Eglevsky, Valentina Blinova, and Ruth Chanova in the Woizikovsky Ballet production of *Les Sylphides*. (*Courtesy of Leda Eglevsky*)

ensemble. The soloists were Anna Pavlova, Tamara Karsavina, Maria Baldina, and Vaslav Nijinsky. Once again the orchestration of two numbers was revised, this time by Igor Stravinsky. This ballet blanc became Fokine's masterpiece of masterpieces, and it continues to be performed all over the world. A principal reason for its deserved success is that Fokine achieved a mood. Every step is in character and flows directly and logically from the preceding; unified ballet is the result. All but one part of the twenty-four minute *Les Sylphides* is in triple time, the tempos are generally moderate, and the tonalities favor the flat keys. The orchestration calls for two flutes, two oboes, two clarinets, two bassoons, four horns, two trumpets, three trombones, percussion, and strings. Although modest in size, this instrumentation effectively enables Chopin's romantic melodies to be heard to best advantage.

Before the curtain rises on a secluded wood scene, the atmosphere is established as the orchestra plays the quiet prelude (op. 28, no. 7) andante in triple time, orchestrated in A flat. With the contemplative nocturne (op. 32, no. 2) in A flat also, slow duple time, orchestrated by Stravinsky, the evocative ballet begins. Integrally conceived to produce a romantic vision, the corps de ballet of sixteen women forming a semicircle tableau around the four soloists at the back of the stage gradually unfolds in forward rippling movements that harmonize perfectly with the mellifluous melody. Each soloist has a brief moment in which attention is claimed, but not forced. At the conclusion of this opening number, the members of the corps de ballet move silently to new positions, preparing for the dance to follow.

The warm valse (op. 70, no. 1) in G flat, is performed by a soloist, generally the third danseuse. Framed by the corps de ballet, and still mysterious, even spiritualized, it is rapid and flowing. The vigorous mazurka (op. 33, no. 3) in D major is generally performed by the leading danseuse who makes a series of entrées welcomed by effective port de bras by the stationary members of the corps de ballet who tilt toward the soloist. During a few measures of introduction (supplied in the several different versions by contemporary musicians familiar with the Chopin style) the corps de ballet again changes its framing positions on the stage; the tempo is accelerated in poetic triple time. There is a gay, lively tone to this joyous number that provides an effective contrast with the previous section, with a most attractive series of jetés and turns.

Next, after the corps de ballet has gracefully assumed a new tableau, comes a slower section, a romantic and difficult solo for the male dancer who is dressed in the manner of a poet. It is performed to the mazurka (op.

67, no. 3) in C major (although on occasion another mazurka has been substituted by Fokine himself).

The prelude of the overture is played once more, now in its original tonality of A major. It is danced by one of the solo danseuses, who enters from the wings and places her hand to her ear to listen before beginning a series of delicate assemblés and dainty steps. As the music is played three times, so quietly the final time that it seems to be an echo, she moves from group to group of the corps de ballet. The wonderfully evocative grand pas de deux for the leading danseuse and her partner is introduced by the etude (op. 25, no. 7); the slow, floating valse (op. 64, no. 2) in c sharp minor is one of the loveliest duets in all ballet, with quiet lifts and gallant sequences alternating with elegant rapid passages.

As the finale Fokine chose Chopin's vivo valse (op. 18, no. 1) in E flat, orchestrated by Stravinsky for the four soloists and the entire ensemble. Each of the soloists takes a phrase of the music to express her or his joie de vivre in leaps and rapid bourrées. The male soloist then gathers the three female soloists around him and the members of the ensemble once more form the semicircle tableau position in which they were first seen, and the curtain falls.

We turn now to Fokine's collaboration with Stravinsky. Before Stravinsky composed *The Firebird* for Diaghilev in 1910, he had written several interesting compositions, but not yet a piece for the stage. *The Firebird* was the beginning of Stravinsky's epoch-making career. The work generally follows the traditional procedure of using numbers (but not actually interrupting the action, following the example of the dramatic flow in *The Sleeping Beauty,* which had numbers just as did *Giselle,* and *Coppélia,* but treated these numbers in a more unified manner). In 1910 Stravinsky's orchestra was very large, including three harps and a stage band— providing great aural variety in the nineteen sections of the score, which Fokine choreographed, bit by bit, carefully, and masterfully. Although it was always very effective, in recent years, except for the incredibly beautiful Royal Ballet revival, *The Firebird* has been performed in con-densed productions based on the composer's 1919 and 1950 suites by Balanchine, whose version we will consider presently, and others. The complete forty-five minute *Firebird* which in 1910 seemed quite advanced because of its exotic harmonies and intricate cross-rhythms and quasi-oriental melodies, today is seen to fit clearly into the Russian nationalist school of which Mussorgsky and Rimsky-Korsakov were probably the greatest masters. To compare Stravinsky's *Firebird* in that composer's oeuvre with Beethoven's First Symphony in the oeuvre of the master symphonist is not to diminish the remarkable place in history or true intrinsic worth of either work. It is rather to appreciate that just as Beethoven later composed a violin concerto and a Ninth Symphony and a group of last quartets, so Stravinsky later composed *Apollo,* and *Oedipus Rex,* and the *Symphonie des Psaumes.*

The thirty-eight minute ballet *Petrouchka* is divided into four sections, but there really are no numbers as such, as even the set pieces are fully integrated. Each section flows directly into the next, with a long drum roll dividing scenes one and two, two and three, and three and four. While vehemently denying the aesthetics of Wagner, Stravinsky adopted some of his predecessor's effective theatrical procedures. For example, his set pieces are so masterfully introduced that they seem to originate without being announced, and they conclude in such a way, as the next section begins, that applause does not interrupt the action. This recalls procedures in Wagner's operas—from *Der fliegende Holländer* to *Parsifal*—in which applause seldom interrupts the spell or the flow of action. The tempos in *Petrouchka* are on the rapid side, the rhythms are more duple than anything else, although polyrhythms also occur, just as do polytonalities. Stravinsky's original orchestration follows the variety of Tchaikovsky and Rimsky-Korsakov, only more so: four flutes, four oboes, four clarinets, four bassoons, four horns, four trumpets, three trombones, tuba, piano, percussion, harp, and strings. In his 1945 version of *Petrouchka* the composer simplified the orchestration.

The story of the creation of the commedia dell'arte like *Petrouchka* has been told by Stravinsky, Benois, and others. Suffice it to say that the preparation of the very effective libretto of this ballet was the joint collaboration of the composer, the designer, and Diaghilev. While Fokine and Stravinsky had worked closely in the creation of *The Firebird,* in the case of *Petrouchka* this procedure was not repeated because Stravinsky fell sick after completing the first two sections of the ballet and was able to deliver the last two sections only a few weeks before the 1913 premiere in Paris. As Lincoln Kirstein pointed out in *Movement and Metaphor* (p. 194), "beginning with *Petrouchka,* Stravinsky did not compose music to accompany the dance, but to direct it." At the first performance Karsavina, Nijinsky, Orlov, and Cecchetti took the leading roles of the Ballerina, Petrouchka, the Moor, and the Showman-magician. Later, Nijinska, Danilova; Massine; Bolm, Balanchine, Dolin, and Eglevsky gave outstanding performances of these parts. Fokine stated that he never had proper rehearsal time to stage the crowd scenes, though Benois helped supervise them very strictly at the Paris premiere. It must be noted, however, that though originally Fokine found Stravinsky's score "undanceable" *whenever* the choreographer rehearsed *Petrouchka* personally it always gleamed, and when he did not, it rarely did. (Although some mention should be made of Nijinsky's three ballets, I must note that having seen only one—*L'Après-midi d'un faune,* long after it was created—I do not feel qualified to comment on his choreography beyond recording the impression that this unique dancer might have contributed masterfully to choreography if he had been given more time to develop.)

Petrouchka is at once an allegory and an attractive depiction of a Russian street fair at shrovetide in 1830. Scene I shows the fair, with its bustling merrymakers out for a good time. Stravinsky uses both French and Russian tunes, dressing them up with his colorful brand of polytonality and polyrhythms. The few set pieces are dealt with imaginatively. The formulas are new, and are used in new ways. The rhythmic, melodic, and harmonic patterns Stravinsky had used in *The Firebird* generally derived from Rimsky-Korsakov. Here they are more personal to Stravinsky, and his masterful orchestration provides all the unity needed or desired. Presently we are introduced to the main characters, the puppets and their master, the tyrant Showman, who touches them and makes them perform, first as puppets, and then amazingly as people.

In Scene II we are in Petrouchka's sparsely furnished room (with a glowering portrait of the Showman on the wall) where he has been tossed by the Showman. The story begins to unfold. Petrouchka is in love with the Ballerina, and she comes to pay him a visit, dancing enticingly on her points to a brash trumpet solo. His joyous over-reaction frightens her, however, and she quickly leaves him. Petrouchka is alone once more, and very, very frustrated.

Scene III takes place in the Moor's garishly luxurious room, in which the Moor performs a routine that betrays his basic simple appetites; he plays with a large coconut until he is visited by the Ballerina. They are attracted to each other, but all of a sudden Petrouchka bursts in. There is a jealous scene during which the Moor chases Petrouchka around and around.

Scene IV shows us the fair at evening. After various solo and ensemble dances, including the attractive Dance of the Nursemaids and the irresistible stomping dance of the Coachmen, the rowdy scruffle between the Moor and Petrouchka becomes violent, and the Moor catches and kills Petrouchka. Alarmed by what it has seen, the crowd calls for the Showman. He picks up the dead Petrouchka, shakes him, and shows that he was only a puppet. But at the quiet ending, when it is beginning to snow and the crowd has dispersed, the soul of Petrouchka appears, leaning over the top of the booth where they had performed, and threatens the Showman, seeming to say, "Life will go on. We will meet again."

At this point it is important to record that Stravinsky was the first composer to break the strait-jacket of ending a ballet scene or act with what is harmonically known as a V–I chord, in music virtually an irrevocable sign of conclusion. This predictable formula was practiced by Lully, Beethoven, Tchaikovsky, and the others. Now there was an alternative, particularly appropriate when choreographer and composer did not wish to imply inevitable resolution, musically or dramatically. Stravinsky's music for *Petrouchka* is marvellously inventive in many, many ways. His final notes in the last scene form a diminished triad plus a normal triad, beginning on C. They are extremely affecting, and unusual, although the student of Wagner's harmony would not be surprised by them.

Two Facets of Massine

Born and trained in Moscow, Leonide Massine (1894–1977) was selected in 1913 by Serge Diaghilev to be a dancer in his company. In 1915 Massine became the third of Diaghilev's five choreographers, with his brilliant first ballet *Soleil de Nuit* that effectively theatricalized Russian folk dances. During a long and eventful career Massine produced over one hundred ballets. As time recedes from the four decades during which we saw his truly extraordinary performing, the significance of his contributions may change, yet in this century a number of his ballets have served as magnificent milestones.

The subject of our essay is the relationships of choreographers and composers. In the case of Massine, however, because of the nature of his position in the history of lyric theatre, as a choreographer totally formed by the ideas of Diaghilev and his circle (whereas both Fokine and Balanchine were formed when they came to Diaghilev), we will consider Massine's work in a somewhat different focus. As a choreographer, his tripartite source of inspiration was the Italian commedia dell'arte (both directly in *Pulcinella,* and through Goldoni, in *Les Femmes de Bonne Humeur* and *Scuolo di Ballo*), the extraordinary effects of the easel painters of the School of Paris (Picasso et al.), and his sensitivity to music of various schools. Thus despite the very definite influence the music of Stravinsky had on him (evident in the three collaborations: *Pulcinella* (Picasso), *Le Sacre du Printemps* (Roerich), and *Le Chant du Rossignol* (Matisse), and also in the two Fokine-Stravinsky ballets in which Massine performed superlatively practically his entire career, *The Firebird* and *Petrouchka*) Massine found in the diverse music of Satie, Falla, Brahms, Hindemith and others outstanding resonances that seemed to bring out his greatest gifts. A few passages from an interview Massine gave in 1932 are revealing:

It is quite individual if I prefer to arrange my ballets to music already written, or to have the music specially composed to my choreographic idea. If I have to work with a new composer, with whose work I am not familiar, I prefer the first way. If, on the other hand, the composer and the style of his music are known to me, I like to get my choreographic idea first and then discuss it with the composer in detail. The next person I consider very important is the designer of the setting and costumes, for, if he is a man of ideas, he can be of great assistance. I keep constantly in touch with my collaborators to ensure the closest coordination of our work, and I discuss all my plans and ideas with them.

The actual scenes and dances I do not work out before I commence my rehearsals; but I generally visualize them in my mind and form just a hazy outline of them, somewhat like the outline of houses seen through a London fog. I do not discuss the ballet with my dancers, unless it is of such unusual character that I find it imperative for them to understand it, in order that they may grasp the situations. I regard the dancers as the elements for the realisation of my ideas, and as such I must be able to inspire them with the same feeling for my work that I have. (Prior to rehearsal, Massine did make voluminous notes concerning movements and ensembles.)

During the rehearsals I create the dances and work out every detail for every member of my company. I prefer modern music to arrange to, but I am also fond of classical music. In some sort my method of arranging ballets has many points of similarity with musical composition. I regard solo dances as melodies written for a single instrument; just as group dances correspond to a piece orchestrated for a given number of instruments. And, just as an orchestration should contain color and contrast, so do I seek to invest my group and mass dances with similar qualities.

In *Le Sacre du Printemps* the predominant element was the music, then the theme; in *Les Femmes de Bonne Humeur* (Scarlatti) the period (Goldoni) was the principal consideration; in *Parade* the music was supreme. Whichever element influences me the most, that is the aspect from which I work.

The ideals to strive for in the production of a ballet are (1) the highest power of expression possible to obtain; (2) the attainment of a perfect balance between dynamic movement and pure *plastique,* and an interesting counterpoint of mass movement as opposed to that of the individual. To my mind the general movement is the most important part of a ballet. Light and shade are essential. My style of ballet-composition is closely connected with the musical theme, and I have my own method for contrasting the movements. If the music does not give it to me, I contrive opportunities for the introduction of light and shade.

Whether I compose an imaginative or a period ballet, I make use of the same method, because these two types are in a sense the same; the only difference is that in the first case the movements are purely imaginative, while in the other they must be controlled by a sense of period.

Among the important ballets of Massine we will be discussing, Brahms's *Choreartium* falls into the imaginative type, while *Parade, Tricorne,* and *Saint Francis* are period works.

Massine's genius as a dancer was discovered when the impressario needed a replacement for the legendary Nijinsky, and his first role in the Diaghilev Ballet was in Fokine's *La Legende de Joseph,* with music by Richard Strauss. Because of his build and his training, Massine was usually at his superb best in character roles that he choreographed for himself *(La Symphonie Fantastique, La Boutique Fantasque, Gaité Parisienne),* but throughout his distinguished career he continued to dance in a number of ballets by Fokine. In 1924 Massine produced for Etienne de Beaumont, as a homage to Johann Strauss, Jr., *Le Beau Danube,* a work which has since been popular throughout the world, one of the very greatest light ballets.

There is enormous variety in the ballets of Massine, even among the four on which he collaborated with Picasso: *Parade* (1917), *Le Tricorne* (1919), *Pulcinella* (1920), and *Mercure* (1924). The music for *Parade* was composed by Erik Satie (1866–1925), an avant-garde Frenchman who also composed the music for *Mercure,* as well as for Jean Borlin's *Relâche* (1925), and scores choreographed by Balanchine, Ashton, Cunningham, Sokolow, and others. In his music he practiced what he preached—brevity, clarity, wit.

While it was not classical ballet, *Parade* certainly provided novelty and controversy when it was first given in 1917. It was Massine's fifth ballet, following four varied, successful works for Diaghilev, two Russian, one Spanish, and one Franco-Italian; all of these were influenced to an extent by the commedia dell'arte mystique. The important French poet Jean Cocteau was the originator of the cubist-surrealist *Parade* (as he had been of the exotic *Le Dieu Bleu,* presented in 1912 by Diaghilev). Certainly Massine's ballets speak for themselves, yet one cannot help noting how many of them have been marvellously decorated by Picasso, Derain, Tchelitchew, Bérard, and Matisse.

Diaghilev began his career as an impressario with the presentation of Russian painting, and opera, and then ballet. When he was isolated in the West as World War I made communication with Russia all but impossible, Diaghilev sought another "tune" to play to make his seasons talked of, and attended. He selected "l'outrage." And it turned out that Diaghilev's new "team of Frenchmen" was admirably suited to the "Realistic" ballet theme of *Parade.* While novel in 1917 it was still popular in 1945, when

Picasso's "Blue" period saltimbanques were transformed into the spare and haunting *Les Forains* by Kochno, Sauguet, Petit, and Bérard.

Parade is the story of contemporary itinerant street players, whose managers present attractions they trust will entice the public into their theatre on a Sunday afternoon. Satie begins with a witty chorale and prelude, starting with a series of deep chords in triple time (perhaps parodying the opening of *Tosca*), and continues with a pastiche of real and imaginary sounds, mostly in duple time, often pseudo-Spanish. Picasso's superbly evocative, somber, neoromantic drop curtain rises to reveal the French Manager in his fantastique oversize cubist, box-like costume, pacing back and forth. He introduces the first act, a mysterious Chinese conjurer in a scarlet costume, pigtail and all, who stalks in to the music of a march and then while circling around, gliding and twitching, performs a number of sleight of hand magic tricks with an egg and fire to pseudo-Oriental music, mostly in duple time.

Having failed to impress, the conjurer disappears into the booth, and the New York Manager, eleven feet high, with megaphone and cowboy boots, appears to announce the second act, the pert little American Girl. She appears in a sailor coat and white skirt to perform a ragtime tap-dance, a movie-routine number that is accompanied by an exotic orchestra that includes a typewriter, pistol shots, and a fog horn.

Her success with "the public" does not exceed that of the conjurer, and the bashful, prancing Horse appears to announce the final act. This is a marvellously most athletic pair of acrobats, clothed in blue and white tights, who perform a circus number with great virtuosity. When no one enters the booth to see the entire show, the Managers and the Actors all parade once more to the strains of the march heard first with the conjurer. No takers? Chords, and collapse—after fourteen minutes of delectable hors d'oeuvres to the á propos ever-changing, irresistible and witty music of Satie that Massine choreographed, in duple or triple time, waltz, ragtime, or free form. Satie's orchestration was for three flutes, three oboes, three clarinets, two bassoons, two horns, three trumpets, three trombones, tuba, percussion, harp, and strings—a large number of instruments, often sparingly, but tellingly, used.

Two years after *Parade* came the colorful *Le Tricorne*. In the course of his career Massine greatly enriched the vocabulary of classic dance with varied elements from folk dance, commedia dell'arte, and American modern dance. (He was exposed to the latter at the time he cast Martha Graham as the Chosen Maiden in his imaginative 1930 production of Stravinsky's *Le Sacre du Printemps,* conducted by Leopold Stokowski.) In particular, Massine mastered the fine points of Spanish dance for theatrical showing probably more thoroughly than anyone else, and he choreographed a number of ballets on Iberian themes.

Le Tricorne, given its premier performance in 1919, was a thirty-minute masterpiece based on a play by Alarcon adapted by Martinez Sierra: the story of a Miller and his Wife who outwit a libidinous and tyrannical local governor. Before Picasso's curtain is seen, the trumpets sound a brilliant fanfare somewhat similar to the one that precedes the entrance of a bullfighter into the arena, followed by the slower beating of the bass drum. Next there is a series of olés, and zapateado and castanet playing. Originally, Picasso's drop-curtain revealed the arena, which helped set the seriousness of the mood; although this has since disappeared, a plaintive chant warns us that we are not to expect a farce.

At the beginning of the action under the brilliant sun in a remote village, the Miller tries to teach his tame bird to sing. He abandons his somewhat comic attempt when, accompanied by a languorous melody, his graceful, attractive Wife appears. They dance and play to the melody of the koradin, then run to their well to draw water. While the Miller is busy, a Dandy crosses the nearby bridge and executes a few steps of the bolero for the special benefit of the Wife, who seems to enjoy the attention. The Miller chases him away, but there is far more serious danger as the vicious Corregidor makes an appearance accompanied by his retinue. He drops his handkerchief, which the Miller's Wife retrieves and presents to him with a curtsy. As soon as the Miller is otherwise occupied, the corrupt Corregidor returns alone, observes the Miller's Wife in her brilliant fandango, and invites the señora to dance the minuet with him.

She soon changes to a faster "Bob-Apple dance." The proud but clumsy Corregidor falls heavily and is picked up by the Miller, but once he turns his back both the Miller and his Wife make fun of him. The Corregidor departs, swearing vengeance, which the happy couple promptly forget. Presently their Neighbors arrive to enjoy a fiesta dancing to the triple time Spanish seguidilla. The Miller then performs his electrifying farucca in triple time. Just as he is receiving congratulations from his comrades the agents of the Corregidor appear with a warrant and arrest him.

In scene II, abandoned by her friends who are frightened by the authorities, the Miller's Wife is attacked by the Corregidor. She repulses him, and knocks him into the stream, but then fearful, helps him out of the water only to be attacked once more. This time she flees. The Corregidor goes into her house to dry off. Now the Miller, who has escaped, returns, and seeing the wet clothes of the Corregidor drying in front of his house sizes up the situation and blithely leaves, taking along the clothes of the tyrant. Meanwhile the Corregidor's henchmen, seeking the Miller, find their master drying in the Miller's clothes and mistakenly start to drag him off to jail.

In scene III the couple is happily reunited and their friends return, determined to help them. The Corregidor flees for his life, the despotic reign of the three-cornered hat over. The effigy of the Corregidor is tossed in a blanket, and the joyous sounds of the duple-time jota complete the festive celebration. Manuel de Falla's orchestra in *Le Tricorne* called for three flutes, three oboes, two clarinets, two bassoons, four horns, three trumpets, three trombones, tuba, *celeste,* piano, percussion (including *castanets*), harp, and strings. Falla's Spanish origin enabled him to bring colorful ethnic touches to the lyric theatre, which he combined with his thorough musicianship, weaving vivid Andalusian dances among a fresh mixture of impressionist and neoclassic idioms.

First performed in 1933, *Choreartium,* to the music of Brahms' Symphony Number 4, had scenery and costumes by Constantine Terechkovich and Eugène Lourié. This, the second of Massine's seven symphonic ballets, is extremely effective. Just as the curtain rises the leading male dancer is in the air with a grand jeté (on occasion this role was danced brilliantly by the choreographer), and the three soloists lead the women and the men in exciting formations backed by a landscape in which one sees a rainbow. In the fresh steps and movements to the music, in sonata form, allegro in duple time in the home tonality of e minor, the number of dancers (from two to twenty-four) changes constantly, with different groupings and exits and entrances forming interesting figures. Seemingly, even the most complex movements are spontaneous (in much the same way they appear to be in *Les Sylphides, Symphony in Three Movements,* and *Apollo*). In both color and design Massine succeeded admirably.

The second movement, andante in E major in duple time, is in sonatina form. At the time of the premier the solo dancer was the intense and sensitive Nina Verchinina, who was called the first symphonic dancer. She led a long chain of dancers costumed in dark crimson against a dark green background. Presently the mourning chorus separates into three groups. They pose, and they move on. Acrobatic and modern dance movements are encompassed within the frame of the classical ballet, but there is no dancing on points. It is somber, and very structured, just like the music. For the lighter third movement, allegro in C major in duple time and sonata form, Massine used background of yellow, beige, and gray, perhaps reminiscent of an Eastern print. In front of this the dancers are dressed in white, pink, and blue. There is a gay tone of popular country enjoyment that the dancers' movements catch very well.

In the finale, with a gloomy gray background, Brahms calls for a majestic allegro in e minor, in triple time; the form is an architectural theme and thirty-four variations in four sections and a faster coda, a chaconne. The brilliant opening, matching the brass of the composer, calls for six male dancers in black to execute a series of tours en l'air successively, followed by an ensemble for the entire male ensemble. The exciting conclusion of the thirty-six minute ballet shows the imaginative, abstract side of Massine's creative work. Brahms' conservative orchestra calls for two flutes, two oboes, two clarinets, three bassoons, four horns, two trumpets, three trombones, timpani, and strings.

The movements Massine used in his symphonic ballets to music by Tchaikovsky, Brahms, Berlioz, Beethoven, Shostakovich, Schubert, and Haydn have in each case a different style, one related to an overall theme the choreographer assigned to the work. Once theme and style were established, Massine proceeded to develop the work in the manner he described in the interview quoted above. Although by no means the first choreographer to produce ballets based on symphonies, Massine was the most systematic in his treatment of the symphony as an integral part of lyric theatre.

Saint Francis (Nobilissima Visione) is a ballet in five scenes with music by Paul Hindemith, sets and costumes by Pavel Tchelitchew, which was first performed in 1938. In his memoirs (see Bibliography) Massine has related that the idea of this ballet was suggested to him in 1937 by the composer: "He had just come from the great church of Santa Croce, which contains the Giotto frescos with scenes of Saint Francis of Assisi." After viewing these moving frescoes together, the composer and the choreographer selected episodes that seemed appropriate for the ballet they began to plan. Massine described his vision of each scene, and Hindemith made notes and then began to play the piano, beginning with various liturgical themes.

Inspired also by the book *The Little Flowers of Saint Francis,* this dramatic choreographic depiction of the life of the Saint (1182–1226) created and preserved an atmosphere of mystical exaltation, following Hindemith's concern for the ethical power of music, for something that would speak authentically to the nobler part of man through the unity of old and new. The composer attempted to delve into areas of experience that are familiar but unfathomable, and Massine matched him every step of the way, deriving dances from the spiritual frescoes he and Hindemith saw. The opportunity to grasp the lasting calm of the man who inspired it, and

Saint Francis. Leonide Massine (Saint Francis) and Nina Theilade (Lady Poverty) in a scene from Massine's ballet. (*Courtesy of the Ballet Russe de Monte Carlo*)

to hold and treasure it is what audiences who saw this ballet were given. I agree completely with the 1938 critic who wrote it was one of the most thrilling ballets ever conceived. Hindemith's music, based on early Italian and French themes and formulas, fits perfectly the "troubadour of God."

François Mauriac has written that Massine expresses what is most beautiful and sacred in the world—the love of God taking possession of the soul of a young man through poverty. The thirty-five-minute ballet opens with Francis Bernadone, living in his father's house (Bernadone père was a wealthy draper who covered his walls with cloth), enjoying idle pleasures with his idle friends. However, after treating a beggar roughly, suddenly Francis runs after him to make amends. Briefly exhilarated by military life, he soon abandons the life of a soldier, as overcome by the cruelty and horror of war, he longs for peace. Fugal frenzy and brutality give way to compassion as the contrasts of the hurly-burly are exchanged for the complements of repose by the musician and choreographer alike.

In scene II, entitled pastorale, Francis meets Poverty, Chastity, and Obedience who reveal to him that destiny has reserved for him a life of piety and self-sacrifice.

During a magnificent marble hall banquet in scene III, Francis gives away everything that belongs to him; and attracted by a procession of monks, pursuing a life of unselfishness, he leaves home with only a few rags left to cover his body.

In scene IV Francis tames a ferocious wolf, and then finally is wedded to Lady Poverty in a moving, simple ceremony.

In the climactic final scene Francis sings a hymn of praise to all; and during the stunning contrapuntal passacaglia, the doves of peace seem to flutter among the company of sisters and brothers. Hindemith's orchestration calls for flute and piccolo, two each of oboes, clarinets, and bassoons, four horns, two trumpets, three trombones, tuba, percussion, and strings.

Massine, like Fokine and many choreographers before him, appears to have preferred period ballets over imaginative ballets. Yet, in many instances, they are not so far apart as one might suppose—at least as he created them.

The Collaborations of George Balanchine and Igor Stravinsky

George Balanchine's place as a twentieth-century choreographer is unique. Like Fokine and Massine, he was a ballet master for Diaghilev and a dancer who performed for many years. His thorough musical training gave him invaluable extra perspectives that have shaped his ballets. Among composers, Balanchine's enduring musical association has been with Igor Stravinsky. (It is noteworthy that Stravinsky's greatest choreographic association was with Balanchine, and that with the exception of Borodin and Glazunov, their musical tastes were very similar; aesthetically, and personally, they had a number of consonances and resonances in common.)

As the confines of this essay permit us to include only a selection of Balanchine's more than 400 ballets, I have chosen to discuss the thirty Stravinsky collaborations, beginning with the Diaghilev revival of *Le Chant du Rossignol* (1925) and continuing through *Perséphone* (1982). Balanchine has changed many of his early ballets, as they were interpreted by succeeding generations of Russian, French, Danish, American, and British dancers. Although *Apollo* is a particular example we will consider when we discuss the Stravinsky ballets chronologically, *The Prodigal Son, Serenade, Le Bourgeois Gentilhomme, Mozartiana* are among the ballets he has rather re-created than revived as new dancers and different national companies presented them.

Balanchine has danced, choreographed, and produced most of Stravinsky's works for the lyric theatre, as well as many of the composer's other works. Their partnership is comparable in history only to that of Lully and Beauchamps. There is significant variety in Stravinsky's lyric compositions for orchestra, and in his choreography Balanchine adapts to it most appropriately. As leading ballerinas in productions of Stravinsky's works he has featured, among many others, Tamara Geva, Alexandra Danilova, Vera Zorina, Maria Tallchief, Tanaquil LeClercq, Tamara Toumanova, and Suzanne Farrell.

To say that neither Stravinsky nor Balanchine would have existed without the other would be absurd, but they have benefitted each other greatly, and all of us have been involved witnesses, rejoicing in what was probably the significant artistic association of the twentieth century, a partnership created and nurtured by Diaghilev, Lincoln Kirstein, and the gods. The fact that this section of our essay occupies about half of the space devoted to twentieth-century forms should not be taken as a value judgment concerning the hierarchy of artistic collaboration, but rather as an opportunity to consider a very special achievement in the history of the lyric theatre.

George Balanchine elects several composers to his musical pantheon—Tchaikovsky from his childhood on, Stravinsky from his coming alive artistically, and Delibes from the years he spent in France. Glinka, Glazunov, and Mozart are also among the composers he admires most. Although he did not choreograph the music of Delibes while he worked with Diaghilev, it was during these years that he gained close acquaintance with a wide variety of classical and modern French music.

In the music of Igor Stravinsky, Balanchine discovered a remarkable mixture of Dionysian and especially Apollonian tendencies. Apollonian characteristics include those of system, moderation, poetic intellectualism, noble restraint. On stage in Lully's ballets Apollonian characteristics were personified by Louis XIV whose favorite ballet role was impersonating Apollo. Later Apollonian characteristics were demonstrated by Mademoiselle Sallé, whose great rival was the Dionysian Mademoiselle Camargo. Dionysian tendencies—effervescence, Bacchic abandon, dramatic exaggeration, animal enthusiasm—have also contributed positively to lyric theatre. Though the Dionysian characteristics were perhaps first seen fully in such nineteenth century works as Wagner's *Tannhäuser,* they contributed to scenes in *Le Ballet Comique de la Reine Louise,* to Lully's *Alceste,* Noverre's *Medea,* Borodin's *Prince Igor,* and so forth. In the composer, Stravinsky, Balanchine found an extraordinary Russian mind with a classical education, with many qualities added through living in France and America that paralleled his own development. How their collaborations were achieved is a fascinating story; the pieces are exciting individually, and together they are significant for all art in this century. The personal relationship between the two has been described as father to son (what with the twenty-two year difference in age), but the working relationship developed into one of organized collaborators each appreciating thoroughly the craft of the other, and not interfering with the scope of the partner's contribution to the work in progress.

Balanchine's initial exposure to the music of Stravinsky occurred about 1918, when, struck by the unusual score of *Le Sacre du Printemps,* he hoped to choreograph music of the composer. In 1921 he planned to choreograph *Pulcinella,* but except for two excerpts this was not to be for another fifty years. From the first Balanchine instinctively was aware that virtually all of Stravinsky's music is danceable. His initial opportunity to choreograph a ballet by Stravinsky was his first assignment as ballet master for Diaghilev. Many years later Balanchine said, "It is because of Diaghilev that I am whatever I am today." While Stravinsky may not have said the same thing, essentially it is as true of the musician as it is of the dancer.

As a choreographer who brought movement and sound together in the music of Stravinsky, perhaps the most influential composer of this century, Balanchine's relationship to that music is clear. The profile of Stravinsky's oeuvre reveals the relative importance he assigned to instrumental and vocal works, stage and concert, solo and ensemble, but through his early identification with Diaghilev, the relationship he formed with theatrical dance became dominant in his works. This is clear when one realizes that of his 109 compositions, 47 have been given major choreographic treatment.

For Balanchine, the choreographic stimulus depends on the music and the dancers available, even when there is a strong mood or story line involved. This clear aim at fidelity and realization of the best possible results under the conditions present as opposed to a so-called masterpiece complex is evidence that Balanchine considers his work a craft rather than a philosophy. If he has created ballets of extraordinary range, from electronic to Vivaldi, from jazz to Brahms, from cabaret to Stravinsky, from movies to Mozart, it is a tribute both to his mind and to the dancers with whom he has worked. That other influences besides the music and the dancers sometimes are present does not distract him; it often extends even further the thrust of his artistic ideas. (His reading of the Bible has often been an important influence.)

Quietly and steadily Balanchine created a varied oeuvre that is broad almost beyond belief. Before we look in perspective at Balanchine's collaboration with Stravinsky, it is imperative that we note the central point of view of the musician. Igor Stravinsky (1882–1971) insisted vehemently on being the most exact composer possible, although the concept "exact" defines an absolute that cannot exist in art or in science, but can only be approached. Stravinsky has described (to me, and to others) wonderfully clearly his approach to composition, "meaning in music." Still, at different times of his life, he shifted the center of his focus, perfectly understandably and logically. For example, at succeeding stages he has altered the instrumentation of his music, changed tempos, and redirected his attitude toward serial music. For a variety of reasons Stravinsky promulgated certain ground rules in connection with the performance of his music; until recently (1966) Balanchine did not have as much control over the performance of his ballets. Stravinsky's rules for the performance of his music were not always observed, but they were there, available to performers, and important in themselves as a guide, which will be used in our consideration of the close creative collaborations of Balanchine and Stravinsky, in an attempt at definition.

Balanchine has declared that all of Stravinsky's music is danceable, that every measure is interesting; and although he has not set out to prove his assertions quantitatively, he has proved it qualitatively through the range of his ballets both to commissioned scores and to works such as the Violin Concerto and the Symphony in Three Movements. The key to their fruitful collaboration is not only their personal relationship but Balanchine's musicality and his musical training which made him unique among choreographers (at least of this century). His understanding of musical form, tempo, and texture was sure. He could well have left his mark as a composer, and even more fame probably would have been his as a pianist or conductor, but as Stravinsky later remarked: "The world is full of pretty good concert pianists but a choreographer such as Balanchine is, after all, the rarest of beings."

As a youth Balanchine observed and enjoyed the aesthetic rewards of Beethoven, whose Sonata Pathétique he had performed on the piano from the age of seven. Rubinstein, Scriabin, Chopin, Ravel, and Milhaud were among the composers whose music he studied after he graduated from the Ballet School into the Russian State Company and simultaneously enrolled as a student in the Leningrad Conservatory (under Glazunov). Once Balanchine tasted the possibilities of choreographing the music of Stravinsky, it was almost inevitable that he be drawn toward a number of that composer's scores. Whatever spiritual and physical roads Balanchine took early in his life, he proved to be the right man at the right place when he was appointed ballet master to Diaghilev in 1925. At age 21 he was an artist worthy of that post.

The order of presentation of the Balanchine-Stravinsky collaborations will be that in which Balanchine produced the "30" scores, rather than the order in which the composer wrote the music. The initial Balanchine-Stravinsky ballet, the 1925 version of *Le Chant du Rossignol,* is a twenty-minute composition dating from 1917, which is a condensation of music from acts II and III of Stravinsky's 1914 opera, *Le Rossignol* (a work the choreographer already knew). In the ballet version the Oriental opera story line was retained, and Stravinsky's colorful score shows both unity and consistency, as the music looks both backward to such works as *Petrouchka* and forward to the *Symphonie des Psaumes.*

There are several ways of approaching the style of Stravinsky's music. One is to try to divide his compositions into periods (nationalist, neoclassic, cosmopolitan, serial, and last phase). Another is to observe the rise and fall of Dionysian and Apollonian principles and techniques. Still another is to approach each work separately, relating its form and substance to the subject at hand, the collaborators, and the circumstances of the composition. In our discussion we will be varying our approach, depending upon the particular work. Stravinsky made a scenario from the Hans Christian Andersen story that goes with the 1920 Massine ballet, *Le Chant du Rossignol.*

1. *The Fête in the Emperor of China's Palace.* In honor of the Nightingale that sings so sweetly, the palace is festively adorned. There is running to and fro. The Nightingale is placed on a golden perch; a Chinese march signals the entrance of the Emperor.
2. *The Two Nightingales.* The Nightingale sings so gloriously that tears come to the Emperor's eyes. The lackeys and chambermaids report that they are satisfied too; and that is saying a good deal, for they are the most difficult to please. Envoys arrive from the Emperor of Japan with the gift of a mechanical nightingale. As soon as the artificial bird is wound up he sings a piece and his tail moves up and down, shining with silver and gold. He is just as successful as the real bird, and is much handsomer to look at. Where is the living Nightingale? No one has noticed that he has flown out of the open window. The fisherman is heard out-of-doors, singing for joy because his bird has returned.
3. *Illness and Recovery of the Emperor of China.* The poor Emperor can scarcely breathe. He opens his eyes and sees that Death is sitting upon his chest. From among the folds of the splendid velvet curtains, strange heads peer forth—these are all the Emperor's bad and good deeds, and they tell him so much that the perspiration runs from his forehead. The mechanical bird refuses to sing, but the little live Nightingale is heard singing outside the window. As he sings the spectres grow paler and paler. Even Death listens, and says, "Go on, little Nightingale, go on!" Death returns each of the Emperor's treasures for a song. The Emperor falls into a sweet slumber. The sun shines on him through the window when he awakes refreshed and restored.
4. *Funeral March.* The courtiers come to look at their dead ruler, and stand astounded when the Emperor says "Good morning!" Meanwhile the Nightingale has flown back to the fisherman who is heard singing his song once more.

When Diaghilev wished to revive the Massine ballet version with sets and costumes by Matisse, he found no one could remember it, and thus it was that Balanchine was asked to choreograph a new version. According to Balanchine, in 1925 scenes one and two were combined. The music is very atmospheric, but relating the details of the story in twenty minutes does present the choreographer with problems. That Balanchine solved the problems to Diaghilev's satisfaction is proved by the fact that this version was kept in the active repertoire for several seasons. The revival presented casting problems because Karsavina was no longer a regular member of Diaghilev's company. The producer had already auditioned young Alicia Markova several times without deciding whether to sign her on. When Diaghilev and Balanchine auditioned her again, the choreographer asked Markova to perform a number of different turns, some acrobatic, and then recommended her. Thus Markova created the role of the Nightingale in Balanchine's version, first danced June 17, 1925, in Paris. The orchestration of *Le Chant du Rossignol* is two flutes, two oboes, two clarinets, two bassoons, four horns, three trumpets, three trombones, tuba, percussion, celeste, piano, two harps, and strings.

Beyond seeing the Stravinsky works in the Diaghilev repertoire, and often performing in such ballets as *The Firebird* and *Petrouchka*,[2] Balanchine had very little to do with the composer until 1927, when Stravinsky began to compose *Apollo,* which was a commission from Elizabeth Sprague Coolidge for production at The Library of Congress.

After his Dionysian period as a modern Russian nationalist in *The Firebird, Petrouchka,* and *Le Sacre,* Igor Stravinsky's aesthetic ideal became formally more classic and more Apollonian. His great passions became more contained. It happened that just as he was completing his great oratorio, *Oedipus Rex,* he was offered this commission to compose a work of his choice for the Library of Congress, providing Stravinsky with precisely the opportunity he hoped for: the composition of a ballet blanc. As the contract specified that the work would be Stravinsky's property following the Washington premiere, it occurred to the composer that it would be appropriate for Serge Lifar and the Diaghilev company. Diaghilev agreed, and as Balanchine was Diaghilev's maître de ballet and choreographer, this led to his historic participation in the European premiere. Thus Balanchine collaborated directly with Stravinsky, learning how to purify his own well-developed style of dealing with complex rhythms in movement. Stravinsky was present at critical rehearsals, and he conducted this production as well as others in later years. Stravinsky has written of his great satisfaction with Balanchine's choreography. Balanchine has described how much this collaboration meant to him, both as an occasion to choreograph some extraordinary music, and to learn how to simplify and at the same time expand the vocabulary of classic steps.

For Balanchine, *Apollo,* "white on white," was the turning point in his artistic life. For Stravinsky, its self-imposed narrow frame posed particular problems, and offered solid and valuable results. Balanchine has written how Stravinsky's approach appealed to him, musically and aesthetically. Stravinsky taught his junior partner much about the craft of an artist: "Be precise, inventive, formal—never attempt to create a masterpiece, only a well made work of art." Instinctively and intellectually, Stravinsky's music appealed to Balanchine, who understood it both as music and as a platform for dancing.

Purely as music this thirty-minute masterpiece is one of the most beautiful works of the twentieth century. As ballet its place is assured; in this most ephemeral of the arts it is likely to last as long as there are dancers to perform it. This collaboration marked the beginning of the close friendship, as Stravinsky realized that Balanchine not only had the professional expertise to train his dancers to execute his visions, he had a technical training in music that enabled him truly to understand Stravinsky's musical ideas and their gestation. Someone has said that Balanchine operated as a prism through which music became visible, and through which one could follow the creative craft of the composer to whatever philosophical conclusions may be involved.

One of Stravinsky's statements in his revealing *Poetics of Music* seems particularly appropriate in connection with *Apollo:* "When variety tempts me, I am uneasy about the facile solutions it offers me. Similarity, on the other hand, poses more difficult problems but also offers results that are more solid and hence more valuable to me."

Balanchine's reactions to the music of *Apollo* (orchestrated for first and second violins, violas, first and second violoncellos, double basses) were classical, and if some have felt he included extraneous material, I, among many, do not. I find it as perfect in its way as *Les Sylphides* is in its way, on a similar level with certain drawings of Leonardo, or lines of Shakespeare, or certain compositions of Mozart or Handel, stripped of the element of display, yet brilliant in the depth of its revealing, inspiring inventiveness, all while being thoroughly classical.

In *Theatre Arts* of November 1947, Lincoln Kirstein wrote that *Apollo* had "introduced to ballet in its time a spirit of traditional classicism absent since Petipa's last compositions almost thirty years before. It demonstrated that tradition is not merely an anchorage to which one returns after eccentric deviations but the very floor which supports the artist, enabling him securely to build upon it elements which may seem at first revolutionary, ugly and new both to him and his audience. *Apollon* has now lost for us the effects which offended, irritated or merely amused an earlier public. We forget that much of the 'modernism' of adagio movement in our classic dance derives directly from *Apollon;* that many ways of lifting women, of turning close to the floor, of subtle syncopation in the use of *pointes,* of a single male dancer supporting three women, were unknown before *Apol-*

lon. These innovations horrified many people at first, but they were so logical an extension of the pure line of Saint-Léon, Petipa, and Ivanov that they were almost immediately absorbed into the tradition of their craft."

Kirstein continued, "Glenway Wescott said that instead of Apollo, Leader of the Muses, the ballet should have been entitled Apollo's Games with the Muses. The mimed athletics, the strenuous atmosphere of violent physicality recall the nervousness of runners before a race. Each variation seems a training for the final translation to Olympus. In the chariot-race finale which evokes memories of the profiles on Roman coins and cameos, and of the decathlon, visualized in the newly extended idiom of Russian ballet, a transformation of the Olympic games into contemporary dancing takes place. Of all Balanchine's works *Apollon* is the most significant historically, the most compact, the most influential. . . ."

The prologue, scene I, is ternary in form, duple in rhythm, and largely alternating between the tonalities of C and D major, which are the primary tonalities in a work also using g minor and G major and E major, and closing again in C and D. In an obscure light, Leto gives birth to Apollo, son of Zeus. With the appearance of Apollo the tempo quickens, and two goddesses come to unravel his swaddling clothes, and Apollo spins free. The goddesses offer him his lute, and the lights brighten.

Scene II, predominantly in duple rhythym, begins with Apollo's first variation, accompanied by a solo violin at first. During the coda of his variation the three Muses enter: Calliope (poetry), Polyhymnia (mime), and Terpsichore (dance). Next comes the pas d'action, in which Apollo presents each muse with a gift symbolic of her vocation: to Calliope, a tablet; to Polyhymnia, a mask; to Terpsichore, a lyre. Stravinsky's use of canon, with the theme developing at different speeds simultaneously, is matched appropriately by the complementary movements that Balanchine gives the individual dancers.

From moderato, the tempo increases for Calliope's variation. The allegretto has a rhythm taken from alexandrine poetry: six iambs, with a caesura in the middle: ._ , ._ , ._ , // ._ , ._ , ._ . Stravinsky does not use the rhythm inexorably, but freely invents and embroiders around a basic pattern, which in fact influences the entire composition. Polyhymnia's variation speeds to allegro, but she is no more successful in pleasing Apollo and reaching the standards he has set for the Muses than was Calliope. The music for Terpsichore returns to allegretto, as she performs a variation basically in triple time which Apollo finds entirely praiseworthy. (One may recall Petipa's series of variations in the prologue to *The Sleeping Beauty.*)

Apollo follows with a majestic variation, lento, basically in triple time. He begins with the wide sweeping arm movements that gloriously reveal and express his godhead, and he closes with the same. In between, his jumps and his smooth enchainements focus on his relationship to ideal form and universal balance. Next comes the pas de deux between Apollo and Terpsichore, adagio, in duple time; a tender sequence with playful touches, such as the "swimming" lesson.

Presently Calliope and Polyhymnia return, and all four dance the vivo coda together (in E Major), with Apollo the leader guiding the Muses and lifting them. In a moment of confidence and repose he rests his head in the cradled hands of the Muses. Then, as the Muses are sitting on the ground each sister raises one leg to form a cone, which Apollo touches with his hand. Finally, Apollo leads the Muses to Olympus, as the strings play the apotheosis, largo e tranquillo, a magnificent, majestic conclusion.

In *Apollo,* the pas of the god with the three Muses was an entirely new creation, a kind of prototype for intimate group (and also ensemble) movement Balanchine used again on appropriate occasions. In *Concerto Barocco,* for example, the involvement of dancers linked by clasped hands offers a continuous plastic unfolding. This characteristic procedure (technique, if you will) of Balanchine often is used in alteration with passages where dancers run in and out in succession until seeming to find each other, and in pairs or in groups they begin a new section. The running on and off, however, is as often as not an integral part of the action, continual seeking, searching.

Although I did not see *Apollo* during the Diaghilev years, when I did see it some years later I recognized it at once as a masterpiece of masterpieces in the canon of Balanchine and Stravinsky alike. I have known and seen all the principals of the premiere on other occasions, and I am compelled to imagine admiringly their contributions to the whole in 1928. By this I do not wish to imply that subsequent collaborations of Balanchine and Stravinsky have been inferior, but I wish to record their achievement together, from their first full collaboration, and to note its significance for the history of performing arts, since *Apollo* has gone through dozens of interpreters and thousands of performances all over the world.

Quite naturally, every artist's aesthetics are influenced by his surroundings—physical and creative. Balanchine has always insisted that ballets must be contemporary, not museum pieces. That was his attitude toward *Swan Lake* when he revised it for the Diaghilev company in 1928, and also when he produced it for the New York City Ballet. Such is also his attitude toward *Apollo,* the ballet he said was a turning point in his career.

As the years have gone by he has simplified certain elements of the *Apollo* story line that no longer seemed relevant to him. First he suppressed the chariot that would take Apollo to Mount Olympus in the finale. Later he discarded the Greek costumes in favor of practice clothes. Most recently, he has felt that the prologue of *Apollo* does not fit in today's world, and he begins the ballet at the moment of the god's birth. Over the years Balanchine has also permitted various dancers to make certain changes. He feels that he must be flexible and alive to what the best presentation is, in concentrated form, under the particular circumstances. (He cut ninety-one measures from *Apollo* for recent performances; would Stravinsky agree?)

We have noted that Balanchine said Stravinsky helped him learn artistic discipline. Stravinsky's method of composition was a model of how to omit extraneous elements in creation and still be complete in the statement of a theme. No doubt this concept has pursued Balanchine, and it probably is responsible for his ability to present the essence of a work, whether short or long, in appropriate fashion. Balanchine began *Apollo* with Lifar, a dancer whose ability was almost godlike, and gave him movements that often were what seem appropriate for gods, as well as some of an athletic nature.

Following another tale by Hans Christian Andersen, Stravinsky composed *Le Baiser de la Fée* for Ida Rubinstein in 1928 as an homage to Tchaikovsky, whose themes he used throughout the four-scene forty-five-minute work. Neither Nijinska's original choreography nor that of Frederick Ashton for Sadler's Wells in 1935 proved memorable. What Balanchine did at the Metropolitan Opera in 1937 and then revived for the Ballet Russe de Monte Carlo in 1940 and for the Paris Opéra in 1947, and the New York City Ballet in 1950, became definitive in the presentation of a moving allegorical story in modern terms, with Balanchine's extraordinarily apt movement supplying the added dimension of meaning rather than merely parallel motion.

Stravinsky saw the allegory of the Fairy kissing the tiny boy whom she would later claim for herself forever as the Muse of Music, claiming Tchaikovsky, and he wove excerpts of nineteen identifiable pieces of Tchaikovsky along with some fifteen themes of his own into the score.

For B. H. Haggin, for me, and for countless others, Balanchine's sensitiveness to this wonderful score remains a fresh miracle of performing art. Edwin Denby expressed brilliantly its fascination: "Its images of destiny, its tragic illuminations are as convincing as any I know in literature. . . . *Baiser de la Fée* is poetic theatre at its truest." (See Bibliography.) The description of this ballet is based on that of Balanchine and remarks by Stravinsky.

Igor Stravinsky and George Balanchine discussing *Le baiser de la Fée* with Alexandra Danilova, Frederic Franklin, and Maria Tallchief (c. 1946). (*Courtesy of Ballet Foundation and Ballet Russe de Monte Carlo*)

In the first scene a mother and her baby are caught in a Swiss mountain snowstorm. The mother dies and the helpless child is rescued and adopted by passing peasants, but only after a beautiful and bewitching fairy, the Ice Maiden, has passed by, picked up the child, and kissed it, thus sealing its destiny.

The second scene takes place at a village festival twenty years later. The boy has grown up and soon is to be married to the miller's daughter. After a sequence of celebrative dances, both solo and ensemble, the handsome bridegroom is left alone and is approached by a gypsy fortuneteller (the Ice Maiden in disguise). He is soon at her mercy, following her in every direction.

The action of the third scene takes place inside the mill. There are several numbers, the most touching of which, musically and choreographically, is the pas de deux for the lovely bride and bridegroom. Presently the bride leaves, only to return shortly with her wedding veil over her face. As the couple dances to the haunting melody of Tchaikovsky's "None But the Lonely Heart," the groom becomes more and more attracted to the bride, but when at last she reveals her face, he recognizes her as the Ice Maiden-Gypsy. Now totally in her power, he lets her lead him away.

The epilogue shows us the same scene, as the bride looks in vain for her fiancé. The wall of the mill dissolves, and we see the young man in the distance, as he climbs upward to reach the Ice Maiden in the sky. Stravinsky's orchestration calls for three flutes, three oboes, three clarinets, two bassoons, four horns, three trumpets, three trombones, tuba, harp, percussion, and strings.

In two of the three seasons the American Ballet was resident at the Metropolitan Opera, important new choreography by Balanchine was presented on festive occasions in addition to occasional ballet evenings and of course, the frequent ballet divertissements called for by the opera repertoire. In 1936 the ballet feature of the season was a completely danced production of Gluck's *Orpheus,* with singers in the pit. In 1937, the first of Balanchine's Stravinsky Festivals, the choreographer revived *Apollo,* choreographed *Le Baiser de la Fée* for the first time, and commissioned the composer to write a new score. This became *Card Party,* premiered April 23, 1937.

It is an amusing twenty-three-minute divertimento-pastiche in three scenes about three deals of poker in which the Joker mischieveously attempts to upset the balance of the hands. Probably because he was such an ardent card player all his life, Stravinsky had long thought of composing a ballet in which the dancers dressed like playing cards would perform as if on a green table. The composer worked out his own libretto, which Balanchine has generally followed. Another of Stravinsky's many creative divertimentos (as opposed to such magna opera as *Oedipus*) in *Card Party* Stravinsky drew on themes by Mussorgsky, Rossini, Messager, Strauss, Stravinsky, and others.

In the first deal, following the introductory parade of the cards presented with a musical fanfare, the Joker's hand has a full house, but he does not win outright. In the second deal the Joker joins four aces to present a victorious five of a kind. In the final deal the hand with the Joker is roundly defeated, this time by a royal flush. There are many possibilities of combining and grouping the twenty-six cards divided into four suits and two sexes, with the Joker as an ever-present interrupter of music and action alike, and sometimes acting almost as the master of ceremonies. Although the Joker is defeated, his Eulenspiegel-like immortality is indicated at the end, and Stravinsky's reiteration of the introductory fanfare theme (inserted as a memory of the composer's early casino days) reminds us that the game is to be continued.

Dramatically, *Card Party* is related to the composer's *L'Histoire du Soldat*, the Joker assuming a role quite similar to that of the devil. Structurally, there is a close relation to *Renard;* tonally, there is a relationship to *Danses Concertantes*. In each case Balanchine's movements are related to Stravinsky's music, which they complete, enlarge, and intensify in meaning—in phrasing and architecture.

Musically, the three sections may be outlined as follows: Deal I: alla breve in B flat major, meno mosso in D flat major, moderato assai in D flat and D major, stringendo in f minor, tranquillo in D flat and F major; Deal II: alla breve in B flat major, marcia in A major (variation I allegretto in B flat major, variation II in A major, variation III in A flat major, variation IV in G major, variation V sostenuto e pesante in E flat major, coda piu mosso in G major), marcia (brief reprise) in A flat major, finale con moto in F major/minor, B minor/major, F major/minor; Deal III: alla breve in B flat major, valse in E flat major, presto in c minor/b minor, finale leggiero grazioso in E major/G major, coda tempo del principio in E major. The orchestration of *Card Party* is two flutes, two oboes, two clarinets, two bassoons, four horns, two trumpets, three trombones, tuba, percussion, and strings.

Although in some circles Colonel Wassily de Basil was regarded more as a questionable businessman than an artist-producer, in 1941 he gave George Balanchine an attractive opportunity: to choreograph *Balustrade* for the Original Ballet Russe using Stravinsky's marvellously astringent Violin Concerto in D. Sets and costumes were designed by Balanchine's longtime trusted collaborator, Pavel Tchelitchew (who provided unforgettable designs for *Concerto* by Mozart, Gluck's *Orpheus,* a revival of *Apollo,* etc.). The four movements of Stravinsky's twenty-two-minute concerto are toccata in moderate tempo, a faster aria I, a slow aria II (in which the choreographer exploited an acrobatic back bend for Toumanova in the pas de deux she danced with Paul Petroff), and concluding with a very fast capriccio. (Among the other new ballets Balanchine choreographed with important roles for Toumanova in the years 1933 to 1947 were *Cotillon, Concurrence, Le Bourgeois Gentilhomme, Mozartiana,* and *Le Palais de Cristal.*)

Written in 1931, the composer states his neoclassic work was not modeled on the standard violin concertos, none of which he particularly liked, although he admitted to the slight influence of Bach's Double Violin Concerto in d minor. Note that Stravinsky composed a double solo in the capriccio movement of his concerto, where one violin from the orchestra joins the soloist in a brief duet. There is no cadenza (as there is none in the Bach), but throughout the solo part is important and difficult. Also, in some passages Stravinsky has used a texture that resembles chamber music rather than orchestral writing.

Planning his choreography of *Balustrade* while listening to a recording of the concerto with Stravinsky, Balanchine fully satisfied the demanding composer in this work. In *Dialogues and a Diary* by Igor Stravinsky and Robert Craft, the composer states, "The result was a dance dialogue in perfect coordination with the dialogues of the music."

The title of this ballet came from Tchelitchew's simple white balustrade stretched across the back of the dark stage. Long a genius at creating costumes and decor, his work with Balanchine was evocative and haunting; here Tchelitchew created sinuous and sexually suggestive patterns of black and white on the costumes of the dancers. *Balustrade* was never revived, and *Violin Concerto* (by Stravinsky) as re-choreographed by Balanchine in 1972 is an entirely different work. The orchestration of *Balustrade* is three flutes, three oboes, three clarinets, three bassoons, four horns, three trumpets, three trombones, tuba, timpani, and strings.

Not all of Balanchine and Stravinsky's collaborations were art with a capital A. In the spring of 1942 The Ringling Brothers, Barnum and Bailey Circus featured "Fifty Elephants and Fifty Beautiful Girls" in Balanchine's choreography for Stravinsky's commissioned *Circus Polka.* This four-minute piece starred the elephant Modoc, whose solo dancing at the circus had already been admired. The neoclassic music is marchlike, and it was successfully performed by the elephants (under protest) 425 times.

There is an amusing anecdote about the exchange of precise boutades by the choreographer and the composer. Balanchine asked if Stravinsky would write music for elephants to dance, and Stravinsky replied, "Yes, if they were very young." Each artist respected the other and each is always as precise as possible, knowing that exactitude is important to the other in his craft as in his creation. On numerous occasions they discussed the lengths of sections in a work and often the lengths have been estimated in seconds, not merely in minutes. The initial orchestration for *Circus Polka* was one flute, two solo clarinets, two clarinets, alto saxophone, baritone saxophone, two solo cornets, three cornets, two baritone cornets, two horns, four trombones, two tubas, and percussion. For the revised version (1966) it is two flutes, two oboes, two clarinets, two bassoons, four horns, two trumpets, three trombones, tuba, percussion, and strings.

During the several years Balanchine served as principal choreographer for Serge Denham's Ballet Russe de Monte Carlo, he prepared his first balletic version of Stravinsky's eminently danceable *Danses Concertantes,* which had been introduced to concert audiences under the direction of the composer in 1942. Balanchine's premiere of this twenty-minute neoclassic work, with brilliant costumes by Eugene Berman, took place on September 10, 1944, in New York City. It was newly produced in 1972 for the New York City Ballet's Stravinsky Festival. This bright, inventive ballet is full of characteristic rhythmic variety in sound and in movement.

All things are related, and it is up to us to see how this is so. Yet when we have observed similarities, it is at once incumbent on us to note differences. How things differ in shape, form, color, and timing gives individuality to a work and makes it interesting and important rather than just another homogeneous unit in a continuum.

There are both formal and tonal relationships between *Danses Concertantes* and other works of Stravinsky. For example, we note that the five sections of *Danses Concertantes,* marche, pas d'action, theme varié (four variations), pas de deux, marche, relate formally to the structure of *Renard.* The composer cast his "ballet for chamber orchestra" in the form of a semiabstract work, providing a march to get the dancers on stage at the beginning, and repeating it at the end to get them off, just as he does in *Renard.* In *Danses Concertantes* the variations are set consecutively to a series of ascending semitones. The theme is in G major, and it is succeeded by variations in A flat, A natural, A natural, and B flat; the variations in *Card*

Party follow a series generally descending in semitones, B flat, A natural, A flat, G natural, E flat, G natural. There is another way in which *Danses Concertantes* resembles *Card Party,* that is, in the way the short sections are built up into larger movements, sometimes with quotations of well known themes. This characteristic of a number of Stravinsky's works of various periods is shared in the same way by Balanchine, who uses certain steps or patterns in works to clarify certain dance relationships. It is the inventive differences, however, which Stravinsky exhibits from *Renard* to *Danses Concertantes* to *Symphony in Three Movements* that Balanchine makes visible and memorable.

Balanchine has noted that he used the bodies of dancers to "feel out" the volatile qualities of Stravinsky's complex rhythms. For his 1972 production of *Danses Concertantes* the choreographer inevitably changed the work he had first given stage life to twenty-eight years earlier. The dancers of the New York City Ballet were well versed in his demands of rapid, chameleon-like changes, and he was able to envisage that marvellous synthesis of novelty and elegance that is his exclusively.

At the beginning of the ballet, four groups of three come on successively to bow and to joke, followed at the climax of the march by the ballerina and her cavalier. This ballet is yet another side of Balanchine's homage to classicism; it is all wit yet never vulgar, whereas his *Ballet Imperial* had been all grandeur, without despotism.

The pas d'action is a rondo dance for all. Next comes the theme and four variations: allegretto, scherzando, andantino, and tempo giusto, each executed by a trio of dancers, with syncopated footwork and jumps following the characteristic ostinato[3] of the composer. In the third variation something of *Concerto Barocco*'s entwined passages involves the trio in leggy steps and configurations while the dancers hold hands. Hopscotch and jazz appear to be the inspiration of composer and choreographer in the final trio variation involving characteristic quick transitions.

The brilliant pas de deux features quick movements, kicks, arabesques, extensions, jumps, and beats, both dignified and playful, and then this contemporary circus of great charm, a friendly, ironic vaudeville, draws to a conclusion with a repeat of the march.

The spare orchestration of *Danses Concertantes* is one flute, oboe, clarinet, bassoon, two horns, trumpet, trombone, timpani, six violins, four violas, three violoncellos, and two double basses.

The next collaboration was the *Elégie* for unaccompanied viola (or violin), which Stravinsky wrote in 1944 and Balanchine choreographed the next year for students at his School of American Ballet. This work lasting four and a half minutes was first performed professionally on April 28, 1948, by the New York City Ballet, with dancers Tanaquil LeClercq and Pat McBride, and with Emmanuel Vardi playing the viola.

In 1948, in *Dance Index,* Balanchine noted that he "tried to reflect the flow and concentrated variety of the music through the interlaced bodies of two dancers rooted to a central spot of the stage." I remember clearly the absolute perfection of these two long-legged dancers executing a difficult and inspiring work that is full of fascinating convolutions performed adagio, with an uninterrupted sequence atune to the music. B. H. Haggin and others have noted how this pas de deux is one of a long series of Balanchine pas de deux that are constantly changing and constantly testing both new choreographic vocabulary and new dancers. In the revised version, presented by the New York City Ballet on June 13, 1982, Suzanne Farrell danced a solo lament of grandeur accompanied by solo viola. She began crouching on her knees. Her twists and turns in place matched the rise and fall of the music. Presently she rose to dance, her back to the audience. At the close she settled back into her initial crouching position.

In a number of compositions Stravinsky uses a cyclic method, with a motif or fanfare introduction and conclusion; these include *Renard, Card Party, Danses Concertantes, L'Histoire du Soldat,* and *Symphony in Three Movements.* Balanchine choreographs Stravinsky's cyclic procedures in variations of a formal parallel nature, introducing the dancers at the beginning, presenting the main part of the work, and bidding them farewell in the reprise of the introduction.

Dating from 1916, Stravinsky's saucy, masque-like *Renard* was choreographed originally for Diaghilev by Nijinska, and later revised by Lifar without great success. Balanchine first presented his imaginative version of this twenty-minute barnyard fable for four dancers and four singers as a Ballet Society production on January 13, 1947, with beautiful sets and costumes by Estaban Francés. We see the "animal dancers" march on, play their irreverent little comedy about how the naive cock is twice lured from his safe perch, overcome by the cunning fox, but rescued by the practical cat and goat, and march off together just as they entered. Stravinsky has not tied the dance characters either to particular vocal voices or to instrumental parts. Thus he retained full control of the musical structure, which is intricate and constantly surprising despite deceptive directness. In a way he complicates his stated purpose, which had been to compose a piece that would suit a small group of performers. Balanchine's choreography was resourcefully effective in its telling of this fairy tale. He did not resort to symbolic or allegorical presentation, but rather hewed brilliantly and steadfastly to the actual story line (and Ramuz's fine text) as it is sung. The spare orchestration of *Renard* is two solo tenors, two solo basses, flute, oboe, clarinet, bassoon, two horns, trumpet, percussion, *cimbalom,* and solo string quintet.

Dating from Hellenic times, the near universal theme of *Orpheus* has continually inspired poets, musicians, and dancers. At the Metropolitan Opera in 1936 Balanchine had choreographed Gluck's opera entirely for dancers, with Pavel Tchelitchew's imaginative visual aids and with the singers in the pit. That Stravinsky should wish to have his say on the theme seems natural and inevitable, particularly after his *Apollo.* The invitation to compose the music for this ballet came from Lincoln Kirstein and George Balanchine.

In many of Stravinsky's ballets one can refer to techniques he had already employed and also to procedures he was to use later. Thus *Orpheus,* first performed April 28, 1948, by Ballet Society, has moments reminding us of *Apollo, Baiser,* and *Scenes de Ballet.* At times the textures of this meditative and mysterious *Orpheus* remind us of those used by Monteverdi in his *Orfeo* (1607). Then again, Stravinsky's *Orpheus* looks forward to some of his later compositions, such as *The Rake's Progress, Monumentum,* and *Movements.*

Balanchine and Stravinsky planned *Orpheus* together in 1947, dividing it into three scenes, the whole lasting thirty-two minutes. Stravinsky has noted the clear yet plaintive quality of his music (beginning in the Phrygian mode and concluding in the Dorian),[4] and he has pointed out the "family relationship" with the String Concerto of a year earlier. The composer felt Noguchi's sets and curtain were extremely successful, although he appreciated the costumes less, noting that Orpheus looked too much like a baseball catcher and that his mask interfered with his vision. Commenting that much of the music is in the nature of mimed song presented as the staged frieze moves before the audience, Stravinsky brought out the tragedy of the lovers in the pas de deux accompanied by strings. He also felt the drama of the first interlude was heightened by the way the harmonic movement and active bass line effectively interrupt the compelling succession of ostinatos, one of Stravinsky's outstanding hallmarks. The composer used the harp as a concertante instrument representing Orpheus's lyre, an eternal element in the intimate story, at the beginning as well as at the end when Orpheus is dead. Ritualistic and subjective, modern and abstract, the ballet was admirable in its low-key approach.

The following synopsis is based on the outline in Stravinsky's score of *Orpheus*. Scene I: Orpheus weeps for Eurydice. His friends offer sympathy. Lento sostenuto. Air de danse. Andante con moto. Dance of the Angel of Death. Andante (on the way to Hades). Interlude. The Angel and Orpheus reappear in Tartarus. Andante. Scene II: Pas des Furies. Agitato. Air de danse (Orpheus). Interlude. Orpheus in Tartarus. L'istesso tempo. Air de danse (Orpheus). Pas d'action. The Furies return Eurydice to Orpheus. Andantino. Pas de deux. The death of Eurydice. Andante. Interlude. Moderato. Pas d'action. The Bacchantes kill Orpheus. Vivace. Scene III: Apotheosis of Orpheus. Apollo. Lento sostenuto. The orchestration of *Orpheus* is three flutes, two oboes, two clarinets, two bassoons, four horns, two trumpets, two trombones, timpani, harp, and strings.

Balanchine's version of Stravinsky's atmospheric *The Firebird* was premiered on November 27, 1949. It is based on the composer's 1945 condensation of the 1910 forty-five-minute score, in which Stravinsky included ten of the original nineteen sections but retained the entire story in two scenes. On May 28, 1970 the New York City Ballet presented a new, more lavish production, for which Jerome Robbins revised the dance of Kastchei's monsters, and Balanchine revised his dance of the Firebird, but much of the remainder of this popular work did not change. The structure is as follows: Introduction (Prelude and Dance of the Firebird). Pantomime. Pas de Deux of the Firebird and Prince Ivan. Pantomime. Scherzo Dance of the Princesses. Pantomime. Rondo (Prince Ivan, Tsarevna, and Princesses). Infernal Dance of Kastchei. Lullaby (solo for the Firebird). Final Hymn.

Balanchine danced in a number of Fokine Ballets in Russia and elsewhere; while he was with Diaghilev in *Firebird* he took the role of the evil Kastchei. However, his purpose was not to recreate Fokine's detailed book or choreography; rather, it was to tell in his own terms the old Russian fairy tale of Prince Ivan hunting in the forest, seeing the Firebird turn and jump in her native habitat, capturing the magical creature, and then taking pity on her and letting her go. In parting she gives him a feather as a pledge of her assistance if he should ever need it. Presently, in Kastchei's garden, Ivan encounters the charming, young princesses, including his destined bride, the Tsarevna, with whom he dances. As dawn breaks the captive princesses must return to Kastchei's castle. Dramatically, Ivan challenges the evil Kastchei, and as the good Firebird comes to his aid and casts a spell of sleep over the infernal grotesque creatures, Ivan kills the monster. This is followed by a hymn of rejoicing and the majestic wedding of Ivan and the Tsarevna. As the Firebird takes her leave she reveals her own very warm, feminine affection for Ivan.

It is appropriate to remember here that Balanchine is a Russian of Georgian blood, as well as a Frenchman by taste and an American by custom. He has always shown his sensitivity to different aspects of contemporary life in these diverse cultures. In *The Firebird* he was concerned with the Eastern tale, but he knew well the world had changed since 1910 when it was premiered, and he presented the story so that audiences in the second half of the twentieth century would be touched by it. Also a consideration was Balanchine's wish to provide a vehicle for Maria Tallchief. His brilliant solution in *The Firebird* of both cultural and practical problems may not efface our memories of the full-length masterpiece (danced by Karsavina, Danilova, and Fonteyn, among others, and which Balanchine himself had arranged for Diaghilev in 1926), yet we shall not deny its effectiveness in its own right. Due to Maria Tallchief's brio in the brilliant solo of the title part, and to Francisco Moncion's extremely fine supporting work as Prince Ivan partnering the Firebird in balanced off-balance steps of the adagio, this version was an immediate success. So it has continued over the years, as many dancers of the New York City Ballet have performed the leads. The orchestration of the 1945 *Firebird* is two flutes, two oboes, two clarinets, two bassoons, four horns, two trumpets, three trombones, tuba, percussion, xylophone, harp, piano, and strings.

The Rake's Progress is a three-act opera in nine scenes with an epilogue, inspired by the famous series of paintings by Hogarth and based on a text by W. H. Auden and Chester Kallman. It was given its premiere performance on September 11, 1951, in Venice, and the New York premiere took place on February 14, 1953, at the Metropolitan Opera House. The latter production was directed by George Balanchine, with crafted, effective scenery and costumes by Horace Armistead. It is the familiar story of a foolish man who inherits immense, undeserved wealth, wastes it, and goes berserk.

Stravinsky conceived of his longest work (150 minutes) as a classic opera with arias, ensembles, choruses, recitatives, and other formalities of eighteenth-century lyric theatre found in Handel and Mozart. However, he used many characteristic modern procedures, and the work is neoclassic in content and outlook, with a preponderance of duple rhythm.

In his *Musical America* review Ronald Eyer expressed my own opinion that however special and imaginative Stravinsky's creation was, it usually was framed by the composer's ballet procedures and instrumental considerations more than by opera and vocal ground rules. (At this time perhaps a caveat about value judgments is in order, as we note that in the canon of Stravinsky's unique compositions, such diverse works as *Apollo* and *Oedipus Rex* are at least as wonderful and evocative, and probably more central to his achievement than many of his most popular works.) The libretto of *The Rake's Progress* is a good one, but in this work text and melody do not unite in the special way they do in the composer's *Oedipus* and *Symphonie des Psaumes*—despite Stravinsky's apparent references to his *Oedipus,* and also to Mozart's *Così fan tutte.*

However, under Balanchine's inspired direction at the Metropolitan, the action flowed exactly at the pace of the music, and the characters were never less than arresting. Balanchine knew when to move his singers and when to have them stand still, something other directors have not well realized; and many of the choruses are dance pieces, which Balanchine took advantage of. Stravinsky's dances—minuet in bedlam, fandango in the graveyard—shine in the hands of Balanchine, also the gigue in scene one, the march in act two, and the fugue in the epilogue. In the brothel scene in act I, where Mother Goose claims Tom Rakewell for herself, the music is 6/8, a danse bretonne, which gives the ballet an expansive opportunity. Thus, throughout Balanchine was acutely observant in his judgment of the character of the music and the interaction of eight solo singers and chorus, always keeping continuity, yet providing effective, logical variety. The orchestration of *The Rake's Progress* is two flutes, two oboes, two clarinets, two bassoons, two horns, two trumpets, cembalo (piano), timpani, and strings—essentially the classic orchestra.

Four years passed before George Balanchine choreographed another Stravinsky score, and this time it was once again a true collaboration. *Agon,* a twenty-minute ballet, was given its stage premiere by the New York City Ballet on December 1, 1957, though it had been performed in concert earlier that year. This typically heterogeneous yet compact work has not a moment of filler. It is a neoclassic ballet in the line of *Apollo* to *Orpheus;* although its title means "contest," it is in no way Greek in inspiration. It is danced in the "uniform" of many great Balanchine ballets—practice clothes. Most of the sections are modeled, through the composer's senses, after seventeenth-century French dances. Much of its music is rapid, and its orchestra is a large one, although it is never used full strength, but rather in varying, interesting combinations.

The composer describes the four sections as follows: I. Pas de Quatre—4 men, beginning with their backs to the audience. Double Pas de Quatre—8 women. Triple Pas de Quatre—a variation of the preceding, 4 men, 8 women. II. Prelude for orchestra. First Pas de Trois—1 man, 2 women.

Saraband–Step–1 man. Gaillarde–2 women. Coda–1 man, 2 women. III. Interlude for orchestra. Second Pas de Trois–2 men, 1 woman. Bransle Simple–2 men. Bransle Gay–1 woman. Bransle de Poitou–2 men, 1 woman. IV. Interlude for orchestra. Pas de Deux–1 man, 1 woman. Variation–1 man. Variation–1 woman. Refrain–1 man. Coda–1 man, 1 woman. A la strette–for orchestra. Danse des Quatre Duos. Danse des Quatre Trios–4 sets of 1 man, 2 women. Coda des 4 trios–near the end the women leave and the men resume their original positions.

A précis of Lincoln Kirstein's penetrating prose on *Agon* is as follows: "*Agon* is a contest without competition, a hymn to endless, tireless struggle; opposition, tension; release; stops, starts; conciliation, mutual consideration, in chancy but designed encounters. Visual and aural asymmetry are its identifying elements along with a unique formal strait jacket. The ballet is more an analysis of time and space than a struggle or a demonstration of competitive virtuosity. Discipline and impersonalization accentuates witty, musical dynamics, with tension and anxiety ever present."

Agon is the first serial composition by Stravinsky that Balanchine choreographed. This late masterpiece becomes doubly creative through the imaginative and calculated vision of Balanchine. The pairing of the contributions of each is so acute it is difficult to realize where the work of one leaves off and the other begins. This ballet is in the same class as the late operas of Monteverdi, Mozart's *The Marriage of Figaro*, Berg's *Wozzeck* for many of the same reasons, including first of all, mastery of old and new techniques. Second, fresh ways of presenting eternal verities are used here with diatonic and chromatic harmonies joined with serial techniques in cyclical forms, and also with the traditional ballet pas de deux, trois, and quatre, sarabande, gaillard, and bransles, along with Balanchine's special acrobatic and chromatic stretching of classic techniques.

The very genius of Stravinsky's rhythm, harmony, and textures is matched creatively by Balanchine's total comprehension of the musical subtleties. The parts are not only perfectly constructed in the first place, but make up a total architecture, abstract despite the balanced sections. Note that the prelude and the interlude, the latter played two different times, are not identical, although they are remarkably similar. As Balanchine modestly observed, "musically it is complicated, somebody had to analyze this; in this case I did." Stravinsky agreed that Balanchine's "plastic realization" matched his "architectonic music."

This rigorous work is like living sculpture as only the very best ballets are. It was recognized immediately by all who saw it as one of the great works of contemporary theatre, a true inspiration, clear and clean. Some have compared it to other ballets by Balanchine, for example *Four Temperaments*. But as we have said, even though one may always find parallels and similarities in works by the same creators (Mozart, Shakespeare, Leonardo), it is rather the differences that make a work of art interesting and important, and here there are far more differences. This wonderfully inventive abstract ballet exploits the designs of the human body danced to spare but evocative and provocative music, with each part extending the dancer to the utmost. There is wit as well as exercise, and there is structure, a combination in which the resulting drama is just as interesting as the architecture itself. Timing and position are all-important, and Balanchine's dancers are trained in a manner ideal for the achievement of this ballet. The orchestration of *Agon* is three flutes, three oboes, three clarinets, three bassoons, four horns, four trumpets, three trombones, harp, *mandoline,* piano, timpani, three *tom-toms, xylophone,* castanets, and strings.

Monumentum is based on an instrumental version of three brief madrigals by Gesualdo (1560–1613) recomposed by Stravinsky in 1960, and first produced by the New York City Ballet on November 16, 1960. Both Stravinsky and Balanchine have a chaste lyric simplicity in their fluid yet formal modern treatment of a four hundred-year-old art form. Balanchine's usual clarity and precision fit exactly the courtly ceremonial style of the dance to this Byzantine chamber music piece of seven minutes, made grandly public by seven couples.

The first stately madrigal (Asciugato i begli occhi, Madrigale XIV, libro quinto) is immediately baroque in texture, with brass and strings featured. There is a close relation between the austere yet surprising chords of Stravinsky and the dancers' mannered steps and walking, delineating Balanchine's clear patterns; and there is twice the imposing, slow arc of the ballerina's supported grand jeté.

The shorter second madrigal, moderato (Ma tu, cagion di quella, Madrigale XVIII, libro quinto) is scored for winds only. The movement is somewhat animated and scurrying, yet abstract.

The third madrigal (Belta poi che t'assenti, Madrigale II, libro sesto), reveals how Balanchine appears to master the time of Gesualdo and Stravinsky, revealing emotion in motion that is theatrical, closing in a long diagonal. The orchestration of *Monumentum* is two oboes, two bassoons, four horns, two trumpets, three trombones, violins I, II, violas, and violoncellos.

On April 9, 1963 Balanchine added the ten-minute *Movements for Piano and Orchestra* (1959) to the repertoire of the New York City Ballet. *Movements* has a lead pair of solo dancers plus two trios of women. In *Theme and Episodes* Stravinsky notes, "To see Balanchine's choreography of *Move-ments* is to hear the music with one's eyes." The depersonalized music is free-ly serial. Its phrases, both visual and auditory, are short yet related, as repeated seeing and hearing reveals. Balanchine helps shape the joining of his lyrical, meticulous choreography to the intense music by emphasis on his dancers' extensions in a number and variety of ways. His patterns are classical, yet with a modern touch we have seen ever since *Apollo*. This modern touch combines with the "fantasie Balanchine" in which I believe he indulged ever since he began to make ballets.[5]

Often led by the piano, but not dominated by it, *Movements* (in five separate sections with four interludes) is cast as a tense "faster-slower-faster" tempo continuum. The lead couple, related to the piano part, and the other dancers explore regions of complex rhythmic variety and har-mony, occasionally pausing in their artistic journey. Balanchine has been creatively sensitive to the pedal-point passage for cellos in the first movement, to the harp tremolo in the second, and the clarinet tremolo in the third, and he has shown us the extended string harmonics in the final sections. (String harmonics, brilliantly used by Stravinsky as early as *The Firebird,* have long been a favorite device with the composer.) This spare and bright essay in suspended human sculptural motion has been com-pared to a "mobile caught in the breath of music" in the *London Times*. The orchestration of *Movements* is piano, and two flutes, oboe, English horn, two clarinets, bassoon, two trumpets, three trombones, harp, celeste, and strings (6-6-4-5-2). These two ballets (*Monumentum* and *Movements*) are now given together, a worthy pair, and an extension from the achieve-ments of *Agon*.

Stravinsky's *Ragtime for Eleven Instruments* (1918) was in some ways a further use of ideas he had employed in *Renard* and also in *L'Histoire du Soldat*. On December 7, 1960, Balanchine introduced this short work into the repertoire of the New York City Ballet as a pas de deux for Diana Adams and Bill Carter; on July 15, 1966, he revised it for Suzanne Farrell and Arthur Mitchell, but although many found it charming as a realistic trifle, it did not make its way into the lasting ballets. Stravinsky's music is faithful to a constant duple, jazzy, march-like rhythm, with a few passages featuring the cimbalom and other soloists. The orchestration is for flute, clarinet, horn, cornet, trombone, percussion, *cimbalom,* two violins, viola, and double bass.

Composed in 1963, *Variations* is a serial composition lasting just under five minutes. On March 31, 1966, Balanchine choreographed this work for the New York City Ballet, playing the music three times, and dividing it into three sections; first for twelve women; then for six men; and finally, a solo for Suzanne Farrell. The theme, stated as a series of chords, is followed by six diverse variations, which are matched splendidly three times in the choreography. Both musically and choreographically there are inventive extensions from *Movements,* although at once *Variations* seems bigger, and the three playings of the music is certainly appropriate for the ballet and for the music itself. (Stravinsky himself advised repeated listenings.) By the third playing we are properly prepared for the abrupt ending, a procedure dear to Stravinsky, and completely realized by Balanchine.

The twelve women dressed in black begin with symmetrical, energetic movements, patterns, and poses, like flowers. In the second part Balanchine divides the six men into two mirror groups. They perform athletically and acrobatically, and with their movements even appear to change the sound of the music as we hear it for the second time.

The third part is for elegant Suzanne Farrell alone, as she seems to comment on the music in the style of extraordinary extension and speed Balanchine has made his hallmark. For Farrell, it is a real tour de force. The ballet is dry only in part, and it is certainly one more proof that Balanchine understands music marvellously, and Stravinsky's inventive music perhaps completely. Its stop-and-start quality is very contemporary and because of its very high density it is not disparate. Stravinsky may not have started out in this case composing *Variations* for the ballet, but as Balanchine characterizes so much of Stravinsky's music, "it is for and of movement." And Balanchine is the choreographer for this music. In a number of instances there are other versions of Stravinsky's scores, but Balanchine's ballets, at least during our lifetime, do not date the way so many other choreographers' works do. This ballet is an excellent example of Balanchine's method in expounding his multiple ideas of spatial form and substance in conjunction with illuminating the aural form and substance of the works of Stravinsky.

On July 2, 1982, the New York City Ballet presented *Variations* as a solo for Suzanne Farrell. In this revision the music was performed once, but the new choreography was intense, concise—with effective stretches and bends during the adagio and with enormously energetic high kicks characteristic of Balanchine's work for Farrell in the swift allegro. The orchestration of *Variations* is three flutes, three oboes, three clarinets, two bassoons, four horns, three trumpets, three trombones, harp, piano, twelve violins, ten violas, eight cellos, and four double basses.

Composed in 1961 and 1962, *Noah and the Flood* is a twenty-four-minute musical play for tenor solo (Lucifer or Satan), two bass soloists (God), and chorus (sopranos, altos, and tenors), with speaking parts for Noah, Noah's Wife, Noah's Sons, and a Narrator (whose lines can be shared with a Caller), and large orchestra. It was first performed on television on June 14, 1962, with choreography by George Balanchine and sets and costumes by Reuben Ter-Arutunian. The conducting was shared by Stravinsky and Robert Craft.

The text, arranged by Craft, was derived from the book of Genesis and the English York and Chester medieval miracle plays, with some additional anonymous material. Of all Stravinsky's serial works, *Noah and the Flood* (based on a twelve-note chord spanning five and one-half octaves, which can be analyzed into six intervals of the fifth) shows some of his strongest feeling for harmony; he often pauses on a C sharp chord. Musically, it can be related to *Agon* and to *Les Noces;* dramatically, this morality play recalls several of Stravinsky's other works of this type— *L'Histoire du Soldat* and *The Rake's Progress*—in which good and evil are balanced.

Balanchine's opinion of how this stimulating project turned into typical television is not flattering to the producers, but early stage presentations also had their problems. I can recall being interested in the television production primarily because of the music, which seems to concur with Balanchine's opinion of the production. Stravinsky's notes on working with Balanchine and Craft are contained in the book, *Dialogues and a Diary* (see Bibliography).

The outline structure of the work is as follows: I. Prelude: i. Instrumental prelude. ii. Te Deum (chorus, in Latin). iii. Melodrama (Narrator). iv. God's Word (2 basses). v. Aria (Lucifer). vi. Melodrama (Narrator). vii. God's Word (concluded). II. The Building of the Ark (choreography). III. The Catalogue of the Animals. Melodrama (Noah and Caller). IV. The Comedy. Melodrama (Noah and his Wife and Sons). V. The Flood (choreography). VI. The Covenant of the Rainbow: i. God's Word (2 basses). ii. Melodrama (Noah). iii. Reprise of the Instrumental prelude. iv. Aria (Lucifer). v. Sanctus (chorus, in Latin).

I am extraordinarily glad to have seen the New York City Ballet production of *Noah and the Flood,* June 11, 1982, a feature of the Stravinsky Festival, staged by Balanchine and Jacques d'Amboise, designed by Ter-Arutunian. It made clear the moving qualities of the music and of Balanchine's admirable conception, and it may take its place as one of the very finest of the Stravinsky-Balanchine collaborations. Full credit should also be given to Robert Craft, whose molding of the biblical and other texts is superb. The naive, realistic production is simple, poetic, and beautiful at all times; the masques for Noah and his family and the cardboard animal figures are beautifully realized. The story of this timely morality play is known to all, yet told in this moving way it reminds us of its universality. It is not repetitive, but is fresh, dramatic, and balanced by the varied choreography. The ingenious music of the flood is dramatically achieved by a billowing cover for the stage on which the furies hold their evil rounds, to be subdued by the coming of the child with the bird.

After the te deum (almost a dance piece), the Narrator begins by informing us that God created the world and Adam and Eve are driven from Eden after Lucifer (then Satan) tempts Eve. Noah gathers his family and the animals in the ark; they survive the flood and are blessed by God.

The orchestration of *Noah and the Flood* is four flutes, three oboes, four clarinets, three bassoons, four horns, three trumpets, three trombones, tuba, timpani, three tom-toms, xylophone, *marimba,* cymbal, bass drum, celeste, piano, harp, and strings.

Jewels was first performed by the New York City Ballet on April 13, 1967. It is made up of three sections: *Emeralds,* to music by Fauré; *Rubies,* to music by Stravinsky; and *Diamonds,* to music by Tchaikovsky. It is a balanced evening-long work.

Each section of the ballet is fascinating in itself, and different from the others. Placed between the gentle *Emeralds* and the majestic *Diamonds,* Stravinsky's Capriccio for Piano and Orchestra (1929) is as brilliant a centerpiece as one can imagine. Balanchine uses Stravinsky's twenty-minute neoclassic, jazzy concerto in a modern, elegant way that is special with this choreographer. Purely as music this work is possibly the finest of the composer's three concertos, and Balanchine has matched the dazzling piano part with parallel brilliance for his dancers.

As always the dancing is inventive, and sharply accented ("quirky but unforced," according to the *New York Times*). There is fantasy and there is fugato; there is wit, and there is seriousness, both aurally and visually.

The opening of *Rubies* relies on Stravinsky's massive chords, fortissimo, tutti, with rushing strings (there are jazz passages that may remind us of *Card Party*). Then, led by the piano in dialogue, in this fast movement a ballerina contrasts sexy vaudeville-like routines with the familiar Balanchine vocabulary, including manipulation of her long limbs by her four male partners. In the coda the tempo slows carefully to a halt as the choreographer matches the composer with acrobatic effects of appropriate weight.

In the andante Balanchine again emphasizes rhapsodic twists, bends and convoluted extensions by the ballerina and her partner, with at times an Oriental feeling both in movement and repose. Then, in contrast, he gives each soloist very forceful sequences of movement.

In the rapid finale rondo (which, incidentally, was the first movement of this work Stravinsky composed) Balanchine has conformed to the structure of the composer by emphasizing the cyclical element in the group led by the leading dancer (a role created brilliantly by Edward Villella). The bouncy, concluding ensemble of *Rubies* is characteristic, provocative, tricky—all in all a major ballet. Balanchine interweaves classic technique and a parody of his own style—brilliant, almost hectic, and American in the same sense that Stravinsky's music is "American." Legs unexpectedly fly at unusual angles, without preparation, and feet are flat when one would anticipate them being pointed. The orchestration of *Rubies* is piano, three flutes, three oboes, three clarinets, two bassoons, four horns, two trumpets, three trombones, tuba, timpani, concertino strings (violin, viola, violoncello, and double bass), and ripieno strings (violins, violas, violoncellos, and double basses).

Like Picasso, Stravinsky sought many sources for self-renewal and renewal in art. Late in his "serial" period (1966), he composed a pithy, accessible fifteen-minute work, *Requiem Canticles,* for soprano, alto, tenor, bass, chorus, and orchestra. With the composer's enthusiastic agreement, this very personal work was danced once by the New York City Ballet on May 2, 1968, in tribute to Martin Luther King, Jr.

Based on two distinct twelve-tone series, both starting on F, much of *Requiem Canticles* is slow, in duple time. It is cast in nine sections, three instrumental and six vocal: a prelude marcato moderato, attractively astringent with four inventions; exaudi, a Webern-like plea by the chorus; dies irae, the chorus remembers God's will; tuba mirum, beginning with a trumpet passage and featuring a bass solo; wind instrumental interlude, by turns chordal and melodic, quiet and moving; rex tremendae, again duple for chorus; lacrimosa for tenor solo, reminding one of *Renard;* libera me, duple, for chorus—the only section where the liturgic text is set complete, the others using only excerpts of the relevant material; and an ingenious and quiet percussion postlude, a coda concluding in a series of chords.

The lyric aspects of Balanchine's choreography are developed in a massed corps de ballet; the dancers are clothed in long white tulle, each carrying a three-stemmed candelabrum. As the illumination dims or swells, the contrast of shadows and lights, so well understood by Balanchine, creates differing moods.

A single dancer continually searches for something. The chorus celebrates the service for this man of God, this man of the poor, this man of peace. There is another single dancer in contrasting purple, who at the conclusion is raised heavenward.[6] The orchestration of *Requiem Canticles* calls for contralto and bass solos, chorus, four flutes, two bassoons, four horns, two trumpets, three trombones, percussion, and strings.

In June 1972 on the first anniversary after the death of Stravinsky, Balanchine led the New York City Ballet in a festival devoted entirely to thirty-six works with music by Stravinsky. Robert Irving was the principal conductor. There were twenty-two ballets. Seven choreographers participated, but indubitably the greatest contributions were made by Balanchine himself, who choreographed seven ballets by his long-time friend and collaborator, and shared the choreography of *Pulcinella* with Jerome Robbins. Audience and critics came from all over the world to take part in this tribute to the extraordinary partnership, which continued even after the death of one of the partners. See chronology in frontmatter.

No one could say Stravinsky (any more than Lully, Handel, Mozart, Tchaikovsky) never repeated himself: repetition is one of the cardinal pillars of style and its recognition. Balanchine, however, has always known how to assimilate both inventiveness and repetitions wherever they occur, and to make an appropriate stylistic contribution to the creativity of the composer.

For the opening of the Stravinsky Festival, June 18, 1972, Balanchine choreographed the rediscovered fragment of a scherzo from a piano sonata in f sharp minor Stravinsky composed in 1903 and 1904. This sonata had been performed in 1905 and then lost. Stravinsky, in *Memories* (see Bibliography) surmised it was an inept imitation of Beethoven. Entitling it *Lost Sonata,* for the Stravinsky Festival, Balanchine choreographed a short, unpretentious, and casual little character dance, according to John Clifford, who danced it with Sara Leland.

Stravinsky's *Symphony in Three Movements* (1945) was first danced by the New York City Ballet on June 18, 1972. This large, complex twenty-four-minute symphony is both Dionysian and Apollonian. At times recalling *Capriccio for Piano and Orchestra,* and alternately *Symphonie des Psaumes,* both in the composer's masterful modern classic style, it is chromatic and through-composed. Despite the composer's characteristic use of ostinato, the center tonally and structurally changes constantly, and so does the focus. Balanchine has realized both the point of view and the procedures of Stravinsky, and his choreography reflects their complexity admirably.

The intense, rapid first movement opens fortissimo, with a diagonal of sixteen women who acrobatically suggest a demonic invocation. The response is not long in coming, in the form of a brilliant solo dancer (originally Helgi Tomasson), soon joined by the danseuses (originally Yourth, then Leland). They execute a number of characteristic stop-and-start sequences, matching the explosive nature of the music against a background of an asymmetrical menacing group from the corps. Gradually, the spacing and the momentum of the dancers increases, and the leading ballerina follows the corps off stage in such a dynamic way that the audience believes the dance must be continuing, wherever the dancers go. Meanwhile, another dancer and his group come into view with rather faster, smaller steps and configurations. The music resembles an adaptation of a toccata fused with the habitual symphonic first movement in sonata form. Balanchine sees the double exposition and brings back the first group in a new series of circular movements, related to their initial architecture yet different, and concluding quietly with a return to the original long diagonal of the "ponytailed" women's corps.

The somewhat agitated yet elegaic second movement features an Eastern pas de deux with suppressed energy, and the langorous intermezzo quality found in the catlike *Renard,* matching the harp and the reduced orchestra. Balanchine's convoluted, romantic pas de deux characteristically matches Stravinsky's structural ostinato and variations.

Continuing without pause, the finale is at the same time a kind of scherzo, in which the six leading soloists, ten secondary soloists, and the entire company take part with aggressive syncopated choreography for the soloists, and constant agitation in the corps. The steps for the feet are small, and the gestures for the arms are large. Though Stravinsky's formal structure appears fluid, one can discern a theme with variations, followed by a fugal conclusion which Balanchine's choreography clearly parallels in complex renderings of the different simultaneous themes, culminating in powerful games and acrobacy. The orchestration is three flutes, two oboes, three clarinets, three bassoons, four horns, three trumpets, three trombones, tuba, percussion, harp, piano, and strings.

Stravinsky's Violin Concerto (1931), which Balanchine choreographed as *Balustrade* in 1941, was given entirely new treatment on June 18, 1972, when it was danced in practice clothes. This version has remained in the New York City Ballet's repertoire.

When the curtain is raised on this cyclic work, Balanchine lets the audience experience the wonderful astringent beginning of the composer before his first ballerina begins explosively in choreographic relation to the inventive neoclassic allegro toccata. Each of the four soloists dances separately in the first movement, accompanied by a corps of four; the total corps de ballet is eight men and eight women. It is amazing how, throughout, Balanchine matches the particular density of Stravinsky, so that regardless of the length of a particular work or movement, the artistic result is formally satisfying. And in the ballet, what is formally satisfying is almost always totally satisfying.

In aria I, begun by the solo violin exactly as in movement one, the orchestration is in another key and there is a convoluted pas de deux for one couple. Each dancer seems to be attempting to escape the other and compete with the other, despite a very close involvement.

In the slower-moving aria II, the violin once more begins on the same notes, though they are held less long, with the orchestra in still another tonality. Here the interweaving partners are in relation to the music, a lamenting couple.

Returning to the original tonality in the finale allegro, the violin begins again with the same notes. Doubly cyclic, Stravinsky uses a rondo form, and Balanchine mirrors this with a pelvic movement, noting wittily when the composer quotes his own *L'Histoire du Soldat* near the conclusion. The orchestration of *Stravinsky Violin Concerto* is three flutes, two oboes, three clarinets, three bassoons, four horns, three trumpets, three trombones, tuba, timpani, and strings.

Stravinsky produced his twenty-minute *Divertimento* from the full *Baiser* (forty-five minutes) in 1934, and although in 1937 Balanchine masterfully choreographed the entire ballet to the complete satisfaction of many, since 1972 he has chosen to present only the *Divertimento* (despite the pleas of B. H. Haggin and others to reinstate the entire work). The *Divertimento,* dealing with love, loss, and destiny in somewhat abstract terms, is exquisite in itself, and probably Balanchine feels that society has changed so much that it often will not exert itself to appreciate extended art if it can get to the heart of the matter in less time. (Also, we noted that Balanchine has cut ninety-one measures of music from the beginning of Stravinsky's *Apollo,* and he has chosen to present shorter versions of several works, such as *The Firebird* and *Swan Lake.*) The orchestration for the *Divertimento from Le Baiser de la Fée* is three flutes, three oboes, three clarinets, two bassoons, four horns, three trumpets, three trombones, tuba, harp, percussion, and strings.

Stravinsky's *Scherzo à la Russe* (1944) was given its premiere by the New York City Ballet on June 21, 1972. It was cast for two ballerinas and sixteen women. The music had been first played in a symphonic jazz arrangement but this was not successful, and it is better known as an orchestral piece. Here, Stravinsky is mainly conservative, in duple rhythm, eight measure phrases, and in ABA form, tonal in G major (with two contrasting trios). Parts of Balanchine's syncopated dances may be related to the Swiss dances in *Le Baiser de la Fée* and to the Russian dance in *Petrouchka.*

Balanchine's uninhibited, gay ballet was amusing for dancers and audiences alike, a charming trifle only four minutes long. It does not end; it just stops, unresolved, in mid-course. The women all wore Karinska's chic waistless, white Russian "nightgowns," and tiara-like headdresses with long ribbons. Balanchine gave them stylish, soft, even childlike movements, with delicious wit, both innocent and sophisticated. The orchestration is three flutes, two oboes, two clarinets, two bassoons, four horns, three trumpets, three trombones, tuba, percussion, piano, harp, and strings.

The sixteen-minute *Duo Concertante* (1932) for violin and piano was first performed by the New York City Ballet on June 22, 1972. There are five movements, in which the free forms of the odd movements frame the pastoral-like folkish strictures of the even movements. *Duo Concertante* is supporting evidence of Stravinsky's feeling for the classics. Lincoln Kirstein has noted the music was inspired by the *Georgics* of Virgil, and the composer himself wrote that while composing this somewhat astringent successor to his Violin Concerto he was reading his friend C. A. Cingra's book on Petrarch.

The work begins with a cantilena in which two contrasting ideas are presented separately and then together. It is not danced; however, with eclogue I (a bagpipe kind of melody), a symbolic love duet is gradually initiated by the two dancers (originally Kay Mazzo and Peter Martins), first tentatively, then ever more positively. Eclogue II (seeming to derive from the arias in the Violin Concerto) introduces ever more flowing movement. There are solos for the man, then the woman. The gigue is a scherzo-like movement with two trios; it is swifter and more pastoral than eclogue I. In the final dithyramb there is a personal, exalted, yet mysterious allegorical feeling, as several of the dancers' movements are repeated. The dancers touch and finally embrace after much ceremony. At the close the choreographer emphasized modulated movements of arms and hands, carefully lit, to mirror the closing music. The original violinist was Lamar Alsop, and the original pianist was Gordon Boelzner.

Stravinsky's witty *Pulcinella* was presented by the New York City Ballet on June 23, 1972. This forty-minute ballet (in eighteen sections) based on themes by Giovanni Battista Pergolesi was imagined jointly by Balanchine and Jerome Robbins, with grand decors and costumes by Eugene Berman. The music is closely based on that of Pergolesi, yet throughout Stravinsky asserts his own melodic, harmonic, and rhythmic inventiveness, at times reminding us of his *Renard*. Stravinsky's music, with choreography by Leonide Massine and decors and costumes by Pablo Picasso, had been first presented on May 15, 1920, by the Diaghilev Ballets Russes in Paris. Leon

Woicikowsky, who danced in this ballet, revived the work briefly in 1935, with André Eglevsky and himself performing the two leads.

Pulcinella is the heart and soul of all commedia dell'arte—the source of Punch and Judy, Shakespeare's *Twelfth Night,* Molière's *Le Bourgeois Gentilhomme,* Mozart's *The Marriage of Figaro,* and Verdi's *Falstaff.* This broadly mimed version has a marked relation to the great Venetian eighteenth-century artist, Domenico Tiepolo, whose favorite secular subject was Pulcinella. Balanchine has noted that he always saw Pulcinella as going to hell for his sins. In his ballet he has made this equivocal by having Pulcinella (Villella) die at the beginning and sell his soul to the devil in order to be reborn. Then, though Pulcinella is still a very nasty character, his sweetheart (Verdy, who has the most attractive dancing in this production) helps him evade his contract. After an immense spaghetti orgy (reminiscent of the riot in act II of *Die Meistersinger*), the devil is bested and thrown into the spaghetti pot. A general celebration follows.

Pulcinella calls for soprano, tenor, and bass, who have no part in the action as such, and a chamber orchestra: two flutes, two oboes, two bassoons, two horns, one trumpet, one trombone, and string quintet (solo and tutti).

Stravinsky's 1956 *Variations on Bach's Von Himmel Hoch* (1746) for mixed chorus and orchestra received its premiere performance by the New York City Ballet on June 25, 1972. This fifteen-minute ballet is comprised of the chorale and five variations, the last four of which use the chorus. (The dancers in this celebration all wear white costumes.) It is a moving procession of tribute ending in a révérence, with solos by leading members of the company as well as ensemble pieces. It was given as the first ballet on the closing night of the 1972 Stravinsky Festival. Forty-six members of the Balanchine complex, ranging from very young students at the School of American Ballet to senior members of the company, took part in a grand defilé (such as one sees at the Paris Opéra) conceived as an integral part of this homage.

After a decade in which he produced a number of new ballets to music by Delibes, Bizet, Gluck, Ravel, Gershwin, and others, and during which time he kept fresh the Stravinsky ballets in the repertoire, Balanchine turned again to creating more works to music by his favored composer. From June 10 to June 18, 1982, the New York City Ballet produced the Stravinsky Centennial Celebration (twenty-five works). Balanchine choreographed two works of Stravinsky for the first time and revived three others. Other new ballets were choreographed by Jerome Robbins, John Taras, Peter Martins, Jacques d'Amboise, and Lew Christensen. Once again, the principal conductor for the Stravinsky Festival was Robert Irving, NYCB's indispensable music director.

We have already discussed Balanchine's restagings of *Elégie, Variations,* and *Noah and the Flood.* Composed in 1940 and scored by the composer in 1953, *Tango* is a short evocative piece of four and one-half minutes in ABCBA form, eighty-eight measures long, in duple time, and eight-measure phrases.

Originally a vocalise and then a piano piece, *Tango* is a witty little number, only occasionally rhythmically true to its name. Balanchine has made an attractive pas de deux that refers one to the night clubs of the 1920s, Escudero, and Valentino, with overtones of the painter Bérard and his chic entourage. *Tango* is scored for four clarinets, bass clarinet, four trumpets, three trombones, *guitar,* three violins, viola, and double bass.

Perséphone, a melodrama in three parts to a text by André Gide, was premiered in 1934 by the Rubinstein Ballet in a production devised by Kurt Jooss; and in 1961 this forty-five-minute dance-pantomime was produced for the Royal Ballet by Frederick Ashton. On June 18, 1982 it was first performed by the New York City Ballet, staged by George Balanchine, John Taras, and Vera Zorina in a production designed by Kermit Love.

The source of Gide's original poem was Homeric, but by the time he and Stravinsky brought this masque-like work to the stage it had acquired layers of humanism that transformed it into rather a Christian nature myth, where pity and concern replaced the Grecian contest of light and dark in the miracle of harvest and rebirth. The dramatic action of the dance pantomime is in the hands of Eumolpus (tenor), a Thracian priest and poet, Perséphone (also narrator), and the choruses. In part I, Perséphone sees a vision of the hopeless shades in the underworld, and goes to bring solace to them. In part II, Perséphone, wed to Pluto, refuses many gifts offered her, and decides to return to her mother, Demeter, and the desolate earth, where she will bring a return of springtime and become the bride of her destined husband, Triptolemus (whom we never see). In part III Perséphone returns from the grave and spring appears on earth. Yet despite her joy at seeing visions of her mother and of her appointed husband, she realizes that nothing will now stop the sequence of seasons, and that her true destiny is to return to the underworld as Pluto's wife for half of each year. Balanchine has invented a number of attractive solo dances and ensembles that highlight the action mostly conveyed in song and choral commentary.

The title role of Perséphone is spoken; the main singer is Eumolpus, who has a number of set pieces as well as dramatic recitatives; the choruses sing both in comment on the action and as the voice of Perséphone's companions, on earth and in the underworld. The work, largely in flat keys, is centered around e minor. Part I has three numbers; part II has nine; and part III, beginning with an important prelude, has five. Stravinsky's use of the various elements is appropriately individual. His choice of instrumental texture shows immense variety; he had ever been selective of particular timbres. Here his fastidiousness is impressive. A number of his characteristics heard in previous works can be detected here, including echoes of *Le Sacre du Printemps, Apollo, Symphonie des Psaumes,* and *Oedipus Rex,* which we now recognize as central works in his entire oeuvre. In this production Perséphone (Zorina) took a leading part in the action as well as in the narration. The orchestration of *Perséphone* is three flutes, three oboes, three clarinets, three bassoons, four horns, three trumpets, three trombones, tuba, percussion, piano, two harps, and strings.

If the overall theme of the 1972 festival by the New York City Ballet was the diversity of the composer and the choreographer, in 1982 the overall impression seemed to be one of unity. In a dozen different works Balanchine has shown the greatly expanded range of ballet through the music of Stravinsky. He has made fast ballets *(Symphony in Three Movements)* and slow ballets *(Monumentum).* He has expanded ballet language from Petipa, making unconventional steps artistic, not shocking—both with muscular preparation and without—in the same way Stravinsky has made unconventional intervals and harmonies acceptable, both with melodic, rhythmic preparation and without.

Their *Noah and the Flood* is a masterpiece of story telling, just as is *Apollo.* Their *Violin Concerto* is a masterpiece of the abstract, just as is *Agon.* Balanchine has shown that ballet dancers are equally effective in largo, moderato, or vivace music. (At this time there may possibly be too much reaction in favor of his revolution, by way of imitation, as four decades ago there was too much resistance to it.) Today we see Balanchine as a shaper of our image of Stravinsky as well as of Stravinsky's music, a mantle he wears modestly, for he shares his responsibility with other producers. Yet Balanchine interprets and analyzes for us both the sight and sound of Stravinsky with superb mastery.

I began this brief summation by noting that the variety in Balanchine's choreographic collaborations with the music of Stravinsky had also an element of appropriate unity; the unity of the composer's works is now seen a decade after his death, and Balanchine's vision has helped clarify that vision.

We can see that all in moving from a post-Rimsky Russian Dionysian, oriental-influenced nationalist position through three decades of French cosmopolitanism finally to Apollonian contemporary pragmatism. Stravinsky was not a chameleon who got a few wild oats out of his youthful system, and in his dozen last years flirted with fragmented ideas of serialism he made totally his own, as was always his wont. Rather simply, he was a Russian pan-cultural modern classicist with music as his mode. (Stravinsky's persisting concern with Greek myths began with his schoolboy Greek language class.)

Stravinsky's true center is found in works like *Apollo* and *Oedipus*—almost half his works foreshadow or echo this productive decade of the 1920s. In his ballets, Balanchine has understood this, and he has helped us to understand it. He has choreographed Stravinsky's music of enormous variety and vitality in a way which has enriched our appreciation of music, of dance, and of drama. (It is not my intention here to make comparative pronouncements concerning great creative figures, yet it may be of interest to note that Balanchine's drawing from the music of Stravinsky a number of eternal aspects of Greek culture, in *Apollo, Agon, Orpheus, Perséphone,* has a parallel in many works of Martha Graham: *Clytemnestra, Errand into the Maze,* etc.)

What conclusions or interpretations can one draw from this discussion of two artists' work together? Certainly each reader will draw his or her own. The record is there, and knowing both creators I would say they would wish it to stand for itself. Both are supreme craftsmen who have been brought together by destiny in the form of Diaghilev, Kirstein, and perhaps others. They have made story ballets, and they have made abstract ballets. They have, along with Picasso and Shaw, helped to make the world of the twentieth century, and above all they have helped to make a better world for us and for our successors. Their thirty collaborations, 1925–1982, have changed the lyric theatre largely through their combined contributions to modern classic dance. As the preeminent collaborator and choreographer of Stravinsky for many years, Balanchine was in a number of ways shaped by the music of Stravinsky as well as by his person. Today many of the ballets of Stravinsky and Balanchine are among our greatest artistic treasures.

In our age of confusion, diversion, and multipurpose it was given to Stravinsky to express much of the age in music that brings order out of chaos. Stravinsky's versatile maîtrise is evident in his elegies, in his

Mikhail Baryshnikov, Christine Spizzo, Cheryl Yeager, and Susan Jaffe in *Apollo* (1980).
Courtesy of Valerie Van Winkle and the American Ballet Theatre)

personal settings of works in four languages (always very personal), in his music for Diaghilev, for God, for Balanchine, for himself, and for others. Stravinsky's artistic integrity matched his diversity, and his works are not only a showcase for what has been vital in his time, but also impressive evidence of his distinctive individuality as an analyst and as a creator, perhaps most notably with his chosen collaborator, Balanchine, with whom, needless to say, he has so often agreed.

Postscript, 30 April, 1983.

Early this morning George Balanchine died at the age of 79; his vision and his work stands as a monument for all of us.

7

The Twentieth Century:
The Other Side

Frederick Ashton and English Poetry

Both of the English choreographers discussed here were discovered by Marie Rambert, the late Polish-born dancer and choreographer who had spent several seasons in the Diaghilev Ballets Russes, and whose name is perpetuated in London with the Ballet Rambert, which she founded and directed for many years.

Born in Ecuador in 1906, Frederick Ashton has made his mark in lyric theatre in this century quite differently from the Russian choreographers who worked with Diaghilev at or near the beginnings of their careers. He has not had the unique plasticity of Michel Fokine, the extraordinary gift of dramatic characterization of Massine, or the imaginative musical sense of Balanchine. Rather, as Anna Kisselgoff has said so well, with Ashton, "Inventiveness is taken for granted in his work. Even his early ballets have extended classical ballet's vocabulary into something beyond the predictable." In a way he combines qualities of all three of the great Russians. Within the language of classical ballet, Ashton's lyrical quality and literary sense suggest dramatic undertones and emotions while he remains always concerned with both the structure and the steps individually. Over and over he has requested his dancers to "show me something." He has then used and elaborated that "something" until the steps or gestures fit into the ballet like a glove, and at the same time always make the dancer "look good." Impelled to become a dancer by his ambition and persistence

161

once he had experienced the magic of Pavlova, Ashton's concern with the craft of choreography makes all of his ballets true experiences for the spectators. David Vaughan noted that the great influence of Pavlova led Ashton to include in most of his ballets a step his dancers called the "Fred step," which he defined as the following sequence: "posé en arabesque, coupé dessous, petit developpé à la seconde, pas de bourrée dessous, pas de chat" (see Bibliography).

The fully developed fresh expressivity of Ashton's characters places his choreography somewhere between that of Balanchine, whose musicality governs the movements he gives his dancers, and Antony Tudor, whose acute sense of dramatic timing governs the movements. Ashton has a very personal and particular sensitivity in his ballets, although that must not be taken to imply that Balanchine and Tudor do not have theirs.

It is difficult to define Ashton's; when it is combined with the musical collaboration of Constant Lambert and the production expertise of Ninette de Valois and the special gifts of his favorite dancers, however, this sensitivity achieves a unifying effect that is both personal and touching. Beginning with Marie Rambert, these dancers have included Alicia Markova, Pearl Argyle, Diana Gould, Lydia Lopokova, Tamara Karsavina, and, for more than twenty-five years, Margot Fonteyn.

Ashton studied with Massine, Nijinska, and above all Marie Rambert, who not only believed in him and his gifts, but presented his first ballets, beginning with *The Tragedy of Fashion* (1926). By 1982 Ashton had produced over one hundred and forty ballets, counting solo dances and musicals, films, and a few operas. Since 1935 most have been given their premiere performances by the Sadler's Wells Ballet, now the Royal Ballet.

Considering specifically Ashton's relation to music, we find he did not concentrate on any one composer. Probably because of his association with Constant Lambert, a codirector of the Sadler's Wells Ballet almost from its inception, Ashton did choreograph music by Franz Liszt, beginning with *Mephisto Waltz,* and because of his early association with Nijinska he choreographed several ballets to music by Stravinsky, including *Perséphone,* and the splendid *Scènes de Ballet.* Over the years he has choreographed a wide variety of music, from many lands and many epochs, including that operatic masterpiece of 1934, *Four Saints in Three Acts* by Virgil Thomson and Gertrude Stein, a revealing revival of Ravel's brilliant *Daphnis et Chloé* (1951), a new production of the ever-charming *La Fille Mal Gardée* (1960), Elgar's evocative *Enigma Variations* (1968), and the witty Stein-Berners *Wedding Bouquet.*

Since its premiere in 1931, Ashton's *Façade,* to clever music by William Walton originally written as a setting for satirical poems by Edith Sitwell, has never been out of the repertoire for long, and it has been performed by companies in Australia, Norway, Belgium, and America. At its first performance *Façade* had seven comic sketches selected from the twenty-nine wonderful numbers Walton composed for Sitwell. In the opening Scotch Rhapsody two women and a man satirize highland dancing and classic ballet. The "Yodelling Song" calls for the Maid (who "milks" a cow) and three men. And there is a gay and brilliant variation on point in the polka, performed by a woman who disrobes and dances her solo in her underwear. The valse is danced by four women performing a frivolous burlesque of classic arm and leg positions. There is "Popular Song," a soft shoe number for two men, and "Tango," with its ridiculous back-bends, a gigolo, and a hesitant debutant in a hilarious dance-floor seduction. In the good-naturedly humourous finale everyone joins in the tarantella. Throughout, the composer is in duple time except for the valse and the "Yodelling Song"; this is splendid divertissement in which all but two of the numbers are fast and five different tonalities are used. At various times Ashton has changed the internal order of the sketches, and he has added three more of Walton's miniatures: nocturne, foxtrot, and country dance. The composer's spare orchestration for *Façade* is two flutes, two oboes, two clarinets, two bassoons, four horns, two trumpets, one trombone, tuba, percussion, and strings. Among the dancers who have performed in *Façade* over the years are, of course Ashton himself, Antony Tudor, Lydia Lopokova, William Chappell, Walter Gore, Alicia Markova, Pearl Argyle, Diana Gould, Mary Honer, Robert Helpmann, Harold Turner, Margot Fonteyn, Pamela May, Richard Ellis, Michael Somes, John Hart, and Moira Shearer—in short, most of the founding generations of British dancers in the twentieth century.

Les Patineurs, to music by Meyerbeer arranged by Constant Lambert, was first performed in London in 1937, and it too has been danced ever since, in Africa, Australia, America, the Near East, Canada, and Germany. Lambert took the music from *Le Prophète* (which has a skating ballet) and from *L'Etoile du Nord.* There are eight sections to this twenty-minute work: the entrée and pas de huit (allegro in E flat in triple time), in which everyone "skates" onto the stage. Next comes the man in blue's solo, still in the same time and key but a little faster. The gentle pas de deux is andante in C, in duple time. There is an ensemble, which returns to allegro, this time in D major, in triple time, very loud, and definite.

This is followed by an enchanting pas de trois; the music is allegretto in g minor and G major, in duple time with an abrupt stop half way through—perhaps a mishap on the ice—but all ends smoothly. There is the pas des patineuses by two women who are then joined by the ensemble. The finale is a galop, allegro in E major, in fast duple time, and at the end everyone "skates off," leaving only the man in blue spinning and spinning. The orchestration for *Les Patineurs* calls for two flutes, two oboes, two clarinets, two bassoons, four horns, two trumpets, three trombones, percussion, harp, and strings.

The *Times* (London) commented after the premiere of this ballet, "*Les Sylphides* is the most perfect example of the divertissement form, and if *Les Patineurs* does not equal that masterpiece it at least has the same coherence and unity. Mr. Frederick Ashton has devised a brilliant choreography based upon the classical technique modified by the movements of skating. The result is novel and beautiful, lit up by flashes of wit, for he has not forgotten the limitations and danger of dancing upon ice in his pre-occupation with its grace and swiftness.

"The most striking dance in the ballet is a variation for Mr. Harold Turner, which one is not afraid to call the most brilliant characteristic solo in the classical style since the dance of Harlequin in *Carnaval*." In my opinion neither *Les Sylphides* nor *Les Patineurs* is a divertissement: the first is a poem, and the second is a short story.

Frederick Ashton has said, "I think ballets, without librettos, popularly known as abstract ballets, though appearing to convey nothing but the exercise of pure dancing, should have a basic idea which is not necessarily apparent to the public, or a personal fount of emotion from which the choreography springs. Otherwise, in my opinion, a cold complexity emerges which ceases to move an audience."

This serves as introduction to our discussion of *Symphonic Variations*, created in 1946 with decors and costumes by Ashton's frequent collaborator and friend, Sophie Fedorovitch. It is set to the music of César Franck's Variations Symphoniques, a fifteen-minute work for piano and orchestra. It has three sections played uninterruptedly; somber allegro, introduction in ABC form; theme and six variations; and a joyous finale.

Neoclassical and plotless, the dancing is quite related to the musical form. It was originally choreographed for Margot Fonteyn, Pamela May, Moira Shearer, Michael Somes, Henry Danton, and Brian Shaw. It flows right along, as one emotional episode seems to merge or diffuse into the next without disruptive jolting. Many persons consider this ballet Ashton's masterpiece, perhaps because, the product of deep thought like most of his works, it is above all a complete ballet simply and truly stated.

Margot Fonteyn and Michael Somes in *Symphonic variations* (c. 1949). *(Courtesy of the Collection of Lily and Baird Hastings)*

After a meditative beginning, the three women who are up front move first. Then, one of three men comes forward from the back of the stage to dance successively with each of the women. Presently the two other men join the first and the women are immobile as the men were earlier. The center man responds to the piano, and the two others to the orchestra. Once more the women come forward, and all dance together. In the theme and variations section, after short solos, the leading danseuse performs a variation, followed by a short romantic pas de deux with her partner. Once more they all dance, not as individuals, but as participants of an ensemble and as couples. At the conclusion, following the joyful strains, the six dancers resume their original positions. Franck's conservative orchestra calls for piano, two flutes, two oboes, two clarinets, two bassoons, four horns, two trumpets, and strings.

A. V. Coton believed that *Symphonic Variations* "satisfied exactly the same desires as *Les Sylphides* and *Apollo*. The curtain rises on a vast stage, and before the deep-set backcloth of sprayed white-and-green are seen six immobile and minute dancers, all clad in white, with a little black relief here and there. Nothing whatever is stated of place, person, condition or circumstance; here we have six living bodies within a prescribed area of space which, throughout the duration of the music, move in splendour and heroism, creating solo, duet, and ensemble dances of a fascinating variety of shapes, emphases, and configurations.

"The disparity between these persons and the vast area of their action proposes an imagery of infinities. . . . We can catch the imagery either as planetary bodies moving with subtle rhythm against cosmic vastness, or the geometric complexities revealed in watching the rapid formation of crystals under a microscope. . . . On analysis it can be seen that no step or movement is daringly new—every part of every pattern is something that one could quickly isolate in that laboratory where a dancing class takes place. Yet the majesty and splendour of this ballet (are) made out of the same kind of simplicities that Fokine and Balanchine both used in their master works. . . . In each of these instances a choreographer of assured mastery, moving perhaps to some degree deliberately, and to some extent intuitively, has re-stated the primary function of theatrical dancing by re-shaping its basic material into a new and exciting assemblage of images."

Antony Tudor and Psychological Ballet

The second important English choreographer to be discovered by Marie Rambert whose work we will discuss is Antony Tudor. He was born in

London in 1909, and after studying with Marie Rambert and dancing in her company, he choreographed his first ballet to music by Frescobaldi, *Cross Gartered* (based on Shakespeare's *Twelfth Night*), which Rambert produced in 1931. Though he has choreographed a wide variety of subjects, in his most important ballets Tudor has chosen themes with intense psychological overtones, and using music of romantic feeling, has created theatrical pieces that have atmospheres close to those produced by modern dance choreographers, and which even use some modern dance techniques. This is all the more remarkable because prior to 1940 he never saw Martha Graham perform, although he was well acquainted with Agnes de Mille somewhat earlier.

In the social tragedy *Jardin aux Lilas* (1936) Tudor developed the psychological ballet in which touching human relationships and complex characters are portrayed in dance. Performed to Chausson's haunting sixteen-minute Poème for violin and orchestra, this passionate yet contained and understated dance drama of manners takes place at an engagement party in a moonlit garden. Two couples, split by a prearranged Edwardian marriage of convenience, attempt to say privately their fond, personal, anguished farewells to loved ones they fear they will never see again. The ability of Tudor to blend natural gesture with dramatic movements of the dance reveals to the audience various processes of the hesitating hearts and minds of the fiancé (and his former mistress) and the fiancée (and her former lover). Through Tudor's use of a wide spectrum of expressive and eloquent movements we are led to empathize instinctively. At a chosen moment Tudor has his dancers stop, immobile—a breathtakingly effective procedure, appropriately used. Edwin Denby has noted that Tudor's nuances in timing and placing of personal visual rhythms moving to music create the desired atmosphere of social tensions. Avoiding obvious virtuosity through delicate, suggestive, laconic pantomime extended from classic ballet, Tudor exposes complex relationships between the four principal characters. With expanded classical grammar and parallel extension from musical structure, his movements seem to transfer emotions to the audience by illustrating human reactions to these emotions in a connected manner that relates the story psychologically: there is anxiety, guilt, apprehension, desire, loss, risk, frustration, regret, rebellion, submission, seeming to draw on Proust, de Maupassant, Freud. Martha Graham uses many of these same emotions in her modern dance movements, but uses them outside the tradition of ballet.

Undertow (1945), to specially commissioned music by William Schuman, is a twenty-five minute ballet symbolic of the birth of man and his emotions, with Freudian interpretation and equation with contemporary myths. As Toby Tobias has noted, the youth's state of mind is revealed with cosmic effect in the final scene, when the dimly lit, solitary figure of the young murderer is dwarfed by the rising backdrop, which unfurls a lurid, jumbled vision of clouds, buildings, huge winged horses, and a woman with flying hair.

While Tudor has given us such other works of lasting value as *Romeo and Juliet* (Delius), *Shadow of the Wind* (Mahler), *Leaves are Falling* (Dvorak), very likely *Pillar of Fire* is his masterpiece. *Pillar of Fire* is an extension of the psychological theme of repression that carries the muted treatment of *Jardin aux Lilas* into open expression and passionate formulation of physical longing (though not explicit illustration, a development that seems to be imminent). The portrayal of the release of powers of sexuality and love was sensitively conveyed in the 1942 production by Ballet Theater with a cast headed by Nora Kaye as Hagar and the choreographer as the Young Man. The splendid decors and character building strait-laced costumes were by Jo Mielziner. The music is by Schoenberg.

About his style Tudor has said, "Acting in ballet, whether small or large, must be clear and the preparation for steps must not be acrobatic, but controlled within the general line." Composed in 1900, this twenty-six-minute work for string orchestra was inspired by "Verklärte Nacht," a poem by the German expressionist Richard Dehmel. Walking hand in hand with her lover in the woods, a woman confesses she is pregnant with another man's child, the product of her wild oats before she reached fulfillment with her true companion. He asserts that in the transfigured night their combined love makes that unborn child his and hers together. Tudor sets it brilliantly, lovingly in *Pillar of Fire,* as the music in five sections proceeds from a slow introduction in d minor in duple time, through many tempo changes, modulations, dynamic changes, and meter shifts to a calm apotheosis in D major, duple time.

The curtain opens as Hagar is sitting outside her house on a town square. On the opposite side of the stage is another, darker house, while in the distance we see other buildings. In this rather oppressive town where everyone's business is known and discussed by one's neighbors, live three sisters. They are respectively, the youthful Younger Sister, attractive and pleasure-loving; the tense, thwarted, middle sister, Hagar, who is on the verge of becoming an old maid; and the possessive Elder Sister, who is already a spinster inside and out. Hagar's spirits soar when a Young Man comes to call, but her timid responses are so equivocal that he turns his attention to the malicious Younger Sister who is superficial and flirtatious.

Pillar of Fire, ballet by Antony Tudor. Group featuring Nora Kaye. *(Courtesy of the Collection of Lily and Baird Hastings)*

Hagar, left alone and desperate in her need to escape a barren future, sees the house across the square now lighted up, in which couples are enjoying themselves to the utmost. She dreams that she will reach fulfillment in joining them and finally succumbs to the sexual advances of the provocative Man Across the Way. When remorseful and unfulfilled Hagar returns home, her sisters shun her with silent disapproval, as in fact does everyone in town. Meanwhile the compassionate Young Man has tired of the shallow Younger Sister, and returns to Hagar, imploring her to forgive his previous callousness. Rejecting her self-deprecation, he takes Hagar's hand, and suddenly, as the buildings in the town seem to dissolve, the true lovers are seen walking hand in hand together in a forest toward a more rewarding relationship, as the music finishes eloquently. During the epilogue the movements of Hagar, previously tight and nervous, become released and ample, and, in ecstasy, she rises on point.

Walter Terry has noted, "During the course of the ballet, two groups, the lovers-in-innocence and the lovers-in-experience, serve as did the choruses of classic Greek drama. They mirror in their actions the shifting desires of Hagar, they omen what is to come, and they comment, through movement, upon the pure beauty of innocent love and the harsh, bright excitement of carnal attraction."

Throughout, Tudor is an intuitive modern, as he translates life movements into steps and dance. His lifts are unlike any others in ballet, and are charged with feeling. His rond de jambe, a sort of signature step, is used emotionally; his arabesques clearly have different meanings, depending on preceding or following circumstances. Because of Tudor's deep concern with movement primarily motivated by interior moods, rather than related to architecture or to rhythmic pulse, he is not generally attracted to the music of Stravinsky or others for whom motor impulse is predominant, or for whom form is capable of being an end in itself. Tudor's choice of music falls usually on romantic composers who inspire the listener's feelings to come easily to the fore—Chausson, Schoenberg, Delius, Koechlin—and infrequently on contemporary music, although he has choreographed scores by William Schuman, Prokofiev, and Weill.

Tudor has stated that his ballets explore emotional, stifling bourgeois, sexually repressed conflict often involving literary drama integrated with technique. Within his choreographic structure, dancers convey bittersweet themes through gestures, about which Proust and Chekhov have written. Tudor's world is neither the fabled world of Petipa nor the abstract world of Balanchine; rather, it is psychological. Also, he has referred to himself as a miniaturist, rooted in English tradition. Always insisting that steps by themselves have little meaning for him, in comedy or tragedy Tudor endows them with expressive meaning, often by means of naturalistic movements for the arms, as the positions of the dancers' feet remain largely formalistic. I think it is fair to say that Tudor's characters usually may be related to a late Victorian or an Edwardian world, even when ostensibly they come from different milieux and different epochs. Controlled and restrained by his mind, Tudor imposes control and restraint on his dancers.

An Interlude

After discussing works by English choreographers nurtured by Marie Rambert, Ashton and Tudor (who with the exception of Ravel's *Pavane* never used the same music), it seems appropriate for two reasons to discuss at least one work by another English choreographer, Ninette de Valois. In the first place, she herself, among a number of repertoire ballets, created *Job* in 1931, a master ballet, perhaps of equal importance to Fokine's *Petrouchka,* which in theme, music, design, and choreography is one glorious piece. In the second place, she nurtured the ballets of Ashton and Tudor, really making possible the fifty-year career of Ashton.

Born Edris Stannus in 1898, she danced with Diaghilev's Ballets Russes and then helped found British ballet in the late 1920s. Her work as a dancer, choreographer, and administrator in England will never be forgotten, any more than will that of Lincoln Kirstein in the United States.

The background of *Job, a masque for dancing* in eight scenes, begins with Geoffrey Keynes, who based it on the biblical drama portrayed in William Blake's *Book of Job,* commissioning music by Ralph Vaughan Williams (1872–1958), and scenery and costumes by Gwendolen Raverat, later replaced with those of John Piper. Because Diaghilev turned down Keynes's initial libretto, Williams's music was given its premiere as a concert piece, but then de Valois persuaded the newly formed Camargo Society of London to sponsor *Job*'s rightful presentation in the lyric theatre. Vaughan Williams was always drawn to traditional song and traditional dance (we have already noted the tradition of English dance stretches back to the Middle Ages) and he uses musical means to suggest the ethical and philosophical values of eternity in pastoral, forceful terms, which in the best Noverre tradition de Valois has matched perfectly. In a sense this close collaboration foreshadowed the magnificent collaboration of Massine, Hindemith, and Tchelitchew, which we noted in our discussion of *Saint Francis.*

Scene from *Job*, featuring Robert Helpmann in the title role (1949).
(Courtesy of the Collection of Lily and Baird Hastings)

A summary of the program of *Job* follows: Scene I. Introduction and saraband of the sons of God: beginning quietly, largo, allegro in triple time, flutes, harps, and violas outline a pastoral dance of Job and his family; Satan appears; the tonality changes from g minor to A major; Job agrees to have his moral nature tested. Scene II. The dance and triumph of Satan, who usurps the throne of Heaven, to brassy accompaniment. Scene III. Minuet of the sons of Job and their wives; at first woodwinds and strings accompany a festive formal dance, and cymbals clash, though when Satan arrives all stops and the dancers fall dead, the minuet turning to an elegy. Scene IV. Job's dream (allegro); Satan's terrifying visions of war, pestilence, and famine, accompanied by pizzicati and crescendos. Scene V. Dance of the three messengers. To soft woodwinds (andante) Job awakens to realize he has lost all, but still blesses the Lord in a cantabile tune; oily saxophones and pizzicato strings suggest hypocritical compassion; cursing Job loses his patience; Satan is revealed on the throne of Heaven; Job and his friends cower. Scene VI. Elihu's dance of beauty; a rhapsodic violin plays a sinuous song; Job perceives his sin; the sons of the morning dance a pavane. Scene VII. Gaillard of the sons of the morning; Job's victory, as Satan is expelled, is celebrated in an altar dance featuring an oboe, allegretto, in triple time; rich chords: the stage darkens, then lightens for the epilogue. Scene VIII. Job blesses his numerous family, as humbled he sits with his wife and friends; gradual fadeout, dying away to soft chords held quietly by the strings.

This forty-minute work is indeed marvellous in the grand manner, and its production was totally realized. The effective orchestra calls for two flutes, two oboes, two clarinets, saxophone, two bassoons, four horns, two trumpets, three trombones, tuba, percussion, harp, and strings (for concert performances the orchestra is somewhat larger).

The second work that helps serve as a transition to our last two figures of the twentieth century is Kurt Jooss's powerful satire *The Green Table* (1932), with effective music by Fritz Cohen (1904–1967), and masks and costumes by Hein Heckroth.

In this century German expressionist painting has taken the role of artistic leader in somewhat the same way German preromantic literature did at the turn of the nineteenth century. And a key figure in dance expressionism (that is, nonimitative exaggeration of movement to help focus on a particular emotion in a dance) has been Kurt Jooss (1901–1979). Jooss was a disciple of the space-movement theories of Rudolf von Laban and Mary Wigman. He achieved remarkable characterization of the mentality and emotional feeling of his protagonists in much the same way

The Green Table, ballet by Kurt Jooss. Opening scene. (*Courtesy of the Collection of Lily and Baird Hastings*)

both Tudor and Graham have, and even Balanchine in such works as *The Prodigal Son* (Prokofiev). He denied the use of artificial conventions found in the pure classical style, the danse d'école founded on the still valid principles of Blasis, but used many steps and structural procedures of classical ballet (particularly in choreographing such works as Stravinsky's *Perséphone*).

Although Fritz Cohen's music for *The Green Table* is not distinguished in its own right (in the sense that Mozart's music for *Les Petits Riens* is), it fits the work of an inspired choreographer in a way comparable to the effective manner with which Louis Horst worked with Martha Graham, and John Cage with Merce Cunningham. I agree wholly with Cyril W. Beaumont that this moving thirty-minute ballet in three scenes (ABA form in nine sections) is a modern dance of death, in which the legendary glory of war is proved to be a hollow concept, a game the diplomatic politicians play, and in which the only winner is death. *The Green Table* is part dance, part dramatic movement, and throughout very contemporary. Both its overall design and its insistent largely duple rhythms further its tragic theme. In dance terms Jooss has matched the tragic atmosphere of the Berg operatic masterpiece, *Wozzeck*.

Scene I finds the diplomats conferring at the long green table to decide the fate of the nations. After heated discussions, arguments, misunderstandings, and reconciliations (to the rhythm of the tango), concord is not achieved, and there is a declaration of war, signaled by a pistol shot. Scene II transports us to where the dance of Death (originally performed by Jooss himself) is a prelude to the Farewells amidst the bustling preparations for war, then the horror of Battle, the agony of the Refugees and the activity of the Profiteer, the passacaglia of the Partisan, the Profiteer and the waltz at the Brothel, and the Aftermath—the whole menaced by the grim figure of Death. Scene III takes us back to the green table where the diplomats in conference resume their tango, to what end? Cohen's orchestration for this contemporary ballet resembles that of his contemporary, Kurt Weill: winds by ones or twos, percussion, and strings; but actually Jooss preferred to present the work accompanied by the original two-piano version. Both *Job* and *The Green Table* are masterpieces of modern lyric theatre, helping to join the spectrum of spectacle entertainment from lavish opera-ballet to the most ascetic of movement forms.

Isadora Duncan (1878–1927) is the third figure to include in this interlude, because of her pioneer work in freeing theatrical dance from overworked formulas to make it more expressive, and because of her audacious choice of music for her dance, including Beethoven and other composers whose works had not been explored by choreographers. Through her example she helped free dancers from stereotyped costuming, and in maintaining that movement was an expression of the mind she helped enlarge the horizon for all dancers. These ideas were interesting to Fokine, who included them in his own canon. They bore even greater fruit in the works of less academic choreographers, such as the modern dancers.

Martha Graham—The High Priestess of Modern Dance

Born in Allegheny, now Pittsburgh, Pennsylvania, in 1894, Martha Graham was trained at the California Denishawn School by Ruth St. Denis and Ted Shawn, and performed with their company until 1923. Ever since 1926 she has represented the American tradition of modern dance, mostly choreographing solo and group works to new music by American composers, including many compositions by her long-time brilliant music director, Louis Horst. Herself one of the greatest performers in the history of dance, Martha Graham has poetic imagination, iron determination, a fertile mind, outstanding intellect, and a hypnotic power over her company and her audiences. She has been a uniquely important force for good in American dance, and very probably the greatest American artist in a humanistic, not nationalistic, sense. Her very full story has been told many times. I value particularly Lincoln Kirstein's summation in his *Dance:*

And Martha Graham from year to year stands as a monument to the pioneer strength of the American dance. Her *Frontier* (1935) is a kinetic statement of Whitman's essence, and her *Letter to the World* (1941) gives us Emily Dickinson in her most precious lyric portrait. Graham has also been occupied with her spiritual sisters, Duncan and St. Denis, with spiritual problems, even at the expense of theater and the sacrifice of spectacle. Now her expression is no longer naive. Her work is as simple as Shaker furniture and the crucifixion of the New Mexican pueblos, and as rugged as a clipper ship's figurehead. She is the center of American dance.

We noted previously how all creative artists, no matter how gifted, original, or productive, depend on their ancestors. For more than half a century Martha Graham has lived the very ideals of freeing the dance to be totally expressive, ideals Duncan promulgated but was too fragmented to achieve, ideals Fokine saw clearly but did not have the proper frame to complete. Graham has done her work through enormous will power and sacrifice. Her achievement has been . . . unique, as in her work she reached past literary sources and past rationality into the center of the psyche. Her works are permanent additions to the repertoire, depending not on her own marvellous performances, but on her powers of invention, controlled by form and structure.

Martha Graham usually choreographs for herself or for her group. Her experiment as the leading dancer in Massine's version of Stravinsky's *Le Sacre du Printemps,* in five performances with the Philadelphia Orchestra under the direction of Leopold Stokowski in Philadelphia and New York in 1930 was only partially successful. Still, she recalled later in a conversation: "I recall the shock I had when I danced in *Le Sacre.* I would like to do it again, for there is something real, deeply Russian in this important work. It had universality, and it did something for me." Massine stated he appreciated working with her.

Another partial success was her collaboration on *Episodes* with George Balanchine. Together they choreographed this remarkable work inspired by Mary, Queen of Scots, to the complete orchestral music of Anton Webern in a presentation lasting barely an hour. Graham did the first part, somewhat biographically and Balanchine concluded with memories of Mary's inner feelings and thoughts.

But even these not fully realized experiences helped Graham advance majestically in her ideals, which have involved ever broadening and deepening relationships between all elements in theatrical dancing, which can be seen even in this short series of selected works among nearly two hundred:

1940   *El Penitente* (Horst-Gilfond)—American Indian customs

1941   *Letter to the World* (Hunter Johnson-Lauterer-Gilfond)—Emily Dickinson

1943   *Deaths and Entrances* (Hunter Johnson-Lauterer-Gilfond)—the Brontë sisters

1945   *Appalachian Spring* (Copland-Noguchi-Gilfond)—American pioneers

1946   *Dark Meadow* (Carlos Chavez-Noguchi-Gilfond)—primitive Greek mythology

1947   *Night Journey* (William Schuman-Noguchi)—the Oedipus story

1955   *Clytemnestra* (Halim El Dabh-Noguchi)—adultery and Greek revenge

1959   *Episodes* (Anton Webern-David Hays)—Mary, Queen of Scots

1975   *Lucifer* (Halim El Dabh-Leonardo Locsin)—the Devil (with Fonteyn and Nureyev)

1978   *Frescoes* (Samuel Barber-Halston)—Antony and Cleopatra

1981   *Acts of Light* (Carl Nielsen-Halston)—lyrical adventures in the Aegean

1982   *Dances of the Golden Hall* (Andre Panufnik-Halston)—Eroticism and union with the divine

Before proceeding to a discussion of several of Graham's works, the following comments she has made are pertinent:

Throughout time dance has not changed in one essential function. The function of dance is communication. The responsibility that dance fulfill its function belongs to us who are dancing today.

A new vitality is possessing us. Certain depths of the intellect are being explored. Great art never ignores human values. Therein lies its roots. This is why forms change.

While the arts do not create change, they register change. I refuse to admit that the dance has limitations that prevent its acceptance and understanding— or that the intrinsic purity of the art itself need be touched.

Artistry lies in restraint as much as in expression. The ideal of technique is the absence of strain.

If you can write the story of your dance, it is a literary thing, but not dancing.

The dance is a universal art, certain aspects of which, basic position in particular, will be found all over the world.

It takes ten years to build a dancer. The body must be tempered . . . the mind enriched.

No artist is ahead of his time. He *is* his time: it is just that others are behind the time.

A dancer on the stage should be in command of all things physical.

I am sorry if I am still obscure, for I do want to be understood, even if I never do have a wide audience. However, I cannot dilute my work, either as I present it, or by putting it into a musical. In fact part of my usefulness consists in shocking.

For my dance I seek to express Life in a moment of evolution—a human being in crisis, at the crossroads: Jocasta, Medea, Emily. The story is not particularly important, but the crossroad is. There is nothing eternal but change. I must explore new possibilities of movement.

Once the inspiration comes I must get in mental condition to prepare a new work. The basic sets and costumes, I think out or work on with Noguchi, who is my favorite designer. Then I begin with the dancers and the music. I never calculate in advance. On occasion I have composed the dance before the music, and in a sense I still do this, but usually the rhythms have already been determined when I start work. The actual sets come only after Noguchi has shown me a model, and he has seen several rehearsals. In *Night Journey* we use a bed made of Male and Female symbols. The *Deaths and Entrances* dress I wear was suggested by an evening dress, and I couldn't establish this character until I had a rehearsal dress made in the same form, though not in the same material, as the costume I was going to wear. To rehearse properly the character and the costume must become one being.

For over a score of years, while Martha Graham was achieving and perfecting her technique, her musical director was Louis Horst: a most professional, modest, compassionate man who has commented as follows:

"Music can underscore or set off the dance, hold it in check, give it a certain boundary, for the body is the most dangerous of instruments and, without the boundary of music and the authority of form, is likely to run riot in emotional expression. Motion is born of emotion (with the experienced dancer the process is sometimes reversed) and both must be kept under control." Horst, whose influence on Graham helps shape her work to this day, saw both the parallels and the differences in form of music and the dance. In his work with Graham he began by accompanying her purely with the piano, then he added woodwinds, as in his own score of *El Penitente,* and later, other instruments.

Martha Graham's *El Penitente,* a beautiful, formal, remote mystery play of the American Southwest about sin and atonement, is in ten episodes, mostly performed without pause. For this simple but passionate, evocative, and tender twenty-five minute work Louis Horst has written a spare score mostly notated in C major, yet, like Hindemith, he has not composed strictly in the notated tonality. Only two of the ten sections have triple time, and only three are slow in tempo. His sparse yet telling ensemble includes flute, oboe, clarinet, bassoon, violin, violoncello, drum, piano, and guitar, which is used in seven interludes.

The three principal dancers arrive, carrying their properties. The naive Penitent beats himself with a rope to drive out the evil and dreams of forgiveness, the Virgin pleads, Christ blesses. The characters march about, the Penitent pulling the Death Cart, the symbol of original sin. The Magdalen seduces the Penitent; Christ condemns them. With the help of the Mother, the Penitent takes the Cross on his back. Atoning by the Crucifixion, he wins salvation. The characters celebrate with a festival dance.

This perfectly framed, perfectly structured somewhat simplistic story has many resonances and overtones. Its success is on several levels— immediate recognition, its intellectual morality, and its transfer of myth. A principal reason Martha Graham has been so extraordinarily revealing in her art is because of her constant concern with presenting her ideas and ideals on the highest possible plane she can conceive (which is also direct), hoping that her audience would join her.

One of the finest scores of Martha Graham's works was provided by Aaron Copland, *Appalachian Spring,* which takes place on and around the porch of a farmhouse in the Pennsylvania hills. It begins with the processional entrance of the members of the pioneer community, the woman, representing the strong future of the promised land, the revivalist and his followers, the bride and her husband.

Copland originally scored the work for thirteen instruments and later expanded it to twenty plus full strings. In this thirty-minute ballet the tonalities move from A major to C major, with many modulations in between. The rhythmic and tempo changes are many and irregular. The balance is almost even between fast, moderate, and slow, which sets a tone of moderation rather than frenzy.

In the slow introduction, the protagonists come on stage, in character, and the story of setting up a new home begins. The second section, in quick tempo, is devoted to the elated feelings and the religious experience of the revivalists. In the moderato duo for bride and groom there is a tender and passionate feeling. To some this scene is more satisfactory than the parallel scene in Stravinsky's ballet *Les Noces.*

The next scene brings the revivalists on in full force, with the music full of folksy square dances and country fiddlers. The joy, fear, wonder of the bride is now depicted in a solo, where she expresses the presentiment of motherhood. There follows a slow section, a sort of transition with music recalling the introduction. Out of this calm of the daily activities of the bride and groom grows a wonderful theme and five variations, beginning with a clarinet solo, in which Copland takes an old Shaker tune, "The Gift to Be Simple," as his text. In the coda to this celebration of spring on the frontier, the bride receives the neighbors, who then leave the happy couple together, and the ending comes hushed and prayerlike.

In *Clytemnestra,* which many persons believe is Graham's masterpiece to date, previous currents in her work were assimilated and combined. As Selma Jeanne Cohen has noted in *Chrysalis* (1958, nos. 5 and 6): "The protagonist, now in the underworld, reviews her past. . . . The characters involved in her fate are seen in unrelated moments. There are intimations

Martha Graham in *Clytemnestra*.
(Courtesy of Anita Galt and the Martha Graham Dance Company)

of jealousy, of plots and danger, but—as in a dream—their total meaning is submerged."

This one hundred minute work is divided into a prologue, two acts, and an epilogue. The Messenger of Death has summoned Clytemnestra to recall her life in the limitless landscape of the mind. She recalls the sack of Troy, the Sacrifice of Iphigenia, the return of Helen, the banishment then return of Electra and Orestes. In the first act there is Clytemnestra's love of Aegisthus, the murder of Agamemnon and his mistress, as she is determined to understand the forces that shaped her fate. In the second act the ghost of Agamemnon plagues her, and she and Aegisthus are in turn killed. Clytemnestra begins to understand the curse. In the epilogue she embarks on a solitary journey toward redemption.

This was the last great role Graham choreographed for herself, and although the work does demand tremendous effort on the part of the audience to follow its deep involvement with layers of meaning, the rewards are commensurate. Typically, *Clytemnestra* involves the fork, the tragic fork, and all that ensues once the choice has been made, left, or right! Since Graham's retirement as a performer and leading dancer in most of her works, this role has been excellently danced by Yuriko. Like many of Horst's scores for Graham, the orchestra Halim El-Dabh uses in *Clytemnestra* is spare—flute, oboe, clarinet, horns, trumpets, percussion, and strings—and often its sections are fragmentary, to match the action. It is difficult to imagine music more suitable, as by turns it is eerie, warm, and inexorable; it contains all the elements that are appropriate to Graham's telling of this infinite Greek tragedy. Part of the score's strength is in the composer's refusal to treat the percussion cliché as the raison d'être. His structure and his melody are far more subtle, and Graham uses this variety in her own unique way.

Episodes was a spectacle-entertainment in two acts using the complete orchestral music of Anton Webern, with costumes by Karinska and lighting by David Hayes. Martha Graham choreographed Passacaglia, op. 1 (1906), and Six Pieces, op. 6 (1910) for Part I, which was biographical, treating the execution of Mary, Queen of Scots; and George Balanchine choreographed Symphony, op. 21 (1928), Five Pieces, op. 10 (1911–1913), Concerto, op. 24 (1934), Variations, op. 30 (1940), and Ricercata in six voices from Bach's Musical Offering (1935), which was very abstract. The work was performed for two seasons in repertory by the New York City Ballet, following which each choreographer took his or her own half, and with changes performed it in his or her own company.

Although there was some interchange of personnel, originally each choreographer created separate entities, which were planned to go together. It was exciting to see the two parts performed together, but each part does have a separate existence that can be fully justified.

In *Repertory in Review,* Nancy Reynolds has summarized the reactions of the critics which have refreshed my own memories of the original production (see Bibliography).

In part I Graham externalized the emotions and memories of Mary in the last moments of her short life. In these sections Webern's orchestra is somewhat less astringent than in the pieces of part II; and while Webern was already under the spell of Schoenberg, his adherence to atonal techniques was not yet total or systematic.

The first section is devoted to Mary's (Graham) final decision that love has no place in destiny. She dismisses Bothwell and steps out of her magnificent regal dress, which remains standing alone. Left in white, Mary reacts in despair and then is clothed with another gown, blood red. As her attendants recede, Mary crosses herself and indicates resignation. There is the tennis match duel with Elizabeth, splendidly danced by Sallie Wilson of New York City Ballet. Then the game is over, the Executioner awaits, and darkness closes in.

Although now the finale of part II, Ricercata, is often performed alone, in 1959 and 1960 there were five sections by Balanchine. His original choreography begins as we hear the spare and fragmentary sounds of Webern's Symphony. Although one might recognize group movements similar to those Balanchine had used in *Four Temperaments,* and also some of the movements Graham had used in part I, mostly this section became new, uncharted territory at once. Five Pieces, with its tiny spurts of provocative, complicated sounds matched by Balanchine's effective groping movements, and with silences and standstills, included a touching pas de deux. Concerto combined a pas de deux with a closing sequence, which was somewhat unusual for Balanchine, with its daisy-chain irrationality. Variations was a solo for Paul Taylor, performed, as Melissa Hayden has said, "Like an octopus. Somehow there was more of him than there really was." (Later this section has been dropped from part II.) Ricercata presented a fascinating contrapuntal finale with fifteen dancers. In his architectural choreography Balanchine somehow brings the audience back to reality. (Recently, it has been danced alone, very effectively; after all, Virgil Thomson has observed that the music of Webern is a dialect of Bach in the unending unfolding of musical forms.)

We can no more summarize the diverse character of Martha Graham than we can list the qualities of the moon or an iceberg. With regard to music she progressed from innocence to experience—from dancing to any number that caught her fancy to choreographing generally commissioned scores by such living American composers as William Schuman, Samuel Barber, and Norman dello Joio, as well as those previously mentioned. Working closely with her musical and visual collaborators, she has usually directed both the style and the contents of the various forms used. She has preferred open, even fragmentary scores (though composed along the dramatic lines she needed to deal with emotional and psychological states) to set forms like waltzes and hymns. Throughout she has known what she needed, and she resists categorization in her music as in all her art.

Reference to Graham's latest works, such as *Dances of the Golden Hall,* is in order. Even with the unexpected symmetry appearing after half a century of upholding modernism's traditional avoidance of the mirror image, Graham continues her search of ourselves as in her work she reaches past the literary and past the rational. She looks for the ultimate in herself, engaging in a never-ending quest that seldom brings more than momentary fulfillment. Turning to Greek and other sources, she makes history, psychology, and mythology contemporary. In the words of Anna Kisselgoff, "Goddess-Mother. Virgin. Repeatedly, Graham heroines are seen in multiple aspects of themselves."

Cunningham, Cage, and the Abstract

The contributions of Merce Cunningham and John Cage to spectacle-entertainment in the twentieth century are like those of no other partnership in lyric theatre history. The continuing story of the more than forty collaborations of Cage and Cunningham began when they met in 1938, and were both introduced to parallels between zen and dadaism. In time this led to Cage's remark that "we are in a multiplicity of centers," and to both adopting chance as a full partner and factor in their creative activity (replacing the previously expressionist frames of their artistic endeavors).

Merce Cunningham, born in Centralia, Washington in 1920, performed on the West Coast before coming to New York where he studied at the School of American Ballet, and danced with Martha Graham for six years prior to starting his own independent career and company. John Cage, born in Los Angeles in 1912, started his amazing career in 1937 with the statement that all conceivable noises would be used to make music. Cage has occasionally used classic procedures in his aural experiments and "happenings," but usually these are almost incidental to his devotion to his stated aims. Cage is one of the few individual musicians of our time not to succumb in one way or another to the intellectual and seductive aura of Stravinsky. His period of study with Arnold Schoenberg may be compared to the learning years Cunningham spent with Martha Graham—no more personal than need be, interesting in themselves, but not central to the main professional activity of the younger artist.

While the Cunningham-Cage artistic partnership may account for only a minority of the works of either man individually, this important minority is the result of an elite relationship that has given effective exposure to the music of one and character to the dances of the other. The designers of their works include Noguchi, Fullemann, Lancaster, and Graves. (Other designers who have made important contributions to dances of Cunningham include such well known artists as Duchamp, Rauschenberg, Stella, Johns, and Warhol.)

Cunningham's long and continuing association with Cage has provided guidance and inspiration in his other collaborations. Cage, in rejecting the credos of Stravinsky and Schoenberg, found considerable strength in the philosophy of the East. His credo has been a kind of controlled nihilism, and as a result Cunningham has usually worked with other musicians who had this same philosophy. Cage approved of the music of Erik Satie, and Cunningham choreographed Satie's *Socrate.* (We have noted that Massine, Ashton, and Tudor were involved with productions using the music of this important French innovator, who said music was disposable, to be listened to or not according to one's mood.) Nearly every other work by Cunningham uses music composed or arranged by living composers, such as David Tudor, Earl Brown, Christian Wolff, Jon Gibson, Martin Kalve, Takehisa Kosugi, Gordon Mumma, Yasunao Tone, most of them influenced by Cage.

Cunningham's background of six years with Martha Graham and her collaborations with Barber, Schuman, Chavez, and Noguchi were important influences musically, scenically, and kinetically, leading him to dramatic freedom, innocence, musical experiment, and visual fragmentation. Cunningham's dances range from short solos to hour-long group happenings. He believes in advanced professional virtuosity and independence in combining performing arts. His role in his company is certainly primus inter pares, but whether the focus is on him personally or on his dancers, the idea of a grand, unified spectacle-entertainment for our time is uppermost in his mind, and, I believe, in the minds of his spectators, whether they are part of his fanatic following or part of the larger public for whom the arts are either an escape or a substitute for religion. In essence, Cunningham has combined in a new and provocative way the virtuosic individualism of Martha Graham and the coordinated achievement of Serge de Diaghilev in creating an expression of the performing and plastic arts of the latter twentieth century, which takes into major account the element of chance and improvisation along with professional responsibility. David Vaughan has noted in his excellent book on Frederick Ashton a resemblance between the structures of certain of Cunningham's works and those of Ashton, in particular Ashton's *Monotones* to music of Satie's Gnossiennes, and for that matter the Franck *Symphonic Variations,* which had no fixed and absolute center, with the ballerina in the middle. (See: Bibliography.)

Where Cunningham and Cage will lead us I do not pretend to predict, but the importance of their work at this time is vital, and it is to be celebrated. Jennifer Dunning noted that Cunningham broke away from Graham so that he might discard the rigid trappings of theme, or plot, music, and decoration and thus emphasize the "kinetic energy of the body." He combined elegance in movement, presented in stage space in such a way as to approximate the unexpectedness and visual complexity of everyday life in our time; and with the young professionals his influence has been increasing rapidly, both among his acolytes and those who are foreign to his particular dialect.

Cunningham is a plastic counterpart to that amazing Cage phenomenon. Cunningham believes dance is vital, something for people who think. He himself is erudite, down-to-earth, and focused, not diffuse. His dance is about discipline, abstract, yet dramatic, always pushing a frontier, just as was that of virtually everyone before him in this field who made a mark for posterity.

Certainly Merce Cunningham has opened audiences' eyes to new movement, and through the music he used he has opened audiences' ears as well. Many of the scores he dances with or to involve various forms of sound manipulation, even distortion, electronic or other. On occasion, distortion is not far away, as in Cage's Fielding Sixes, although the original starting place was Irish fiddle tunes.

Cunningham's attitude toward life involves the constant of unpredictability and multiplicity of collage, or chance. Thus the component parts of his work in the performing arts coexist in time and space, but except for a defined time space they do not relate to each other. Music, dance, decor are separate and equal, and once they are "mated" in his works they operate as a unit, if not as a unity. Music is not accompaniment to his dance, nor is his dance illustration to his music; kinetic and musical phrases are not purposely coordinated. This is particularly evident in Cunningham's more than three hundred *Events*—full evening-length improvisations involving his entire company, in which the performers draw freely on previous Cunningham works and on new ideas as well.

Anna Kisselgoff has indicated that Cunningham applied Cubist principles, offering a radical vision of traditional forms, breaking them up into different segments than we usually observe, making clear to us relationships we had never dreamed of or had failed to comprehend. But with all his rhythmic analysis to simplify and make art seem more direct, Cunningham does retain limits, as in fact any artist must, whatever the medium. Just as Denishawn spawned Martha Graham, Martha Graham spawned Cunningham, so he too now has direct artistic descendants to the right and to the left, some more structured and some less.

Cunningham's devotion to advanced elements in contemporary music and art brings dance spectacle to a new horizon that we will attempt to define in a few of his many works. One of Cunningham's 1947 works (which should be revived for the generation who has not seen it) is his eighteen-minute ballet, *The Seasons* (Cage-Noguchi). Cage scored the work for forty-three players, with an orchestra in which there are no physical or electronic alterations for the instruments or their basic sounds (such as "preparing" a piano, a procedure of which Cage is fond). In spite of the music being nearly "normal" to our ears, it is personal and characteristic of Cage, with pauses, totally unprepared cadences, and weird progressions. Cunningham has an answer in movement for the variety of Cage's procedures, various rather simple and brief musical effects appearing only to metamorphose into other effects, other colors, or to disappear totally. The transformation of the musical ideas is more often graceful than rough, and it is not difficult to follow the relationships of the dance and the music or the sequence of the seasons, which Cage tells us have marked Indian aesthetic connotations. Surrounded in 1947 by the excellent dancers of Ballet Society, Cunningham himself took a leading role as sort of catalyst for the others and for all the action in a cohesive, integrated way, rather than as a ringmaster in a divertissement.

Winter (Quiescence) begins mysteriously, in a quiet opening for strings in slow duple time, succeeded by a flute solo which introduces alternating surges of sound and near silences. At one point it suggests the prelude to act III of *Tristan und Isolde,* though with more of a French feeling. Spring (Creation) is a longer section, beginning moderately in duple time, rippling like a brook generally more active. A calculated small explosion heralds its arrival. Summer (Preservation) is in moderate tempo, in triple time. It seems to stretch the basic rhythmic count—one and, two and, three. Strings dominate, with woodwinds, brass, percussion, and celeste also involved. Fall (Destruction), moderate, in duple time, begins with woodwinds, then becomes percussive and very rhythmic, before dissolving finally once more into the prelude to Winter. The orchestra calls for woodwinds and brass by twos, percussion, keyboard, and strings.

In *The Seasons* Cunningham combines modern dance, ballet, and theatrical devices in a variety of effects aimed at reflecting changing moods of the music of Cage, suggesting metamorphosis in weather, time of day, and elemental aspects. Images of moving fire, snow crystals, and water drops are projected against a transparent backdrop. Masks and properties are added to basic striped costumes. Reflections of sprigs of dogwood, butterfly nets, and a kite all pass in front of our eyes as the seasons progress. Colors are used in sharp, controlled accents in much the same way the music is orchestrated and shaped. The dancing seems deliberately playful, gay, yet serious. At the end the outlined symbol of a large crystal geometrical form fills the entire scene as Winter returns.

Some years later, in 1966, Cunningham's *Summerspace, a Lyric Dance,* which he had presented with his own company in 1958, was performed by New York City Ballet. The music that played while the dancers moved was Morton Feldman's Ixion, and the pointillist decors and costumes were the work of Robert Rauschenberg. Although this characteristic Cunningham theatrical dance event was well performed and well received, it did not remain in the repertoire beyond one season. (In 1982 Cunningham's *Duets* was performed by American Ballet Theatre.) Among the wonderful dancers who have appeared with Cunningham, specific mention may be made of several who provide female interest as a contrast to Cunningham—Viola Farber, Carolyn Brown, Lisa Friedman, Karole Armitage, Ellen Cornfield, all of whom have given years of devoted service on the Cunningham team.

In all his dances Cunningham continues to explore movement, its sources and its effects. In *10s with Sixes* (1981) (Kalve-Lancaster) he uses a phrase of ten counts for the dancers, varying a set phrase with elements of surprise, a technique basic to his collaborations with Cage; Martin Kalve's score, All Happy Workers Babies & Dogs, contrasts with the costumes of black body suits for four men and three women, and gives the piece a lightness that makes it very unlike Massine's *Rouge et Noir* (1939) (Shostakovitch-Matisse).

Merce Cunningham in *Tango* (1981).
Photographer: Nathaniel Tileston. Courtesy of David Vaughan and the Merce Cunningham Dance Company)

Tango (1978) is noted in the program as by "John Cage: a letter to Erik Satie, with Sound anonymously Received; visual elements are by Mark Lancaster," the current artistic advisor of the Cunningham Company. *Tango* is a twenty-minute solo performed by Cunningham in a plain studio in which four television screens reflect images of Cunningham that may provide unity to the apparently improvisatory nature of the dance. Without suggesting any ethnic resemblance, comparing it to a Spanish number gives one an idea of the nature of this dance (performed in practice clothes, black tight trousers, white shirt, and white shoes).

It is acute, complex, varied and unpredictable. Although it may not be possible to define the theme of *Tango* accurately, the movement phrases (sometimes repeated in the multiple television screens positioned around the stage) do establish shading and character, with spurts in the music which are reflected in movement, or vice versa. Occasionally, Cunningham seems to be engaged in conversation, occasionally demonstration, occasionally exhortation. Recognizable sequences are varied with totally original ones. Playful gestures alternate with portentous ones, often idiosyncratically, nonmusically.

Locale (1979) uses Takehisa Kosugi's score, *Interspersion,* and has design and lighting by Charles Atlas. For the entire company of fourteen (without Cunningham), this is a stage version of a work originally choreographed for film (shot as a film under the direction of Atlas). This is a fast workout for the company, with front-side-back traveling jumps, combined often with ballet steps in Cunningham's choreography and sometimes at odds with Cage's dour music.

Among Cunningham's other significant works, mention may be made of *Fielding Sixes* (1980), in decor by Fullemann and *Roadrunners.* The latter with music by Tone for viola, piano, and narrator, and decors by Lancaster gives evidence of his continuing concern with ideas and aesthetics of the East, as well as aleatory procedures, which he combines in art to make the best of two worlds. First performed in 1979, this work for his full company is quirky, whimsical, and charming, without social connotations. In "fortune-cookie English" the score gives directions for far away places, and relays what Confucius said in response to some rather unusual questions. Much of Cunningham's choreography is two-dimensional, posed, with odd angles. The impact of music and dance combined is cryptic, and somewhat mystical although abstract, but not architectural in the way Balanchine's ballets are. Dance can never be totally abstract, as human bodies are always involved, yet in many of Cunningham's works there is an attempt at the purely visual, which seems to approach painting.

Earlier works by Cunningham, which fortunately he still revives, are: *Rainforest* (1968) (Tudor-Warhol); *Galaxy* (1956), music by Earl Brown; *Place* (1966), music by Gordon Mumma; and *Tread* (1970), music by Christian Wolff. For Cunningham as for Cage life and art are one, an eternal quest, an experiment, rarely a definition.

We began this historical essay on the relationships of theatrical dance and music by noting the interdependence of the two means of artistic communication. This interdependence has survived six centuries of revolutions against the church, the state, the forms, the manners, and powerful personalities. The influence of Stravinsky has created a remarkable family relationship and unifying element in the performing arts of this century, even among those who have not found his music stimulating and satisfying.

As we conclude, it may be argued by some that Merce Cunningham has truly embarked on a new track, as he rebelled against forms, ballet, Graham, and Stravinsky in favor of ideology that John Cage finds less structured. Yet Cunningham has choreographed the music of Stravinsky, a fact that automatically relates him to many other choreographers. Cunningham may even have tried to revolt from the tyranny of the human body, the most efficient machine we know, and to many the most beautiful. Yet, true to himself, Cunningham is still here, experimenting wonderfully with everything he believes is appropriate. In a Cageian mood, perhaps, one day we will see relationships between the Bible and the comic strip.

Whatever, whenever, whichever—qui vivra, verra!

Appendixes

Appendix 1.
Dances of the Middle Ages

Ballata—A two- or three-voice fourteenth-century Italian song form in several sections. Usually duple time.

Caccia—A three-voice fourteenth-century Italian song form, also called a chace, or an early madrigal. Its text involves hunting, fires, street cries, and the like. The upper parts are in strict canon, the second part beginning six or more measures after the first; this is followed by a ritornello that is sometimes canonic. Throughout there is a third part, a tenor, which is noncanonic. At times the upper parts are coloratura. Duple or triple.

Canzona—An Italian song related to the troubadour canzo, sometimes danced. In duple time.

Carole—A round dance apparently originating in Provence and northern Italy, alternating verse and refrain. Usually duple.

Conductus—A two- or three-voice thirteenth-century Latin contrapuntal strophic song, often used as an introduction, suitable for processions. Either duple or triple.

Estampie—A thirteenth-century instrumental gliding dance form (also called stantipes) deriving from the sequence, and consisting of four to seven puncta (phrases), each repeated. Originally monophonic, it later had three voices. (The similar ductia has four or fewer puncta.) Usually triple.

Frottola—A type of fifteenth-century Italian strophic song often danced. Duple time.

Hymn—A church form used on many occasions. Originally monophonic, it expanded to four voices. Either duple or triple.

Lamento—A three-voice fourteenth-century Italian dance in triple time.

March—A binary dance form, such as a processional entrée to a ballet, used to regulate movement of a group of individuals, mostly in duple time. In

194

later times two contrasting trios were often added to extend its structure, also variations.

Reigen—A stately German round dance, usually in duple time.

Rondel—A Latin song often danced, an ancestor of the French rondeau. Usually in triple time.

Rota—A fourteenth-century Italian "after" dance in duple time. Also called a ripresa.

Saltarello—A fourteenth-century dance in triple, or occasionally duple time, linked with the pas de Brabant of the Renaissance. The music is like a gaillard, but with small leaps indicated rather than the large steps of the gaillard. At first the saltarello was paired with the rota, and then later with the gaillard. Often the order of the dances was basse danse-quaternia, saltarello.

Trotta—A fourteenth-century stepping dance from Italy. Usually duple.

There were numerous musical forms in late medieval times that were danced on occasion, but whose relationship to the consecutive development of the classic theatrical dance has not yet been clarified. Readers who wish further information on this aspect of our subject are referred to two splendid studies by Gustave Reese listed in the Bibliography: *Music in the Middle Ages* and *Music in the Renaissance.*

Appendix 2.
Dances of the Renaissance

Allemande–A moderately slow dance in duple time often with a short up-beat; of sixteenth-century German origin, it is heavier than the gaillard, and frequently is followed by a jumping dance in triple time.

Basse danse (danza bassa)—Often in four sections (branle, reprise, second reprise, tordion). The earliest preserved basse danse for court performances was composed about 1450, probably of Italian origin. The name refers to the fact that the feet were barely lifted from the ground. Although there is controversy as to whether the basse danses were originally in triple or duple time, most authorities incline toward the latter. The written notes of the extant examples of basse danse manuscripts are "tenors" (tenere, to hold) serving as foundations played by the ancient slide trumpets above which the shawms improvised. Each note of the tenor is equal to a step unit of dance (described in Arbeau's *Orchésographie*). The dance steps follow the upper melody rather than the melody of the tenor. The basse danse developed into a popular model for the dance suite as variations to the basic melody and basic steps were added by the time of Arbeau. Percussion, viols, and other instruments were used to play the accompaniment. Later the basse danse was contrasted with the danse haute, the former being sliding steps, the latter being jumping steps. One can trace the basse danse forward to the German hoftanz, the French minuet, and on to eighteenth-century virtuosity.

Ballo–Originally an imaginative, pantomimic Italian dance in free rhythm (often sung), it came to be the same as balletto, which in the seventeenth century was a duple-time, bipartite dance resembling the allemande. Although Guglielmo Ebreo listed the ballo as a closed form, for some choreographers it continued to be a free form.

Branle–Developing from a "step" into a sung dance which included swaying of the body, it was rapid and pantomimic. There were more than twenty varieties of the Breton dance in which the steps went alternately from left to right. The slower varieties of branles (simple and double) were duple time; the branle gai was faster, in triple time.

Bergamasca–A rapid dance in duple time originating in northern Italy.

Bicinium–A sixteenth-century dance in two voices, popular in Italy, Germany, and later, France.

Pas de Brabant–A rapid French dance often in triple time; related to the Italian saltarello and to the gaillard.

Bouffons–A rapid pantomimic dance in duple time, related to the moresca.

Brando–An Italian branle, similar to a moresca.

Calata–An interweaving dance in duple time of Italian origin, similar to the basse danse.

Canaries–A lively French masqued dance in duple time, imitating the natives of the Canary Islands.

Chaconne–A stately dance with a continuous variation on a pattern of harmonies; in moderate triple time, it probably came originally from Mexico via Spain as an unbridled dance. The faster, related passacaglia was also a dance or a march based on variation, of a defined, repeated pattern of notes (ostinato). The sarabande, also related, was slower in tempo.

Courante–A rapid or moderate French dance in triple time, later popular in Italy also.

Canzona–A fanfare form for processions, alternating between duple and triple time; in the Baroque period it led to the keyboard fugue and the instrumental sonata.

Dreh tanz–A German dance in triple time, a precursor of the ländler.

Farandole–An ancient Provençal street dance in duple time in which the participants hold hands, performing figures while weaving in and out.

Gaillard (gagliardo)—Originally a rapid Italian dance in duple time (6/8) with leaping steps, more vigorous than the saltarello or the sarabande. The gaillard uses Arbeau's five basic steps; the leap on the fifth beat of the measure is higher for the gaillard than for the saltarello; the pattern of the steps (left-right-left-right) involves a forward thrust of alternate legs at the same time the opposite foot executes a bounce with a leap on the fifth beat and a hold on the sixth beat, though at times improvisation provides a contrast from the above.

Gavotte–A gay dance from Dauphiné in duple time, usually with two notes of up beat.

Gigue–An Irish or English jig, or Italian giga, in two sections, which in France developed into a fast duple dance with numerous jumps.

Hay (or hey)—A serpentine country dance in duple time (often with performers ranged in two rows), perhaps related to the bouffons, branle, or reel.

La manfredina–A northern Italian country dance in duple time.

Masque–A mimed scene or production in which performers, often masked, mime a scenario to the accompaniment of a ballo.

Moresca (morisque, mauresco, morris dance)–Of Moorish inspiration, if not origin, in moderate triple time; originally a sword dance with a jigging step.

Nizzarda–A moderate dance performed in northern Italy.

Passamezzo–A duple-time dance from Italy, faster than the pavane, usually coupled with a saltarello, gaillard, or pavane, sometimes set as variations on a ground.

Padoana–An Italian dance related to the pavane.

Pavane–A slow Italian or Spanish dance in duple time, often followed by a gaillard. Spagnolettas and pavaniglias were among the many pavanes.

Pie de Jibao–A sixteenth-century dance from Spain.

Piva–A sixteenth-century Italian dance in duple time, using series of leaps and turns.

Prinzen tanz–A slow German dance in duple time followed by the proportz, fast in triple time.

Recoupe–Similar to a saltarello, binary in form, a middle section of the basse danse sequence.

Sàrabande–A dignified dance in triple time, slower than the minuet, originally of exotic origin.

Tordion–The third section of the basse danse, a binary form of gaillard with less elevation.

Triori–A gay, fast dance from Brittany, a kind of branle in duple time.

Villanos–A moderate Spanish dance in duple time.

Volte–A rapid, duple time dance of Provençal origin in which the female dancer is lifted into the air by her partner.

Acknowledgements for some entries to Arbeau's *Orchésographie*, 1588.

Appendix 3.
Dances of the Seventeenth Century

Lully and his choreographers made effective musical and dramatic use of the established dance forms, and also were open to new forms, some of them adapted for theatrical use from peasant dances originating in the French provinces. They preserved what was effective and useful from the past, and at the same time pointed to the future. Lully's works include the following new forms:

Anglaise—A quick dance in duple time, beginning on the bar (no upbeat).

Bourrée—A very quick dance in duple time, beginning on the third beat of the bar, in binary form. Coming from Dauphiné, or Savoie, often it was used alternately with the minuet.

Loure—A slow dance from Normandy in triple time, found in Lully's *Alceste.*

Minuet—A moderate dance from Poitou (possibly having a Spanish ancestor) in triple time (quicker than the passacaglia, passecaille), a form increasingly popular in Lully's works.

Passacaglia—A moderate dance of Spanish origin in triple time, related to the slower chaconne and to the still slower sarabande.

Passepied—A gracious dance in triple time, originally a Breton sailor's dance, quicker than the minuet.

Rigaudon—A moderately rapid dance of southern origin in duple time, in several sections.

Pastorale—A slow dance in duple time.

Sicilienne—A moderately slow dance in dotted duple time.

In the 1650s the order of popularity in Lully's works was: minuet, sarabande, gavotte (including the related form la mariée), chaconne. In the 1660s the order of popularity of dance forms was: minuet, bourrée, sarabande. In the 1670s the order of popularity was: minuet, bourrée, chaconne, canaries, sarabande. Lully also used the gaillard, pavane, and allemande, in addition to those mentioned above, although some of the forms changed greatly during his lifetime. Generally the initial entrée began with dotted rhythm, often a march for men, with intricate figures. As the work progressed the dances mostly became lighter and faster (with the frequent exception of a stately conclusion). It is important to note a parallel development in nontheatrical music, echos of which were in fact felt in the lyric theatre. During the seventeenth century composers increasingly began to write instrumental suites for keyboard or ensembles which were performed without vocal or terpsichorean collaboration. For the most part these suites used dance forms of the Renaissance and Baroque according to the following sequence: allemande, courante, sarabande, optional, gigue; the optional movement usually was chosen from among those dance forms discussed. La Bourgogne was a particular suite of dances made up of the courante, bourrée, sarabande, and passepied.

Appendix 4.
Dances of the Classical Age

In the Classical Age choreographers had available the various dance forms we have noted, and they soon added another dozen or more. The following are the new forms found in various stage works:

Air de caractère–A mixed dance, entry of beggars, entry of winds, etc.

Contre danse (contradance, country dance)–Usually a moderate dance in duple time, it formed the basis for the later quadrille, and elaborate ensemble finales; probably of English origin. In much the same way folk dances contributed steps, the country dance contributed form.

Fandango–A moderate Spanish dance in triple time, used by Gluck, Mozart, and others.

Forlana–A rapid dance in duple time of northern Italian origin, found in Campra's *Les Fêtes Venitiennes,* also called La Conty, or La Venitienne.

Hornpipe–A varied sailor's dance in duple time probably of English origin used by Handel (originally in triple time).

Musette–A moderate French peasant dance in duple time, a form of the shepherd's bagpipe dance, somewhat similar to the gavotte.

Polo–An Andalusian dance in triple time.

Polonaise–A moderate Polish processional dance in triple time; originally it was a peasant dance taken up at court.

Tambourin–A rapid dance in duple time with a drum bass from Provence, found in Rameau's *Les Fêtes d'Hébé.*

Teutsche (or deutsche)–A rapid German dance usually in triple time, developing from the Renaissance tedesco.

Toccata–A rapid dance in duple time, related to the forlana.

"Tricotets"–A rapid French dance in duple time, related to the allemande.

201

Among the most popular dances in duple rhythm in the lyric works of
Jean-Philippe Rameau were: gavotte (indicated when Amour appears), bourrée,
rigaudon, loure, gigue, and march. In triple rhythm the following dances
appear most frequently; sarabande (noble, elegiac, meditative), chaconne (used
in Greek and battle scenes), passacaglia or passecaille (used in important
dramatic scenes), minuet, passepied (which Rameau used more often than the
minuet, particularly in scenes of sport and pleasure).

Generally the lyric works of Rameau were very good for dancing. His use of
key changes and varied rhythms gave vital dramatic thrust to scenes that
otherwise might have been purely decorative and static. Rameau really did
employ the dance for dramatic purposes, and in some of his "operas" the dances
were half the music. Yet despite this fact, and the fact that his orchestra was both
fuller and more varied than Lully's, many of his works for lyric theatre have not
been revived. Primarily because of serious deficiencies in the story line, and also
because the form of opera ballet is now obsolete, it is extremely difficult to stage
them for the public of today, uninformed as it is on the stage conventions of the
period.

Typical Rameau orchestration called for two flutes and piccolos, three or more
oboes, two bassoons, musettes, horns, trumpets, percussion, continuo, and
strings, always idiomatically employed, although somewhat less contrapuntally
than those of Rameau's contemporaries Bach and Handel.

Appendix 5.
Dances of the Nineteenth Century

Bolero–A moderate Spanish dance of eighteenth century folk origin, often in triple time, somewhat similar to the cachucha accompanied by castanets; composed by Beethoven, Auber, Weber, Offenbach, and Verdi.

Cachucha–A lively Andalusian dance in triple time, first danced by Fanny Elssler in *Le Diable Boiteux* by Casimir Gide (1845).

Cancan–A rapid French group dance in duple time; composed by Offenbach.

Csardas–A rapid Hungarian dance in duple time, a derivative of the verbunkos; composed by Delibes.

Ecossaise–A rapid dance in duple time, probably deriving from the English country dance rather than from Scotland (used in both versions of *La Sylphide,* along with reels and highland flings).

Galop–A rapid German round dance in duple time (hopser), used in many ballets (e.g., *Giselle*).

Grossvater tanz–A moderate German ceremonial dance in duple time (in Tchaikovsky's *The Nutcracker*).

Krakowiak–A Polish dance of moderate tempo in duple time, danced by Elssler in *La Gypsy* by A. Thomas (1839).

Ländler–An Austrian peasant dance in slow waltz time, usually involving turning couples.

Lezginka–A Russian folk dance composed by Glinka, Anton Rubinstein and others, in duple time.

Malaguena–A moderate Spanish folk dance in triple time.

Mazurka–A genre of Polish triple time folk dance, including Kujawiaks and Obertas, ranging from moderate to fast.

Polka–A rapid Bohemian dance in duple time.

Quadrille–A type of square dance in duple time for four or eight dancers (originally a group of four to twelve dancers in an entrée of French seventeenth- and early eighteenth-century ballets).

Redowa—A rapid Bohemian dance in triple time, similar to the mazurka.

Sardana—A moderate Spanish folk dance usually in triple time.

Schottische—A moderate German dance in duple time.

Seguidilla—A varied Spanish dance in moderate triple time, used in Petipa's *Don Quixote*.

Slovanka—A varied Slavonic dance for couples.

Sonata—An instrumental form in duple or triple time, used by Mozart, Beethoven, and many others.

Tarantella—A rapid Neapolitan dance in duple time, used in Coralli's *La Tarantulle* and Bournonville's *Napoli*.

Tyrolienne—A moderate dance in triple time from Austria.

Varsovienne—A slow Polish dance in tripe time, related to the mazurka.

Waltz—A popular Austrian dance in triple time, first seen in Pierre Gardel's *Dansomanie*.

Appendix 6.
Dances of the Current Period

Conga—A chain dance of African origin in duple time using syncopation.

Disco—Such nonstop choreographers as Molissa Fenlay have found inspiration in the insistent duple time of this new form.

Farucca—A traditional, rapid Spanish folk dance in duple time; used in Massine's *Le Tricorne*.

Foxtrot—A rapid duple time dance; used in Ashton's *Façade*.

Jota—A traditional, northern Spanish folk dance in triple time.

Jazz—Syncopated dance music, usually in duple time; used in Jooss's *The Big City* and Robbins's *Fancy Free*.

Koradin—A traditional Spanish dance.

Ragtime—A syncopated jazz dance in duple time; used in Massine's *Parade*.

Rhumba—An Afro-Cuban syncopated dance in duple time.

Rock—Twyla Tharp has adpted the duple time twisty-slinky forms in several of her works.

Samba—A syncopated Brazilian folk dance in duple time.

Tango—A syncopated dance in duple time, of African origin, nurtured in Central America; used in Ashton's *Facade*.

Appendix 7.
Table of Orchestrations Used by Composers of Works for the Lyric Theatre

Medieval ensembles—One recorder, one trumpet, one lute, organ, percussion (varied), and two violas.

Renaissance ensembles—Recorder, shawm, trumpet, lutes, harp, harpsichord, percussion, and strings.

Early Baroque—Recorder (flute), oboes, trumpets, trombones, lutes, organs, harpsichord, harps, percussion, two violins, two violas, and two double basses.

Lully and his contemporaries—Two flutes (recorders), two oboes, two bassoons, two trumpets, four trombones, harp, harpsichord, percussion, and five string parts.

Early eighteenth-century composers—Two flutes, two oboes, two bassoons, two horns, three trumpets, three trombones, harpsichord, harp, percussion, and strings.

Late eighteenth-century composers—Two flutes, two oboes, two clarinets, two bassoons, two horns, three trumpets, three trombones, harpsichord, harp, percussion, and strings.

Beethoven and his contemporaries—Two flutes, two oboes, two clarinets, two bassoons, four horns, three trumpets, three trombones, percussion, and strings.

Adam and his contemporaries—Two flutes, two oboes, two clarinets, two bassoons, four horns, three trumpets, three trombones, tuba, harp, percussion, and strings.

Tchaikovsky and his contemporaries—Three flutes, three oboes, three clarinets, two to three bassoons, four horns, four trumpets, three trombones, tuba, harp, piano, percussion, and strings.

Stravinsky—Four flutes, four oboes, four clarinets, four bassoons, four horns, four trumpets, three trombones, tuba, two harps, piano, percussion, and strings.

Notes

Chapter 1–The Beginnings and Medieval Times

1. Duple time or duple meter signifies a rhythm in which the basic pulse is two or a multiple of two in a measure (bar), such as 1, 2; 1, 2, 3, 4; 1, 2, 3–4, 5, 6. Triple time or triple meter signifies a rhythm in which the basic pulse is three or a multiple of three in a measure, such as 1, 2, 3; 1, 2, 3–4, 5, 6–7, 8, 9.

Chapter 2–The Renaissance

1. Repeated figures for the ensemble have been used throughout ballet history, in the chaconnes of Lully and Beauchamps, in the works of Gluck, in such nineteenth-century ballets as *Giselle, Swan Lake, La Bayadère,* and in Balanchine's twentieth-century *Union Jack.*

2. Translated by Cyril W. Beaumont, Arbeau's *Orchésographie* is available in a paperback edition listed in the bibliography; its importance has been properly evaluated by Lincoln Kirstein in his indispensable *Dance,* also listed in the bibliography.

Chapter 3–The Seventeenth Century

1. Pierre Rameau, *Le Maître à Danser.* Paris 1725. A reprint edition is available.

2. *La Délivrance de Renaud,* produced by the Duc de Luynes in 1617.

3. *Le Ballet de la Foire de Saint Germain,* produced by the Prince de Condé in 1606, with music by A. Boësset.

4. Although the collaboration of Jonson and Jones produced fifteen masterful masques, both the writer and the architect had illustrious careers on their own; in all, Jones designed some forty productions.

5. Beating time vigorously with his cane, according to his usual practice, Lully struck his foot imperiously. As he neglected to treat a relatively minor injury, a serious abscess developed. He refused amputation, and shortly all other treatment was of no avail.

6. A composition in binary form is divided into two sections, usually repeated.

7. It is interesting to observe how a dance form could control an entire work. Delalande's *Ballet de la Jeunesse* (1686), a three-scene ballet based on a poem of 250 lines, had at its very center a chaconne with a total of sixty-one variations built on the eight-measure bass phrase; in the post-Lully period this unifying procedure in a divertissement was used frequently by Campra and others.

8. C. F. Menestrier, *Des Ballets anciens et modernes*. Paris 1682 (reprint edition). T. Lajarte, *Bibliothèque Musicale du Théâtre de l'Opéra*. Paris 1878.

9. The French overture, as defined by Lully, was usually ABA in form: slow in dotted rhythm, rapid, fugal, slow, conclusion. The Italian overture, as defined by Alessandro Scarlatti, was usually ABA in form: fast, slow, fast; it was the forerunner of the sonata form.

Chapter 4—The Eighteenth Century: The Classical Age

1. Ballet had been introduced in Russia by Peter the Great (1672–1725) and was continued under succeeding monarchs. A school was established in 1735. With the coronation of Catherine in 1763, Russian ballet began to take itself seriously, and choreographers, dancers, and composers began to be imported regularly.

2. Through-composed (*durchkomponiert* in German) applies to music in which there is no repetition (such as ABA). Each section (A,B,C, etc.) is followed by a section of new music, until the end of the piece or movement.

Chapter 5—The Nineteenth Century

1. Beginning with chamber music (sonatas, quartets) created well within the boundaries familiar to Haydn and Mozart, Beethoven moved to an originality of form, sonority, melody, and harmony that gave convincing individuality and incredible freshness and freedom from formula to all the works he composed after he was thirty. In his mature music Beethoven moved away from set pieces, like the minuet, toward a freedom of form and sonority already suggested by Cherubini and Méhul, toward enlarged symphonic procedures that defy stereotyping. Gradually, his expansionist procedures were introduced into lyric theatre by Rossini, Meyerbeer, Gounod, Delibes, Bizet, Wagner, Tchaikovsky, Stravinsky, and others.

2. Although earlier Grisi had sung, as well as danced, successfully in London, henceforth her professional engagements were completely confined to the dance.

3. Lucille Grahn capped a distinguished career as a ballerina by becoming ballet mistress in Munich, where she choreographed Wagner's *Tannhäuser.*

4. Tchaikovsky (1840–1893) composed many songs, chamber music, symphonic works, and operas as well as the music for three great ballets. These ballets have been termed symphonic, both in praise and in censure. The apellation "symphonic" was applied in previous times to ballets by Lully, Rameau, Gluck, and so on.

Chapter 6–The Twentieth Century: Three Great Russians

1. The succession of Diaghilev's choreographer-ballet masters was as follows: Fokine—1909–1912; 1914–1915; Nijinsky—1912–1913, 1914; Massine—1915–1921; 1924–1925; Nijinska—1921–1924; Balanchine—1925–1929.

2. It is a matter of record that Balanchine once substituted for Markova in *Le Chant du Rossignol.*

3. A figure in the bass, constantly repeated, forming a foundation for varied upper elements.

4. Stravinsky uses the Phrygian and Dorian scales as practiced in medieval times. The original Phrygian mode (scale), D to D in G clef in ancient times became E to E in medieval times. The original Dorian mode, E to E in G clef in ancient times became D to D in medieval times.

5. Balanchine has often stretched the Petipa vocabulary he learned as a student with unusual movements and combinations, some taken from life, some from acrobats, some imagined. His response to quarreling questioners is illustrated by his reply to the man who asked, "Who ever saw Apollo on his knees?"—"Who ever saw Apollo?" At any rate, his comrade in art since their schooldays together, Alexandra Danilova saw his originality and eagerly embraced it from the first, pointing out his many fresh ideas in *Apollo,* where for example the ballerinas danced on point *and* flat foot, perfectly matching Stravinsky's innovations. She commented, "I never knew we were making history."

6. Although the New York City Ballet did dance this work once more, in the Stravinsky Festival of 1972, the choreography was by Jerome Robbins.

Selected Bibliography

Aldrich, Putnam. *Rhythm in Seventeenth Century Monody.* New York: Norton, 1966.

Angiolini, Gaspare. *Dissertations.* Vienna: Trasterne, 1765.

Anthony, James. *French Baroque Music.* New York: Norton, 1978.

Arbeau, Thoinot. *Orchésographie.* Translated by Cyril W. Beaumont. London: Beaumont, 1925.

Arvey, Verna. *Choreographic Music.* New York: Dutton, 1941.

Aubry, P., and Dacier, E. *Les Caractères de la danse.* Paris: Champion, 1905.

Balanchine, George. *New Complete Stories of the Great Ballets.* Edited by Francis Mason. New York: Doubleday, 1968.

Beaujoyeux, Balthasar de. *Le Ballet Comique de la Reine Louise.* Paris: Adrian Le Roy, Robert Ballart, and Mamert Patisson, 1582.

Beaumont, Cyril W. *The Ballet Called Giselle.* London: Beaumont, 1944.

————. *The Ballet Called Swan Lake.* London: Beaumont, 1952.

————. *Ballet Design, Past and Present.* London: The Studio, 1946.

————. *A Bibliography of Dancing.* London: Dancing Times, 1929.

————. *Complete Book of Ballets.* New York: Putnam's Sons, 1938.

————. *The Diaghilev Ballet in London.* London: Beaumont, 1940.

————. *Three French Dancers of the Eighteenth Century.* London: Beaumont, 1934.

Benois, Alexandre. *Reminiscences of the Russian Ballet.* London: Putnam's Sons, 1941.

Bie, Oskar. *Tanzmusik.* Berlin: Bard, Marquardt, 1907.

Blasis, Carlo. *The Code of Terpsichore.* Turin, 1830. Reprint. New York: Dance Horizons, 1975.

Bournonville, August. *My Theatre Life.* Translated by P. N. McAndrew. Middletown, Conn.: Wesleyan University Press, 1979.

Buckle, Richard. *Diaghilev.* New York: Atheneum, 1980.

213

Burney, Charles. *A General History of Music.* Reprint. New York: Dover, 1957.

Bukofzer, Manfred. *Studies in Medieval and Renaissance Music.* New York: Norton, 1947.

Calvocoressi, Michel. *Music and Ballet.* London: Faber and Faber, 1933.

Caroso, M. F. *Il Ballerino.* Facsimile of Venice 1581 edition. New York: Broude Bros., 1967.

Carse, Adam. *The History of Orchestration.* London: Kegan, Paul, 1925.

Christout, Marie Francoise. *Le ballet de cour de Louis XIV.* Paris: Picard, 1967.

Chrysalis. New York, 1948–1961.

Clarke, M., and Crisp, C. *Ballet.* London: A. and C. Black, 1973.

Clement, F., and Larousse, P. *Dictionnaire des Opéras.* Paris: Larousse, 1897.

Crane, F. *Materials for the Study of the Fifteenth Century Basse Danse.* Brooklyn: Inst. of Med. Mus., 1968.

Crosten, W. L. *French Grand Opera.* New York: King's Crown, 1948.

Dance Index. New York, 1942–1948.

Demuth, Norman. *French Opera.* Sussex: Artemis Press, 1963.

Dent, E. J. *The Foundations of English Opera.* Cambridge: Cambridge University, 1928.

Denby, Edwin. *Looking at the Dance.* New York: Pellegrini and Cudahy, 1948.

Dolmetsch, Mabel. *Dances of Spain and Italy.* London: Routledge and Paul, 1934.

Eaton, Quaintance. *Opera Production.* Minneapolis: University of Minnesota, 1961.

————. *Opera Production,* II. Minneapolis: University of Minnesota, 1974.

Fokine, Michel. *Memoirs of a Ballet Master.* Boston: Little, Brown, 1961.

Grigoriev, Serge. *The Diaghilev Ballet.* London: Constable, 1953.

Guest, Ivor. *The Romantic Ballet in Paris.* Middletown, Conn.: Wesleyan University Press, 1966.

Haggin, B. H. *Ballet Chronicle.* New York: Horizon Press, 1970.

Haskell, A. L. *Diaghileff.* New York: Simon and Schuster, 1935.

Hastings, Baird. "Gluck and Angiolini." *American Dancer,* October, 1941.

Hauser, Arnold. *Social History of Art.* 4 vols. New York, Knopf, 1951.

Hilton, Wendy. *Dances of Court and Theater,* 1690–1725. Princeton, N.J.: Princeton Book, 1981.

Horst, Louis. *The Pre-Classic Dance Forms.* Reprint. New York: Dance Horizons, 1968.

Kindeldey, Otto, ed. *A Renaissance Dancing Master.* New York: Freidus Memorial, 1929.

Kirstein, Lincoln. *Dance.* New York: Putnam's Sons, 1935.

————. *Movement and Metaphor.* New York: Praeger, 1970.

————. *Thirty Years: The New York City Ballet.* New York: Knopf, 1978.

Knight, Judyth. *Ballet and Its Music.* London: Eur. Am. Mus., 1973.

Kunzle, Regine. "Pierre Beauchamps." *Dance Scope* 8/9 (1974/75).

Lajarte, T. *Bibliothèque Musicale du Théâtre de l'Opéra.* Paris: Librairie des Bibliophiles, 1879.

Lambranzi, G. *New and Curious School of Theatrical Dancing.* Translated by D. de Moroda. London: Beaumont, 1928.

Lauze, F. de. *Apologie de la Danse.* 1623. Reprint. London, Muller, 1952.

Ledermann, Minna, ed. *Stravinsky in the Theatre.* New York: Pellegrini and Cudahy, 1949.

Loewenberg, Alfred. *Annals of Opera.* Cambridge: Heffer, 1943.

Lloyd, Margaret. *The Borzoi Book of Modern Dance.* New York: Knopf, 1949.

Lynham, Derek. *The Chevalier Noverre.* London: Sylvan Press, 1950.

Magriel, Paul. *A Bibliography of Dancing.* New York: Wilson, 1936.

Massine, Leonide. *My Life in Ballet.* London: Macmillan, 1968.

Masson, P. M. *L'Opéra de Rameau.* Paris: Laurens, 1930.

Molière. *Oeuvres.* 3 vols. Paris: Garnier, 1934.

Moore, Lillian. *Artists of the Dance.* New York: Crowell, 1938.

Nagler, A. M. *Sources of Theatrical History.* New York: Theatre Annual, 1952.

Nettl, Paul. *The Dance in Classical Music.* New York: Philosophical Library, 1963.

Noverre, Jean-Georges. *Lettres sur la Danse.* 1760. Reprint. Paris: Lieutier, 1952.

Orgel, Stephen. *The Jonsonian Masque.* Berkeley, Calif.: University of California Press, 1980.

Petipa, Marius. *Memoirs.* Edited by Lillian Moore. New York: Macmillan, 1959.

Prunières, Henri. *Le Ballet de Cour en France avant Benserade et Lully.* Paris: Laurens, 1914.

Rameau, Pierre. *Le Maître à Danser.* Paris: Villette, 1725.

Reese, Gustave. *Music in the Middle Ages.* New York: Norton, 1940.

———. *Music in the Renaissance.* New York: Norton, 1954.

Reynolds, Nancy. *Repertory in Review.* New York: Dial Press, 1977.

Robinson, Michael. *Opera Before Mozart.* London: Hutchinson, 1966.

Sachs, Curt. *World History of the Dance.* New York: Norton, 1937.

Scholz, Janos, ed. *Baroque and Romantic Stage Design.* New York: Dutton, 1962.

Searle, H. *Ballet Music.* 2d ed. New York: Dover, 1973.

Silin, Charles. *Benserade and His Ballets de Cour.* Baltimore: Johns Hopkins Press, 1940.

The Simon and Schuster Book of the Ballet. New York: Simon and Schuster, 1980.

Stravinsky, Igor. *Chroniques de ma vie.* Paris: Denoel et Steele, 1935.

———. *Poétique Musicale.* Cambridge: Harvard University Press, 1942.

Stravinsky, Igor, and Craft, Robert. *Conversations with Igor Stravinsky.* New York: Doubleday, 1959.

————. *Dialogues and a Diary.* New York: Doubleday, 1963.

————. *Expositions and Developments.* New York: Doubleday, 1962.

————. *Memories and Commentaries.* New York: Doubleday, 1960.

————. *Retrospectives and Conclusions.* New York: Knopf, 1969.

————. *Themes and Episodes.* New York: Norton, 1950.

Strunk, Oliver, ed. *Source Readings in Music History.* New York: Norton, 1950.

Swift, M. G. *A Loftier Flight: Charles-Louis Didelot.* Middletown, Conn.: Wesleyan University Press, 1980.

Taper, Bernard. *Balanchine.* New York: Macmillan, 1968.

Temko, Allan. *Notre-Dame of Paris.* New York: Knopf, 1959.

Terry, Walter. *Ballet.* New York: Dell, 1959.

Thomson, Virgil. *American Music since 1910.* London: Weidenfeld, 1971.

"Interview with Antony Tudor." *Dance Scope* (1978).

Vaughan, David. *Frederick Ashton.* New York: Knopf, 1977.

Welsford, Enid. *The Court Masque.* London: Russell, 1927.

White, E. W. *Stravinsky.* Berkeley, Calif.: University of California, 1966.

Wilson, G. B. L. *A Dictionary of Ballet.* London: Penguin, 1957.

Wilson, Jean. *Entertainments for Elizabeth I.* New York:, Rowman, 1982.

Winter, Marian. *The Pre-Romantic Ballet.* London: Pitman, 1974.

Index

About the Author

Baird Hastings was born in New York City. He took his undergraduate degree at Harvard, his master's at Queens College, and doctorate at Sussex College. Special studies at the Paris Conservatory and the University of Paris were followed by study at Salzburg, Tanglewood, and a Fulbright fellowship. His teachers have included Yella Pessl, Boris Goldovsky, and Dean Dixon.

In 1942 he was, together with Paul Magriel, a founding editor of Lincoln Kirstein's *Dance Index*. He and his wife, Lily, established *Chrysalis,* a review of the arts, in 1948 and guided it until it ceased publication in 1961. Since 1960 he has been the conductor of the Mozart Festival Orchestra. In addition, he has been guest conductor of the American Symphony, Eglevsky Ballet, the Dessoff Choirs, and the Hartford Symphony, and for Margot Fonteyn.

From 1965 to 1970 he was Director of Instrumental Music, Trinity College, Hartford and the assistant music critic of the Hartford Times 1967–1970. Since 1973 he has been associated with the Juilliard School in New York as Orchestra Administrator and Librarian and as music advisor to Martha Hill, director of the Juilliard Dance Department. He is music advisor for the annual School of American Ballet workshops.

He has contributed over four hundred reviews, articles, and translations to arts publications on both music and dance, and has been a guest lecturer at Harvard University, New York University, Tufts College, and the New York Public Library. This is his eighth book.